Slavery and
the Catholic Tradition

American University Studies

Series V
Philosophy
Vol. 157

PETER LANG
New York • Washington, D.C./Baltimore • San Francisco
Bern • Frankfurt am Main • Berlin • Vienna • Paris

Stephen F. Brett

Slavery and the Catholic Tradition

Rights in the Balance

PETER LANG
New York • Washington, D.C./Baltimore • San Francisco
Bern • Frankfurt am Main • Berlin • Vienna • Paris

Library of Congress Cataloging-in-Publication Data

Brett, Stephen F. (Stephen Francis).
 Slavery and the Catholic tradition: rights in the balance / Stephen F.
Brett.
  p.   cm. — (American university studies. Series V, Philosophy;
vol. 157)
 Includes bibliographical references
 1. Thomas, Aquinas, Saint, 1225?–1249—Views on slavery.
2. Salamanca school (Catholic theology). 3. Slavery and the church—
Catholic Church. I. Title. II. Series.
BR765.T54B74   1994   261.8'34567—dc20   93-42798
ISBN 0-8204-2358-0   CIP
ISSN 0739-6392

Die Deutsche Bibliothek-CIP-Einheitsaufnahme

Brett, Stephen F.:
Slavery and the catholic tradition: rights in the balance / Stephen F. Brett.
- New York; Washington, D.C./Baltimore; San Francisco; Bern; Frankfurt am
Main; Berlin; Vienna; Paris: Lang, 1994
 (American university studies: Ser. 5, Philosophy; Vol. 157)
 ISBN 0-8204-2358-0
NE: American university studies / 05

The paper in this book meets the guidelines for permanence and durability of
the Committee on Production Guidelines for Book Longevity of the
Council on Library Resources.

To Edmund L. Brett and Marie K. Brett,

my parents, in abiding gratitude

for their lifelong generosity and love

Preface

In the thirteenth century Saint Thomas Aquinas wrote about rights, duties and justice in a political context that could not imagine the trajectory of modern democracy. The kind of race-based slavery practiced in the New World after the arrival of Columbus and European colonialism was hardly what Aquinas meant when he wrote of *servitus*. Still, he made it plain that servitude of any sort is repugnant to the plan of God and human wisdom.

The basis for the judgments of Aquinas was divine revelation and human reason. In contrast, the basis for the ethical reflections of Francisco Vitoria and Domingo de Soto in the sixteenth century was still revelation and reason but an ungainly body of canonical and civil laws that had grown enormously from the time of the Roman Empire skewed first principles discerned for Aquinas by metaphysical clarity. As churchmen and scholars, Vitoria and Soto were forced to confront the enslavement of human beings by profit-seeking countrymen. The link between evangelization and slavery tormented their sense of right and wrong but they could not find the tools to disentangle the practice of slavery from the tradition of law.

The three centuries that separate the medieval era of Aquinas from Spanish colonialism marked a revolution in the developments of law, philosophy and international commerce. More and more weight attached to the rights of governments to enact laws to which their subjects would be answerable. This invocation of the *jus gentium*, the power of nations to rule, included the rights of owners to enslave. It allowed for gaps between reason and power, divine justice and human politics, rights and duties, ownership and dignity. The writings of Vitoria and Soto were powerful antidotes to the venom of slavery, but they were not sufficient. Their allegiance to theories which upheld the power of civil legislation led them to flawed and fateful compromises. Their well-meaning and comprehensive scholarship was marked by an inability to confront the threshold question of whether any system which repudiates freedom and dignity can warrant the protection of civil laws.

Change in vocabulary over three centuries is predictable. But much more than language separates Aquinas from his two sixteenth century disciples. The nominalist revolution in philosophy changed more than names. It changed the context of moral decision-making in politics, economics and commerce. Generations of slaves lost their rights because of theories upheld by well-meaning but critically inadequate scholarship.

It is my hope that theories of human rights today will take into sufficient account fundamental truths that flow from the wisdom and kindness of a God in Whose image we are created. Theories of human rights are not fashioned only in libraries but are forged through the generosity and prescience of saints and heroes. Few are as noble as the selfless band of priests and brothers known as the Josephites.

For more than a century a small band of religious men, black and white, of several nationalities, has labored in behalf of Christ's message for the African-American community in the United States. This community, the Josephites, has struggled with the onus and bitter fruit of racism in any number of churches and communities. Their efforts—heroic, imaginative, and productive—have lightened the burdens of many individuals victimized by different types of injustice.

As a Josephite, I cannot personally claim the asceticism of earlier generations, but I acknowledge their work with honor and fraternal pride. Through their support I was able to study the perspectives of three distinguished theologians on the subject of slavery—Thomas Aquinas, Francisco Vitoria, Domingo de Soto. Each recognized the bedrock reality of human dignity. The translation of this fundamental theological truth into political realities was a task for them as it continues to be for us. It is my hope that the examination of their views will illuminate more clearly the fragile link between law, justice and dignity.

I want to thank many people whose affirmation of my work was invaluable. Father Charles McMahon, S.S.J. supported my efforts during our assignment together while serving the community as an exemplary religious superior. Father Thomas Kane, O.P., the director of my dissertation, enforced disciplined writing habits with a well-hewn "tough love" and provided indispensable help in exploring the ever creative insights of the Angelic Doctor. Dr. William May contributed generously of his time and critical judgment. Father Matthew O'Rourke, S.S.J., directed me to undertake doctoral studies shortly my ordination to the Catholic priesthood. For his unfailing support and astute judgments born of intelligence and experience I am most grateful.

For any lapses of logic or fact contained herein, I hold only myself responsible. For much love and support which made this book possible, I hold many in deep esteem.

Slavery and
the Catholic Tradition

Introduction

In a truly monumental exploration of ethics and jurisprudence, Hadley Arkes calls attention to a judicial opinion written by Joseph Story in the case of *La Jeune Eugénie* in 1822:

[The trade in slaves] is repugnant to the great principles of Christian duty, the dictates of natural religion, the obligations of good faith and morality, and the eternal maxims of social justice. When any trade can be truly said to have these ingredients, it is impossible that it can be consistent with any system of law, that purports to rest on the authority of reason or revelation. And it is sufficient to stamp any trade as interdicted by public law, when it can be justly affirmed, that it is repugnant to the general principles of justice and humanity.*

Yet it was this same eminent jurist, whose lapidary commentary on American constitutional law has instructed generations of lawyers and legal scholars, who later upheld the right of a slave owner to recapture a fugitive slave. Story's defense of the fugitive slave act was based on his understanding of federalism. His opinion in *Prigg v. Pennsylvania (1842)* was charged with the ambivalence of a jurist who detested slavery but who felt constrained to give legal effect to the political consensus of a community.

Story's dilemma had a long pedigree. Philosophers and jurists who wrote eloquently about human reason and the dignity of individuals nonetheless succeeded in justifying the institution of slavery because respectable authorities had sanctioned it. They predicated their defense of a repellent practice on a theory of natural law jurisprudence, appealing either to biblical theories of sin and its consequences or to the rights of legislatures to construct rights determined by political judgments seemingly impervious to challenge.

We turn now to the theological roots of the dilemma.

---

* Hadley Arkes, *First Things: An Inquiry into the First Principles of Morals and Justice* (Princeton, New Jersey: Princeton University Press, 1986), p. 134.

CHAPTER ONE

St. Thomas Aquinas and Slavery:
Rights and Dominion as Key Concepts

1. The Meaning of Right:

The term *jus* is generally translated as "right." St. Thomas makes it clear that rights and fairness are inseparable, understood best under the rubric of the virtue of justice. The term *jus* stands for "the right" as such, "the just," "the just thing," and as such is the object of the virtue of justice:

> A thing is said to be just, as having the rectitude of justice, without taking into account the way in which it is done by the agent: whereas in the other virtues nothing is declared to be right unless it is done in a certain way by the agent. For this reason justice has its own special proper object over and above the other virtues, and this object is called the just, which is the same as right. Hence it is evident that right is the object of justice.[1]

Since the notion of *jus* as the object of justice stands at the very threshold of Thomas' analysis of justice (*ST.*, 2a2ae. qq. 57-62), one cannot overlook its critical importance for everything that follows. The object of justice, the *jus* or *justum*, exists in itself, in a state of unalterable independence:

> There is something positive, which seems to consist precisely in a definite relationship with others, and not with the acting subject. If the debt is so much, that is the amount which the just man pays. The intensity of his justice is of no importance in determining the amount of his commitment. He will not have to pay more because he is more just.[2]

It is clear at the outset that two aspects characterize Thomas' understanding of justice: (a) it is an objective reality; (b) it entails a relation with another.

Jean Tonneau further provides a valuable analysis of the scope of *jus* as "the right," the object of justice. He concludes with a tightly argued syllogism:

> Right refers primarily to the things themselves. Things (as opposed to persons) are the object of right (as opposed to the subjects of right). This object can be a deed, whether voluntary or not, or an act, or an abstention, or it can be a material thing considered as the object of an act, the matter of the deed, etc. For example, if I am a seller, I consider the payment as my right. It is the proper object of justice to regulate relations with our neighbors. But right is the order of relations with our neighbors. Therefore right is the proper object of justice.[3]

It is critical to a proper understanding of St. Thomas to recall that, in his approach, human acts are specified by their end. He makes this point at the beginning of the *Prima Secundae* (1a2ae. q.1, a.3). Under the heading of "end," we can understand either the end of the work (*finis operis*) or the end of the agent (*finis operantis*). The will of the moral agent, intending an end, is adapted and proportioned, shaped and likened to the will, through the influence of the end as it is apprehended and proposed by the intellect (*finis in intentione*). Moreover, this adaptation and proportioning of the will leads to the attainment of the end (*finis in executione*).

The very existence of a just action implies an essential relationship in two orders: (a) between the end of the agent who intends to be just and the just act, (b) between the agent who acts justly and the other party to whom his just deed is due.[4]

Since our inquiry concerns the status of the relation between a master and a slave, we shall focus particularly on the kind of relation which St. Thomas understood to be present in the *dominus-servus* relationship.

When St. Thomas defines *jus*—the "just thing," the object of justice—to be an objective reality, he thereby establishes a relation between the moral agent whose end is that which is just, *justum*, and another party whose due (*debitum*) must be realized for a just order to exist. We must inquire first, whether the relation between the parties is real or only logical, and secondly, if it is real, whether it is transcendental (i.e., essential, absolute and necessary) or merely predicamental (i.e., contingent).

To sharpen our focus in examining the meaning of *jus*, we can make six observations at the threshold of definition: (1) *Jus* always points to the existence of a real relation; (2) The real relation involved is transcendental; (3) the realm of *jus* is not positive or court-made law; (4) *jus* is not a subjective power or faculty; (5) *jus* and *lex* do not have the same meaning in Thomas' usage; (6) the notion of subjective power is an *effect* of *jus*, not an element of it. Let us specify these points.

First, in the work of St. Thomas, it is always the case that *jus*, the reality of a just order, necessarily entails the existence of a real relation. In his earlier works St. Thomas takes the position that a relation is real because it is in a real category.[5] Starting, however, in his *De Potentia Dei*, he provides a far more fundamental reason—namely, a real relation exists when there is a real order.[6] It is clear from St. Thomas' reflections on the meaning of relation found in his *De Potentia* that a real relation exists whenever there is an ordering of terms in objective reality:

Now if relation had no objective reality, it would not be placed among the predicaments. Moreover, the perfection and goodness that are in things outside the mind are ascribed not only to something absolute and inherent to things but also to the order between one thing and another: thus the good of an army consists in the mutual ordering of its parts, to which good the Philosopher (*Metaph.* x) compares the good of the universe. Consequently there must be order in things themselves, and this order is a kind of relation. Wherefore there must be relations in things themselves, whereby one is ordered to another. Now one thing is ordered to another either as to quantity or as to active or passive power: for on these two counts alone can we find in a thing something whereby we compare it with another. Accordingly, things that are ordered to something must be really related to it, and this relation must be some real thing in them.[7]

Since *jus* stands for an objectively just order between at least two parties, it pertains to the order of reality and not merely intention. It thus entails the existence of real relations.

St. Thomas was conversant with Aristotle's position that the relation of a father to son is a real relation. With precision and consistency he proceeds in his commentaries on the works of Aristotle to clarify the meaning of a real relation.

Following the lead of Aristotle, St. Thomas held, as we saw, that a real relation is founded either on quantity, *actio* or *passio*. In the case of father-son and master-slave, there is a real relation, based on the accident of *actio-passio*.[8]

This explicit analogy of the relation of father-son to that of master-slave foreshadows, from a metaphysical standpoint, what is perhaps the most critical text of the Thomistic corpus on slavery, *ST*, 2a2ae. q.57, a.4, where the same analogy (father:son :: master:slave) is reiterated. We shall argue that these real relations provide the foundation for the critical analogy of *jus paternum* and *jus dominativum*.

Second, the real relation entailed by *jus* is transcendental and can only be understood against the background of the Aristotelian notion of transcendentals. Having established that the kind of relationship which the *jus* or the objectively just ordering of individuals entails is a real one, we must now press on to see whether this real relation is transcendental or merely predicamental. The distinction is important because it logically determines the nature of the real relationship of the parties. A good sketch of the transcendental relation is provided by P. Coffey:

An essential or transcendental relation is one which is involved in the very essence itself of the related thing. It enters into and is inseparable from the concept of the latter. Thus in the concept of the creature as such there is involved an essential relation of the latter's dependence on the Creator. So too, every individual reality involves essential relations of identity with itself and distinction from other things, and essential relations of truth and goodness to the Divine Mind and created minds. Knowledge involves an essential relation to a known object. Accidents involve the essential relation of an aptitude to inhere in substances. *Actio* involves an essential relation to an *agens*, and *passio* to a *patiens*; matter to form and form to matter. And so on. In general, wherever any subject has an intrinsic and essential exigence or aptitude or inclination, whereby there is established a connexion of this subject with, or a reference to, something else, an ordination or *ordo* to something else, there we have an 'essential' relation. Such a relation is termed 'transcendental' because it can be verified of a subject in any category; and, since it adds nothing real to its subject it does not of itself constitute any new category of real being.[9]

If we use this sketch of a transcendental relation as the basis for our inquiry, we quickly see that any just relation is transcendental for three fundamental reasons: (a) an ordering of persons is involved; (b) some real need or existential exigency is also involved; (c) justice is identified with truth, a transcendental concept.

Citations from St. Thomas demonstrate the existence of these three critical aspects—order, need and truth—in the virtue of justice, manifesting its character as a transcendental relation.

First, justice is intrinsically connected with order in creation: "The order of the universe demonstrates the justice of God, as the order of any kind of multitude evidences the justice of its government" (*ST*, 1a. q.21, a.1).

Second, a just relationship is intrinsically connected with the existence of a need or duty (*debitum*): "Justice alone of all the virtues implies the notion of debt" (*ST*, 1a2ae. q.99, a.5 *ad* 1).

Third, justice is in a sense equivalent to truth: "Since the will is the rational appetite, when the rectitude of reason which is called truth is imprinted on the will on account of its nearness to reason, this imprint retains the name of truth. Hence justice sometimes goes by the name of truth" (*ST*, 2a2ae. q.58, a.4 *ad* 1).

These aspects of a just relation—order, need and truth—combine to specify any truly just relationship among parties as a relation among equals, ordered to each other in a truthful manner, discharging their respective debts: "There cannot be a true 'adaequation' where there is not a true reason of justice, but only where there is some manner of justice" (*In Sent*. IV, d. 14, q.1, a. 1).

This connection of order, need and truth under the rubric of equality underscores the fact that a just relation is a transcendental relation of equality, for the *jus* entails something which is due to another individual according to a relationship of equality: "That which is just is a work which is adjusted to another person according to some kind of equality" (*ST*, 2a2ae. q.57, a. 2). That Thomas has in mind concrete transactions, and not merely an abstract relationship, is evident in the use of the term *opus*, which literally means "work": "That in our work is said to be just which responds in some way to the equality of another" (*ST*, 2a2ae. q.57, a. 1).

According to Laurent Clement, the term "work" (*opus*) in this context is best understood as "due" or "duty." Clement's insight is quite pertinent because he examines the meaning of the *jus gentium*, which will be cited as the justification for slavery.[10] In the spirit of Thomas, *jus* is never separated from *debitum*: "*ratio debiti ex quo constituitur ratio justitiae*" (*ST*, 1a2ae. q.60, a. 3 *corp*. and *ad* 1, 2, 3). Citing Isidore of Seville, Thomas holds that *jus* is so named because it is "the just," *justum* (*ST*, 2a2ae. q.57, a.1 *sed contra*). True justice—that which is specified by its object, *jus*, "the right"—has for its mission the rendering to each that which is his due according to some measure of equality.

As the object toward which a just *opus*—whether deed, act, duty, omission, etc.—is directed, the term *jus* signifies the relation of the parties to one another in a real, transcendental relationship:

> The essential character of justice consists in rendering to another his due according to equality.[11]

Jus binds together all of the constituent elements of a just relationship: (a) something due, (b) an apt subject to whom the *opus* is due, and (c) a proportion of equality which characterizes the rendering of the *debitum*.

Although *jus* can readily be perceived as the unifying focus of these elements of justice, confusion and disagreement have surrounded the term *jus* because some theologians have rendered it as "law" and others as "right." Since we will be particularly concerned with the understanding of *jus* on the part of Vitoria and Soto in the sixteenth century, it is instructive to consider the wide range of meanings attached to the term in their era. A detailed study of the Spanish authors of the *De Justitia et Jure* treatises in the sixteenth and seventeenth centuries indicates that five different meanings were attached to the term *jus*: (a) a just debt owed to someone, the object of justice; (b) *lex*, the reason and rule of justice; (c) jurisprudence, the science and art of justice; (d) the place or tribunal where justice is administered; (e) the decree of a court.[12]

Some scholars hold that there is generally no significant difference between *lex* and *jus* in St. Thomas, even though Thomas makes it clear in the first article of the first question of the *De Jure* treatise that *lex* and *jus* are quite distinct.[13]

In taking note of the Folgado study, cited *supra*, we saw that the term *jus* admitted of at least five different meanings among the Spanish theologians of the sixteenth century. Laurent Clement has catalogued more contemporary meanings attached to *jus* in a magisterial study of the *jus gentium*. Clement's study has distilled four major meanings which overlap somewhat with the five meanings presented by Folgado:

(1) a power which is possessed by a physical or moral person;

(2) an objective norm to which individual acts ought to conform (e.g., eternal law, natural law, positive law);

(3) an assortment of laws classified according to a specific category or field of interest (e.g., civil, canonical, constitutional); and finally,

(4) the science of jurisprudence.[14]

J. T. Delos has identified two extremely critical problems which underlie any attempt to define the meaning of *jus* in St. Thomas: (a) tacit presuppositions which are latent in the disciplines of the scholars making the study; (b) ambiguous or inconsistent use of the analogical nature of *jus*.

The first problem stems from the fact that the language of *jus* and *lex* is used by philosophers, jurists and theologians alike. The use of identical language does not, however, assure the acceptance of the same meaning of the terms employed:

> Some jurists who use positivism, juridic formalism, durkheimian sociology or intellectualist philosophy can apparently pose the problem in [their own] terms. In reality they do not come to terms with the underlying premises. The agreement is only verbal and the discussion quickly reveals its artificial character. The words do not have the same meaning or even content, and the inquirers do not esteem the same methods of inquiry.[15]

Delos describes the second problem of the ambiguous use of the analogical meaning of *jus*. The notion of "right," "the right thing," "just," or "the just thing"—the commonly accepted translation of *jus*—(corresponding to the Greek *dike*, or *dikaion*) is analogical. The meaning of *lex* is likewise analogical. Efforts to understand the analogical meaning of both *jus* (*droit*, *derecho*) and *lex* (*loi*, *ley*) can fail to reckon with the pluriformity of these related but distinct terms. Delos stresses that their relationship is analogical, not univocal: "These primary notions designate analogical realities, too rich in properties to be understood in the same sense.[16]

In a slightly different context, Jean Tonneau touches on the different meanings which have historically been attributed to *jus* and concludes that *jus* in the tradition of St. Thomas has both a broad and a strict meaning:

> There is, roughly, a wide meaning. Whatever is correct is right; right corresponds to all moral rectitude, to virtuous righteousness in the ensemble of behavior. This is a general conformity to the order, to the rule. In Christian language the just man and justice require perfection in all relations. Then there is a strict meaning. Virtuous rectitude specified by right is characterized by the fact that it is established in relations with others. This feature is essential and constitutive.[17]

Notwithstanding the problems of definition which flow from the presence of contrasting philosophical presuppositions, often unstated, and the analogical character of *jus* itself, we can ascertain a clearer picture of Thomas' understanding of *jus* by delineating what it is not.

Third, commentators after Thomas tended to see *jus* as simply the decree of a court or legislature. The positive law overrode and recast natural law. Thomas made it clear that he did *not* regard *jus* as the product resulting from decisions handed down by courts of law. Thomas observes that patterns of language can twist (*detorqueantur*) the meaning of terms, such as "medicine" and "law." He analogizes the change in meaning ascribed to *jus* to the change in meaning of the term "medicine." The term "medicine" was first used to describe the healing remedy and then broadened to encompass the very art of healing. Just as health is antecedent to any human effort to regain it, and antecedent to the science which is established to spread and recapture health and well-being, so *jus* or "the just," as an exterior, objective state of things which can be perceived as a reality which either exists or ought to exist, is antecedent to any effort to attain justice. Just as the physician does not create biochemical reactions *ex nihilo* but rather discovers and promotes these reactions for the benefit of a patient, so a jurist does not invent justice but seeks to discover and strengthen it in reciprocal relationships which already exist in reality. It is this objective reality which constitutes justice for Thomas.

The comparison which Thomas makes at the beginning of his treatise *De Jure* between health and the just, on the one hand, and the physician and student of justice (whether jurist or philosopher), on the other hand, is instructive for several reasons. It is noteworthy in the first place that Thomas has already used the relationship of a physician to health in the *Prima Pars* (I, q.13, a.6), making the identical point that medical science is posterior to the existence of health in the nature of people and things. In the very same article (I, q.13, a.6), he formally introduces and discusses the analogical use of terms which can be predicated both of God and creatures. We can thus observe that Thomas has the use of analogical terms in mind when he compares the role of a jurist with that of a physician. Not only does he analogize between the two professions, but it becomes clear that one must adopt an analogical framework, as distinct from a univocal or equivocal view, to understand the broad but nevertheless consistent use of *jus* which Thomas makes.

Fourth, jus is not a subjective power or faculty. In recognizing this reality, we dispose of a notion of *jus* which is inconsistent with Thomas' perspective. This is the notion of *jus* as a subjective right or moral faculty—an understanding which will predominate in the thinking of late medieval jurists and the manualist tradition.[18] We can exclude this notion of *jus* as a subjective right or moral faculty because Thomas nowhere alludes to such an understanding as a possibility. He uses *ST.* 2a2ae, q.57, a.1 to enumerate the diverse meanings of the term and does not even conceive of "subjective right" within the range of derived meanings. To express the idea of subjective power or moral faculty, Thomas uses the terms *dominium*, *licitum* and *potestas*.[19]

Fifth, jus and *lex* are distinct in his treatise *De Jure*. Having seen that *jus* is understood by Thomas to be neither the product of jurisprudence nor a subjective faculty, we can now turn to a third possible meaning which Thomas also rejects in a decisive manner. Can *jus* be considered synonymous with *lex*? Thomas makes it clear that for him *lex* is a rule or a measure. It is a work of reason, residing in the intent of the legislator. Whereas *jus* inheres in concrete realities and reciprocal relationships, *lex* emerges from the human mind as a measure or ordinance designed to foster the common good (*ST*. 1a2ae. q.94, a.1).

All just human laws are derived from "the first rule of reason," which for Thomas means natural law, and the force of all human laws flows from the natural law (1a2ae. q.95, a.2). A law is a *ratio*, an intellectual measure which can be applied to individual acts (1a2ae. q.90, a.1). Law or *lex* has as its final cause the common good of society and as its efficient cause, the reason of those primarily responsible for the conduct of society toward the common good (1a2ae. q.90, a.2). The law as an idea or *ratio* is an intentional reality which is externalized in words and texts, i.e., legislation.

In contradistinction, *jus* stands for an ordering of parties based on reason and need, a relation of equals which ordains people to each other through an adjustment or adaequation (*ad-aequare*) of their respective claims. It is not merely a logical relation, but presents an objective condition, a reality to be done. By constituting a *mensura mensurans*, *jus*, the object of justice, stands for an objective ordering among individuals in some way equal, and adapts their mutual relationships in respect of the due (*suum unicuique*) to which each individual is entitled.

St. Thomas uses a powerful image of the artistic conception vis-à-vis an artistic product to describe the relationship of *jus* and *lex*:

> In the same way that exterior works which the artist produces preexist
> in the spirit of the artist according to a certain notion which is called the
> rule of art, so the just work, which reason determines, preexists in the
> spirit according to a certain notion which is in some way the rule of

prudence. And if this preexisting conception is written, it is called *lex*, for *lex* is, according to Isidore, a 'written constitution.'[20]

We can conclude from Thomas' description of this relationship, presented in substantially the same form in the *Prima Pars* and in *ST.* 2a2ae. q.57, that *lex* is the formal extrinsic cause of *jus*.

Sixth, the notion of subjective power is an effect of a *jus*. In view of the central importance of the term *jus*, we need to look at the connection between the idea of subjective power and *jus*. Having ruled it out as a possible meaning of *jus* because of Thomas' exclusion (and not merely omission) of such a derivation in his enumeration of meanings, we must clarify what the notion of a moral faculty or subjective right, so widely used in the *De Justitia et Jure* treatises and by the manualists after Thomas, actually is and not merely state that it is distinct from *jus*. Again, L. Clement provides a vital clarification:

> It must be remarked that the moral faculty, while being an eminently correct expression, is not a right, properly speaking, i.e., the objective right of that which is due to another according to a relationship of equality, but it *proceeds as an effect or a natural consequence.* (Emphasis added)[21]

A subjective right is thus seen to be distinct from *jus*, which counts as an objective reality. Subjective rights proceed from the external reality as effects or natural consequences. Indeed the exercise of a subjective right presupposes the existence of an external reality (*objectum*) of justice, viz., a *jus* or that which is just.

We are indebted to L. Clement for showing that the exercise of a subjective right is far more dependent on reason than on right, although it presupposes the objective existence of a right. This thomistic distinction can be illustrated as follows: one has a right, *ceteris paribus*, to paint a portrait, but the exercise of the right is more immediately contingent upon reason (the talent of the artist) than upon the right or power of a citizen to engage in self-expression.

What are the elements of a just relationship? Because *jus* plays so critical a role in establishing a relation of equality among parties, we can profit from a consideration of its metaphysical meaning *qua* relation. The reflections of Jean Tonneau are both relevant and valuable, and warrant extensive citation:

> *Jus* is that ensemble of relations in which our rectitude is established in regard to others...The question is one of an order of relations...In relationship there are two aspects to consider. Like every 'accident,' the relationship *inheres*, as we say, in a subject; without this it does not exist. But this relationship is formally constituted by a 'reference,' a correspondence. We know, however, that the relationship is only presented in some predicaments that are capable of establishing a relationship by putting a subject in relation to another thing...The active and passive power, the act of doing or of suffering, naturally establishes the subject in relation to something other than himself. Other predicates (the place, the site, the when) derive from relations rather than establishing them.
>
> 1. From the existential point of view, the relation in which *jus* consists is created by the disposing act of reason, exercised under the realizing impulse of the will and the moral virtues or more precisely by the consecutive decision in the choice. If the juridical order conceived by a mind does not arrive at this degree of realization, it is as though it did not exist. It is chimerical, utopian, adorned perhaps, like the legendary dream, with the rarest qualities, but remaining in the limbo of the possible.
>
> 2. In itself, in its formal, specific reality, the relation of *jus*...includes analytically the two ideas, closely connected, of equality and *altérité* between the two equal terms at the same time that it specifies this *altérité*.[22]

We shall now examine the constituent elements of the just relationship: (a) the *debitum*, that which is due the other; (b) the subject of the *jus*, viz., the person (*ad alterum*) to whom the debitum is owed; (c) the aspect of equality which characterizes the relation.

First, something is due to another. Since Thomas defines *jus* as an *opus* (whether act, service or object) due to another according to a certain relationship of equality, we can isolate and analyze the constitutive elements of the just or "juridical relation," a phrase used by J. Delos to describe a relationship where a *jus* or *jura* are present.[23]

The idea of *jus* necessarily entails a due or *debitum*, as we saw earlier ("*Ratio debiti ex quo constituitur ratio justitiae*," *ST*. 1a2ae. q.60, a.3). The notion of a due implies immediately the existence of a need or necessity on the part of a subject: "In the word 'debt,' therefore, is implied a certain exigence or necessity of the thing to which it is directed" (*ST*. I, q.21, a. 1 *ad* 3. Elsewhere, however, Thomas seems to limit the idea of *debitum* to the moral sphere, e.g., in *De Potentia*, q.10, a. 4, *ad* 8).

The etymology of the term *debitum* can shed much light on the meaning of "due," its derivative. Philologists hold that the Latin term *debitum* comes from the verb *debere*, meaning "ought to," or "must," which is itself a composition of *dehabere*, "to have something belonging to another"—*habere* (*aliquid*) *de* (*aliquo*). In this sense a "due" is *res debita*, something that one has which belongs to another.[24]

It can be argued that the etymology of *debitum* is quite significant, in light of usage subsequent to Thomas, of the term *jus*. Thomas invariably speaks of a *jus* which exists in the objective order of things, an exterior condition or measure of reciprocal relationships. Many theologians who come after Thomas will not speak of a *jus* which exists (objective significance) but of a person who has a *jus* (subjective significance). This is especially true in regard to the distinction of *jus ad rem* and *jus in re*, which became a staple of the manualist tradition.[25]

When Thomas says that a *jus* exists, it means *eo ipso* that a *debitum* exists, or that someone "has" something belonging to another—*habere* (*aliquid*) *de* (*aliquo*). From these roots came expressions such as *habeo facere* and *habeo reddere*, viz., "I have to do something," "I have to return something." This is the essence of Thomas' meaning of *jus*: "something must be done, something must be rendered." Specifically the *suum unicuique* must be rendered. Thomas will not use *jus* in the subjective sense ("I have a right."—*habere jus*) because the meaning of *jus* already contains the verb "to have" in the inherent notion of *debitum—habere (aliquid) de (aliquo)*. The later subjective meaning ascribed to *jus* does not have the same linguistic lineage (or one could argue more strongly, justification) that the objective meaning has.

If a subject can be said to be due something, he has a need or exigency which must be fulfilled as a matter of justice. The one to whom something is due is the subject of a *jus*. The nature of the *jus* holds the measure of the content and scope of that due and establishes the parties who are subject to the *jus*, i.e., those who must render what is due.

The good reputation of an individual affords an example. Everyone is due the respect associated with a good reputation; everyone is the subject of the *jus* or objective interest of a good name. All others are obligated to render what is due, i.e., to respect and promote one's good name. The *jus* of a good reputation, its measure, is both objective and contingent. It inheres in the objective right of all individuals to a freedom from disrespect, slander and cruelty. But it is contingent on the truth: a policeman who testifies against a burglar does not violate the burglar's due of a good name. The *debitum* is contingent upon objective reality, including truth as well as charity. By committing a burglary, one drastically reduces the scope of the *debitum* of a good name to which he is entitled as a matter of justice.

Positive law must take into account the ontological character of fundamental human needs. If human legislation seeks to alter through abridgement or destruction the sphere of human needs which cause *debita* to arise, it violates the *lex aeterna* because it seeks to alter the human constitution of rational created beings in contravention of the divine providential design. Human legislation cannot ignore or violate ontological needs and still constitute a just law, since beings do not have this kind of power, according to Thomas, over the fundamental constitution of their nature (*ST*. 1a2ae. q.93, a.4). Laws which seek to regulate the activities in the moral or legal order must respect the constitution of the ontological order from which all human rights originate. Legislative enactments regulate the voluntary actions of individuals (*agere per voluntatem*) rather than their ontological character (*agere per naturam*).

While St. Thomas approves the traditional definition of justice given by Ulpian as "the constant and perpetual will to render to everyone what is his due,"(*ST*. 2a2ae. q.58, a.1), the arena or field of operation of justice is in exterior actions, which "take their species, not from the internal passions but from external things as being their objects,"(*ST*. 2a2ae. q.58, a.9 *ad* 2). The focus on external realities reinforces the point already made about justice entailing a relationship toward another. The attitude of seeking to render to each that which is due flows from the will, the seat of justice (*ST*. 2a2ae, q.58, a.4), but finds its expression in external actions. Justice has for its particular function the orientation of individuals to each other through their actions (*ST*., 2a2ae, q.57, a. 1).

The fact that the arena of justice is external actions means that the significance of those actions can be measured, and the measure is always a proportion of equality:

> The subject matter of justice, however, is an external deed insofar as the doing or employing of something is duly proportionate to another person. So therefore the mean of justice lies in a certain proportion matching or equalizing the external work to an external person... The objectively real mean of justice is also the mean of reason, and so justice keeps the character of a moral virtue.[26]

Equality holds a special place in Thomas' consideration of the virtue of justice: it is the mean of the virtue of justice (*medium justitiae*). This is very important for two reasons, one pertaining to the distinctiveness of justice as a moral virtue, and the other in regard to our specific consideration of slavery.

First, while all moral virtues strike a *medium rationis*, a balance between an extreme of excess and deficiency, only justice strikes a *medium rei*, "an equilibrium in our social environment through our outward deeds and use of things" (*ST.*, III, q.85, a. 3 *ad* 2). Thus equality is the mean of the one virtue which establishes an objective mean between persons or parties.

The second reason why the notion of equality is so important in our examination of Thomas' understanding of justice is that subsequent consideration of the meaning of *jus* tends to eviscerate the inherent emphasis on equality as the measure of the relationship between one having a *jus* and one subject to a *jus*. Emphasis upon equality as an inherent feature of justice would have been subversive of the rationale supporting slavery in the New World, which was clearly predicated upon an *unequal* status of master and slave.[27]

Since the relationship of *dominus-servus* is a priori one of unequals, the aspect of equality was lost sight of in the manualist tradition. Even when the manuals deferred to the existence of positive laws permitting and regulating slavery, granting slavery the "*vim legis*" ("force of law") of which St. Thomas speaks cautiously, they could have modified the scope of the legislation and tempered the effect of slavery by underscoring the point that any just relationship entails a relation of equality.[28]

The intrinsic connection which Thomas establishes between justice and equality applies a fortiori to *jus*, the object of justice. Insofar as justice is a virtue, it receives its modality from *jus*, its specifying object.

Thus the objective significance of *jus* as a measure of equality confirms its status as a relation between terms. *Jus* not only formally specifies the content and modalities of justice, but it also establishes a relation between terms, viz., human goods, and their possessors, individuals within the human community. This objective and relational meaning of *jus* will be seen to contrast sharply with the subjective and individualist notion of *jus* into which the thought of Thomas is recast. It remains for us to explore the kind of equality intended and the species under which it can be expressed. But before undertaking that task we must look at the subject of the *debitum*, the "other" to whom something is due.

The person or party to whom justice is directed is for St. Thomas not merely an object of justice, but in a sense, its subject. The term *jus* is always *ad alterum*. Justice is specifically ordained to the interests, needs and rights of another. This relationship of equality designates the "other" as a subject:

> It is proper to justice, as compared with the other virtues, to direct man in his relations with others: because it denotes a kind of equality, as its very name implies; indeed we are used to saying that things are adjusted when they are made equal, for equality is in reference of one thing to some other.[29]

Among all of the moral virtues only justice seeks the right ordering of relationships among individuals rather than the personal perfection of the agent (*ST.*, 2a2ae. q.57, a.1). In this sense the virtue of justice and its formal object, *jus*, are essentially altruistic. To speak of *jus* as a *debitum* means that there is someone obligated to discharge the *debitum* and someone to whom the *debitum* ("due" or *opus*) is owed. This latter party is the subject of the *jus*.

St. Thomas composed the *Secunda Secundae* in the years 1271-1272 in Paris. His *Commentary* on the *Nicomachean Ethics* of Aristotle was written in the same period.[30] It discloses his adaptation and transformation of Aristotle's notion of a mean:

> In the question of the 'mean' of virtue the transformation goes deep. While both agree that fundamentally a virtue makes a man good and makes him do his work well (*Ethics* II,6.1106a23; 2a2ae. 56.3), for Aristotle, observing a mean is of the very essence of virtue, whereas St. Thomas describes it as a property (1a2ae. 64, prologue). As a property

a mean is not a factor in the nature of the virtue itself, but rather is a relation of that nature to its existential situation.[31]

Thus the due or *debitum* specified by *jus*, the object of the virtue, is an instance of ordered equality, the mean both of reality and reason in a given setting. The meaning of justice resides in the relationship between the two persons and the "things" (whether services, objects or actions) or human goods which are instrumental to the attainment of a just relationship:

> Justice regards matters as more or less in accord with what is the mean, somewhat extrinsic as it were, but it regards two things and two persons as if intrinsic, whereby justice is in fact constituted.[32]

In his later treatise *De Jure* Thomas again holds that "justice of its nature bears a relationship to another, for something is equal to another, not to itself" (*ST.*, 2a2ae. q.58, a.2). Thomas accepts Aristotle's view that one can speak metaphorically of one's passions as diverse agents but, strictly speaking, "justice requires a diversity of persons, and accordingly it is only of one man toward another" (*ST.*, 2a2ae. q.58, a.2).

Thomas thus excludes animals or subrational creatures from being the subjects of a *jus*. A "right" is a moral entity and exists only within the moral order. It is thus the exclusive endowment of free and rational creatures. The animal, deprived of will and reason, cannot share in this prerogative, as Laurent Clement explains:

> Only the rational creature, who has universal ideas and knows the essence of things, understands right and is fully conscious of that which is due him. Having a proper and immediate end, i.e., God, the rational creature can, in the name of its liberty and dignity, claim as its own the cooperation of inferior creatures and even the activity or aid of his equals to attain his end.[33]

The exclusion of animals as possible subjects of a *jus* will be challenged in the fourteenth century by the nominalist view that all creatures exercise some sort of *dominium* in nature and are, therefore, subjects of (or have a "title" to) *jura*. This exclusion directly contradicts the notion of "animal rights," a view which again today claims some influential adherents. It is revealing that the nominalist tide which swept over the thomistic synthesis in the fourteenth century likewise believed that animals have rights. To deny that animals have rights, as Thomas manifestly does, is not to deny that human beings should treat all creation, and all creatures, with respect and charity. Thomas thus accomplishes the objectives of the "animals rights" movement without sacrificing his rigorous logical and personalist foundations. Reverence toward creation and creaturely goods is a just disposition of the soul, or virtue. To hold that animals can be subjects of *dominium* requires either that we sever it from rational conduct (which was the approach taken by slaveholders who excused unreasonable behavior on the pretext that custom or law justified an exception to reason), or that we attribute rational behavior to subhuman animals, an attribution without empirical warrant. [34]

The proposition of Thomas that only a rational creature, i.e., a person, can be the subject of a *jus* was undisputed in the debate over slavery in sixteenth-century Spain, but sharply at issue would be the rational or subrational status of the Indians of the New World. If they could be shown not to be endowed with reason and free will, they could be forced to aid the conquistadores in colonization. Thomas'clarity did not stop the coercion.

It is clear in Thomas' thought that justice and its formal object, *jus*, cannot be purely individual; justice requires that at least two persons or parties have some relationship with each other (*"non est [justitia] nisi unius hominis ad alium"* ST. 2a2ae. q.58, a. 2). It is also clear that the *jus* measures the actions or claims which constitute the instrumental goods of the persons involved. Justice pertains to realities in which the interests of people may in a sense be opposed to each other, e.g., buyer and seller. Justice orders the equitable relation of those interests by mediating (as both *medium rationis* and *medium rei*) their nature, scope and consequences upon each other.

One can by contrasting the thomistic view of the virtues of charity and justice obtain a better understanding of the focus of each virtue, as the insightful work of Jean Tonneau again demonstrates:

> Charity is fundamentally a friendship of love, and friendship achieves such a blending of two friends that my friend is another myself. I love him as if he were myself, and the good which I desire for him is 'my' good...The same cannot be said of justice. For this concerns man toward whom it is exercised essentially as by an 'other,' opposed to oneself, with an opposition which however does not imply any hostility, since one owes justice even to one's enemy. It is based upon a relationship of otherness and not of identity. Its object is the right done to others, rendered in equality. And one of the degrees of distinction between the virtues attached to justice is precisely the quality of this right: legally, it lays the foundation of the principal virtue of justice; morally, it serves as a basis for more of the 'social' virtues. Even 'religion' will be opposed to charity in its consideration of God not as the friend whose life is communicated to us, but as the Supreme Being to Whom the creature presents with fear and trembling the homages that are necessarily unequal to His infinite majesty.[35]

Love, friendship and charity produce a union and unity directly between two persons; justice produces an equilibrium which revolves around an object exterior to the persons.[36]

There is an explicit reference to slavery in Thomas' consideration of the nature of justice as *ad alterum*. It occurs in *ST*. 2a2ae. q.57.a. 4, where he analogizes the relationship of a slave and master to that of a son and his father:

> Being another can be taken in two ways. First, quite simply as being wholly distinct, as, for example, two people neither of whom is subject

to the other, though both are under the same ruler of the State. Between such lies right in the unqualified sense of the term according to Aristotle. Second, as being of another not quite simply, but as belonging in some way. Thus humanly speaking a son belongs to his father as being in a sense a part of him...and a slave belongs to his master as being his instrument, to quote the *Politics*. Accordingly the relationship of father to son is not as to one who is utterly distinct from him; on this account the right there involved in not right pure and simply, but a sort of right, namely paternal right. *A like reason holds for the dominative right between lord and servant.* (Emphasis added)[37]

This appears to be a very serious modification of the scope of *jus* brought about by the modified nature of the *alterum*—son or slave. In neither the father—son nor master—servant relationship is there said to be a *jus* "pure and simple." It is only a *sort* of right (*quoddam justum*). Thomas makes the analogy explicit by concluding that the *jus dominativum* of the master over his servant is only a *sort* of right.

It is almost impossible to overemphasize the importance of this analogy. The servant is "part of" his master (not entirely *ad alterum*) in the same way that a son is "part of" his father. A convergence of interests between the parties is present which attenuates the normal applicability of the principles of strict justice.

Even more illuminating is the comparison of the relationship of a husband and wife vis-à-vis that of the master and slave which Thomas makes in article 4 of question 57:

A wife, however, though she is part of her husband, since she is to be cherished by him as his own body, as St. Paul commands, is nevertheless *more distinct from him than a child from a parent and a slave from a master.* She is gathered into a society, that of the social life of marriage. Consequently, as Aristotle observes, the notion of right is found more fully there than it is between father and son, and master and slave. (Emphasis added)

In view of the fact that husband and wife are part of a social, and not merely a domestic relationship, they are each more fully *ad alterum* to one another than are a child to a parent and a slave to a master. In these latter relationships Thomas follows the lead of Aristotle in considering them within a domestic context, entailing a *jus oeconomicum* (*dikaion oikonomikon* or *dikaion patrikon*) rather than a *jus* in strict justice (*jus simpliciter*). Thomas thus holds that in one sense there is less of an "otherness" between master and slave (as well as parent and child) than there is between husband and wife. There is less "otherness" because in these relationships one is more a "part of" the other than one spouse is of the other. This is tantamount to saying that there is, in a sense, a greater convergence of interests on the part of master and slave than there is between husband and wife. Those interests are certainly not as intense as the interests of the marital union, but they are less distinctly different, revolving around the same exterior *opera* (human actions or possessions—*res debita*).

This illustrates again the difference between the virtues of friendship, love and charity, on the one hand (characterizing the marital relationship), which lead to a direct union and unity of two persons, and the virtue of justice, on the other hand (characterizing for Thomas the master-servant relationship), which leads to an indirect or intermediate unity, a convergence of interests relative to human goods such as actions or possessions. In none of the three relationships which Thomas analogizes is there a *jus* in the strict sense (*justum simpliciter*) present, but only a "sort" of right (*quoddam justum*).

Thomas elaborates on this distinction in *ST.*, q.57, a. 4 *ad* 2 and 3. He makes it clear that the absence of a relationship of strict justice between father and child, on the one hand, and master and slave, on the other hand, does not mean the absence of other virtues or moral imperatives:

A child precisely as such belongs to the father, and a slave precisely as such belongs to the master. All the same, each, taken as an individual human being, subsists in himself and is distinct from others. Each accordingly is an object of justice in some manner, inasumch as each is a human being. Accordingly laws (*leges*) are laid down regulating the dealings of father and child, and of master and slave. But to the extent that each belongs to another the full character of the right and just is lacking.

Because the child is "part of" his father, and a slave "part of" his master, there is lacking that *altérité* or "otherness" necessary for one to be a subject of a *jus*. It must be clearly noted that this statement does not say that a child or a slave is incapable of being or can never be the subject of a *jus*. It is far more limited and far more specific in its scope. Thomas says that a child cannot be the subject of a *jus* only on the basis of his relation with his father. But he can be the subject of a *jus* on the basis of something else, viz., his dignity as a human being: *et ideo inquantum uterque est homo, aliquo modo ad eos est justitia.*

In explicitly affirming the human dignity of the slave, Thomas likewise holds that the slave cannot be the subject of a *jus* simply on the strength of his relationship to his master, for there is lacking that *altérité* or "otherness" needed for strict justice. But a slave can be the subject of a *jus* on the basis of his human nature and the dignity attendant upon human identity.[38]

No one can logically infer that the absence of strict justice in the parent—child relationship signifies that moral imperatives are missing or that other virtues are excluded. Clearly the virtue of love describes and regulates the attitude and behavior of a parent to a child and the virtues of love and filial piety describe the attitude and behavior of the child toward the parent. To the extent that a child as a human being is an end in himself, he or she is the subject of *jura*. But the close relationship of child and parent (*aliquid alterius*) moves the context of virtues away from strict justice and into the framework of love, friendship and piety.

Similarly the slave as a human being (explicitly acknowledged by Thomas) is an end in himself and the subject of *jura*. As *aliquid alterius* vis-à-vis his master, however, his relationship will not be governed by strict justice (*adaequatione rerum*) but by virtues, such as friendship (*adaequatione quantum ad affectum*), a point that Thomas had emphasized earlier in his *Commentary on the Sentences* (III *Sent.*, d. 28, q.1, a. 6, *ad* 4).

Is the thought of Thomas incompatible with modern considerations of human rights? Several facts dispel such a charge: (a) Thomas considers the slave as a human being with legal rights, not a property right of another; (b) the analogy of the relationship of child and slave to the *paterfamilias* clearly indicates that the slave is not intended solely to promote the private good of the master but that an identity of interests and goods is envisioned; (c) since slavery is incidental to the promotion of virtue and efficiency in the domestic economy, any change in the domestic economy necessarily alters the relevance, if not justification of slavery. In short, Thomas' reflections on what he saw in the medieval system, where a *servus* or bondservant was an integral part of a household, cannot logically be extrapolated to justify a system where the domestic economy had been replaced by a modern industrial society.[39]

Any consideration of the view of Aquinas on human rights must account for his understanding of *'jus'* as always entailing a relation of equality. We have already examined equality as an aspect of the *debitum* of a just relationship; now we shall examine it as an integral aspect of the relation itself. It can be said that while *jus* represents a *mensura mensurans*, a "reality to be done," in Tonneau's phrase, equality represents a *mensura mensurata*, that which is ad-*jus*-ted between the parties by the object of justice.

The thought of Aristotle clearly discloses an understanding of justice as a kind of equality which is established in things, a balance between excess and defect, whereby the equality in things corresponds to an equality in persons:

> Since in all action there is an excess and a defect, there must also be an equity and equality. Since the equal is a milieu (between excess and

defect), *dikaion* is as a consequence a certain milieu...*Dikaion* is at the same time a milieu and an equality. Insofar as it is a milieu it is the milieu of two extremes which are the excess and defect. Insofar as it is equality, it occurs between two persons. According as it is *dikaion*, it is the right of someone.[40]

Thomas restates this view in his *Commentary on the Ethics*:

If then injustice is inequality, right (*jus*) will be equality...And since equality is a milieu between an excess and a defect, the right as a consequence will be a certain milieu.[41]

There occurs within this milieu an adjustment (*ad-aequare*) of the claims of persons so that an equality of persons accompanies the equality achieved among things. That Thomas had developed the link between justice and equality early in his work is shown by other commentaries on Book V of the *Nicomachean Ethics*.[42]

This equality of persons marks the *ad alterum* aspect of the relationship as discussed above. Justice is not proportionate to another because something is due him but, inversely, something is due the subject of the *jus* because it is somehow "equal" ("*aliquem aequalitatis modum*") to him or proportionate to a claim which is his. Justice is a perfection which accomplishes the "ad*jus*tment" of his claims and rights according to some objective measure of proportionality.

Louis Lachance concludes from his study of Thomas that equality is the raison d'être for the *jus* of justice, arguing that just as *lex* is above all else an element of reason and principle of order which serves as the basis for any commandment enacted by a legislator, so equality is the measure or standard of proportionality which serves as the basis for the *jus* in the relationship of justice.[43]

Thomas' consideration of the two quasi-integral parts of justice (in 2a2ae. q.79, a.1), viz., the pursuit of good and the avoidance of evil, which follows his treatise *De Jure*, bears out the view of Lachance that it is equality which is the foundation for the *debitum*. Thomas speaks of constituting and establishing equality as the specific task of the virtue of justice. Toward the end of his treatment of justice as a virtue(*ST.* 2a2ae, q.79, a.1 and *ad* 1), he connects special and general justice by their respective objects of establishing equality:

> It belongs to special justice to do good considered as due to one's neighbor, and to avoid the opposite evil, that, namely, which is hurtful to one's neighbor; while it belongs to general justice to do good in relation to the community or in relation to God, and to avoid the opposite evil...For it belongs to justice to establish equality in our relations with others...Now a person establishes the equality of justice by doing good, i.e. by rendering to another his due...Justice is concerned with operations and external things, wherein to establish equality is one thing, and not to disturb the equality established is another.

The parallel structure of "establishing equality" (*facere aequalitatem*) and "doing good" (*facere bonum*) stands out in bold relief. It thus appears that the *debitum* is motivated by the need for equality and ordained (i.e., ordered) to the *telos* of accomplishing equality (*facere aequalitatem*), without which the due would not be necessary. The object of justice, *jus*, must be specifically constituted by equality.

In his treatise on *jus*, Thomas speaks of "*adaequatum*," "*adaequatio*" and "*adaequantur*" six times; "*commensuratum*," and"*commensurationem*" seven times; and "*aequalitas*" six times, a total of nineteen references to equality in four articles.

In his magisterial study of *jus*, Louis Lachance moves from the position that equality constitutes the form of *jus* to the conclusion that in virtue of this connection of equality and *jus*, *jus* is essentially and specifically a relation among terms which it unites or compares:

In the word 'equality' we find the idea of relation. In saying that *jus* is an equality, we affirm at the same time that it is within the genus of relation.[44]

We have seen above that *jus* can be understood as a transcendental relation, since it necessarily entails need, order and truth. Lachance concludes similarly that *jus* is a transcendental relation, stressing in his exhaustive study that the aspect of equality provides the basis for a relation.

Lachance examines the categories of Aristotle used by St. Thomas and applies Thomas' thought to the aspect of equality in a just relationship. Following Aristotle, Thomas held that substance is the basis for relations of identity or diversity, quality the basis for relations of similarity and dissimilarity, and quantity the basis for relations of equality or inequality.[45]

According to the *Commentary on the Metaphysics*, equality is the equivalence of quantities, which means that the equality of a just relation must be based on some sort of quantity. Thomas is clear that when he speaks of the equality of a just relation that he does not intend a mathematical equality, for he speaks of some sort of equality present in the circumstances of the relationship among the parties: *aliquem aequalitatis modum*, such as, for example, an equivalence of virtue or custom (*ST.*, 2a2ae. q.57, a. 2).

One can ask whether the focus on quantity as the category which provides the foundation for the relation of equality does not in some way reduce virtues or human perfections to the level of mathematical proportion. Our inquiry quickly discloses, as Lachance demonstrates, that no such reduction occurs. By writing in this vein, Thomas is not "quantifying" intangible realities, such as, power or perfection, but is using the term "*quantitas*" in a broad and indeed analogical sense. In view of the fact that justice pertains to the realm of human activity (*agere per voluntatem*), it is clear that Thomas understands the kind of quantity involved to be moral rather than physical, metaphysical or symbolic. The relationship of equality established between two persons (or parties), moral entities, is a moral equality.

This moral equality among the parties in a just relationship has its foundation in the ontological order. Actions which occur directly in the moral sphere (*agere per voluntatem*) presuppose and are derived from the ontological identity of humanity (*agere per naturam*). We have seen that in Thomas' schema no just human legislation can contravene in the moral order what is established by the *lex aeterna* at the ontological level. The equality of the slave with his master is a pointed illustration of this. To the extent that legislation obscures or abridges that equality, to that extent it is violative of the *lex aeterna* and disruptive of the schema of moral equality which is so central to St. Thomas' conception of justice.

One of the most important features of Thomas' thought is the analogical character of "*jus*." We shall now conclude our study of *jus* by attempting to show conclusively that the term is inherently analogical in St. Thomas' theology and that any departure from that analogical usage is a departure from the fundamental ideas of St. Thomas on rights, responsibilities, freedom and human dignity.

In view of the fact that Thomas is generally careful to distinguish between the etymology of a term, i.e., its construction, and the nominal definition of a term, i.e., its application to a context (*ST*. 2a2ae, q.92, a. 1 *ad* 2), it is appropriate that he should make use of Aristotle's nominal definition of *dikaion*. He will do this in his *Commentary* on Aristotle's *Nicomachean Ethics*. We can profitably turn to a study of Aristotle's definition of *dikaion* (*jus* or *justum*) and then examine Thomas' application of it later (c. 1272) in the *Secunda Secundae*. One study has compared the aristotelian and thomistic notions of right:

According to Aristotle the thing signified by *dikaion* has been so called because it is *dike*. What people mean by *dikaion* they call by this name, because it is *dike*...[which] is an adverb meaning doubly or twofold. But as *dikaion* is a noun and not an adverb, Aristotle, to show that we should take the meaning of this adverb as if it were a noun, added in the conditional mood: 'As if we said *dikaion*, inventing and creating for a moment, just for the sake of clarity, the noun *dikaion*, which is non-existent, from the existing adverb *dike*.' Briefly, according to Aristotle the meaning of *dikaion* corresponds to that of *dike*, taken as a noun. We could translate: 'By a right we mean something twofold or equally divided, as if we said equal or just.'[46]

Louis Lachance applies the nominal definition of Aristotle to the thought of Aquinas:

This word [*dikaion*] contains two things: first it implies a relation; for a thing is not said to be just in relation to itself but in comparison to something else to which it is related[...]In the second place, the fact that *dikaion* is a derivative of *dike* reveals that the object measured from which it springs is an intermediary. The word *dike* is an adverb which indicates the idea of sharing. A sharing is at least between two. As such, remarks Aristotle, the word means the measure of that which one shares between several, the attribution to each of that which responds to his conditions. Thus one sees that in its original meaning the word (*jus*) meant a demarcation, among several terms, of that which is just, a balancing in the collective relations, in service of a goal.[47]

In the *ST*, toward the end of q.58 (a. 11), Thomas incorporates the constitutive elements of a relationship of justice in a formal definition of justice as the virtue of rendering to each that which is his due. These elements are placed in a framework which highlights the proportion of equality that exists between the parties in the juridical relationship:

The subject matter of justice is what we outwardly do, according as the doing or the thing we employ is proportionate to the other person who lays claim to our justice. Now each person's own is that which is due to him in proportion to making things even. That is why the proper activity of justice is none other than to render to each his own.

We have seen that the due (*debitum*) which is "each person's own" (his *suum*) always occurs within an order of need or necessity to which it is ordained (*ST.*, 1a. q.21, a. 1 *ad* 3). By making explicit the sense of the argument which Thomas has constructed, we can establish that for him the due or *debitum* is that which is "each person's own" or *suum*, which is ordained toward another (*ad alterum*) according to a relation of equality determined by the objective order of need. In his earlier cited work, Zammit puts this schematically as follows: *Debitum* = "*suum*" = *ordinatio* = *relatio secundum esse* = *ordo exigentiae*.[48]

It is clear that the relation of equality present in the just relationship is not a formal or absolute equality based on the identity of the parties (i.e. not *simpliciter*) but is contingent upon the order of need which exists between the parties (i.e. *secundum ordinem exigentiae*) for its identity.

Zammit offers an example to illustrate his understanding of the relation of equality. A sick person summons a doctor who prescribes an appropriate dosage of tablets, according to the need of the patient. In considering the four parties or variables present—the doctor, the patient, the medicine or tablets, and the dosage—Zammit concludes that only the dosage stands for the *jus*:

> Right is not represented by the tablets, but by the dose or quantity or measure of them. This dose corresponds to the need of the patient, and hence it may be called equal, adequate or commensurate to him, i.e. to his need. When the patient adequates [sic] his action to that dose, by taking the quantity of tablets prescribed, he is said to be equal or adjusted to his measure.[49]

This example illustrates the proportion of equality which characterizes not only the thing in question (*res debita*) but the relation between the parties themselves. The dosage is "equal" or "adequate" (*ad-aequare*) to the needs of the patient in the same way that the doctor who prescribed the medication is "equal" or "adequate" to the claim of the patient to medical treatment. The "equality" of the doctor to the patient in this example is not based on income or medical ability or even a shared human dignity but emerges from (and is proportional to) the "equality" or adequacy of the medicine prescribed. The doctor is equal to the patient's needs in proportion to the "adequacy" (i.e. correct choice plus exact dosage) of the medicine.

This proportion of equality is made explicit by Thomas in his discussion of distributive justice. This is extremely important for our inquiry on the subject of slavery, since the end of distributive justice is the common good of society, the same *telos* used by Thomas to justify slavery under certain conditions. A complete look at Thomas' precise wording in the second article of question 61 is in order:

> The virtuous mean is taken in distributive justice, not according to an equality between thing and thing, but according to a proportion between things and persons, and in such a way that even as one person exceeds another so also that which is meted out to him exceeds that which is meted out to the other. Accordingly Aristotle describes the mean here as being 'according to geometric proportionality,' in which *the even balance or equality lies in a comparative relation, not in a fixed quantity.* (Emphasis added)

In a study devoted to the implications and distinctions of general and particular justice, P.D. Dognin schematizes relations as follows: *persona/persona = res/res*: things are related to each other in a manner analogous to the relationship that people have toward each other. Distributive justice has for its task the reproduction in things of the relation of equality found in the objective order of personal relationships.[50]

Although a difference of opinion exists among thomistic scholars as to the *kind* of relation of equality which exists in a just relationship (i.e., what we have called a "juridical relationship"), the language of St. Thomas is quite explicit on the point that a proportion of equality characterizes distributive justice, the sphere of our inquiry pertinent to the question of slavery (cf. ST. 2a2ae.61).[51]

This proportion of equality entails a relationship both of persons and things and can be summarized by the schema of P.D. Dognin cited above: person:person :: thing:thing. When we schematize the relationship in this manner we recognize the classic form of an analogy of proper proportionality. At the conclusion of our study we will analyze the scope and content of this analogy of proper proportionality in detail. At this point we intend only to advert to its existence. The existence of a *jus* entails necessarily the existence of an analogy of proper proportionality between the parties involved in the relation.

2. The Meaning of the *Jus Gentium*

A leading authority on the meaning of law and right in St. Thomas has written that the Angelic Doctor did not leave us with a very precise idea of what he intended by the *jus gentium*. In modern terminology the *jus gentium* is considered to be synonymous with international public law, but a study of the sources used and comments made by St. Thomas makes it clear that "not only does St. Thomas not attach this meaning to it, [but] he makes appeal...to a classification which can only perplex modern minds."[52]

Dating back to the period of classical antiquity, the concept of *jus gentium* has been considerably modified by jurists, philosophers, theologians and diplomats. G. Del Vecchio, a jurist of this century, has identified the roots of the *jus gentium* as a fusion of Roman experience with Greek philosophy:

> At first, the Romans did not perceive the *jus gentium* to be superior to
> the civil law, but rather to be a brute and elementary law. The study
> of Greek philosophy made them reassess in this simplicity of links the

meaning of nature, the reflection of the natural law. From this point on they discovered an element of superiority. The *jus gentium* was considered as an expression of primordial exigencies common to all people, as the most direct disclosure of universal reason. They understood the *jus gentium* as a positive law common to all peoples, '*quasi quo jure omnes gentes utuntur.*' Thus a fact of experience acquired little by little a philosophical significance, completing the trichotomy: natural law—universal, identical, perpetual; jus gentium—common elements found in the diverse positive laws; civil law—having particularities, which are only the subsequent determinations of its precedents.[53]

The Romans considered the *jus gentium*, the law of the peoples, to be universal in scope, yet having elements in the positive laws of all peoples. This seemingly contrary aspect of the jus gentium—universal because found in all societies, but particular because it is found in specific enactments of positive law—led different commentators to emphasize either its universal scope or particular application as they might prefer.

The broadest possible construction of the *jus gentium* would be to identify it with the *jus naturale*. Del Vecchio dismisses any such attempt to equate the *jus gentium* with the *jus naturale* as unwarranted in view of its historical development:

The *jus gentium* is often confused with the *jus naturale*. But the first is an essentially Roman concept, born of the historic experience of the Romans; the second is a concept proper to Greek philosophy. The two certainly tend to meet and sometimes even appear to coincide. *Nevertheless they have a different meaning, and sometimes are opposed*, so that it is not possible to accept the thesis that they are at bottom one and the same thing.[54] (Emphasis added)

Del Vecchio goes on to identify one issue on which the *jus naturale* and the *jus gentium* were in sharp opposition—slavery. We will examine this clash from the standpoint of Thomas' understanding of the factors involved.

Writing in the second century, the Roman jurist Gaius (c. 150-180) reflected the widespread view of Roman jurisprudence that the *jus gentium* is that body of law proper to the human species—*humani generis proprium*. He termed it "that which natural reason has established among all men, equally observed by all, and called the law of peoples, which all peoples use."[55]

It is clear that Gaius holds the *jus gentium* to be far more than simply the enactments of positive law. His position is much more universalist. Although he neither differentiates between the *jus naturale* and the *jus gentium* nor endeavors to identify them, he adopts the position that the *jus gentium* is a natural law specifically human: *jus naturale humani generis proprium*.

Gaius will enjoy the distinction of having his definition of the *jus gentium* quoted verbatim in the *Institutes*, a systematized manual of "edicts, rescripts and imperial constitutions," which were commissioned in the sixth century by the Emperor Justinian. The *Institutes* were recovered in the twelfth century and had a profound influence upon canonical and theological reflection both in the thirteenth and sixteenth centuries.

Moreover Gaius will be cited explicitly by Thomas in his most complete treatment of the *jus gentium* in ST. 2a2ae. q.57, a.3. Thomas uses twice the phrase *naturalis ratio* which Gaius employs in lieu of *lex naturalis*. We shall see that perhaps the most distinguished thomistic scholar to study the question, Dom Odon Lottin, OSB, believed that Thomas subtly indicated his preference for the position of Gaius that the *jus gentium* is the natural law (or *naturalis ratio*) common to the human species. This view is in contrast to that of Ulpian and Isidore of Seville, as we shall see. Both Ulpian and Isidore are cited by Thomas in the same text but there is evidence to suggest that Thomas was not satisfied with the position of either.

Writing almost a century after Gaius, Domitius Ulpianus (d. 228) furnished a definition of the natural law which would become famous: natural law is that which nature taught all animals.[56]   While the *jus naturale* is that which nature taught all animals, both human and subhuman, it is unclear in Ulpian whether the *jus gentium* is part of the *jus naturale* or an addition to it.   T. Gilby notes:

> If...Ulpian's description of natural law was allowed, namely that it is what nature teaches all animals, then the *Jus Gentium* represented rational additions to natural law to meet the stresses of social life more or less everywhere; these, when accepted by the State, became part of the *Jus Civile*.[57]

Although Ulpian explicitly distinguishes the *jus gentium* from the *jus naturale*, and is alone among the Roman jurists in so doing, he does not explain the nature of their relationship.   He does express accord with the view of Gaius that only humans participate in the *jus gentium* and uses nearly identical language to make this point.   The language is so close that Ulpian might run afoul of charges of plagiarism: Gaius states, "...*vocaturque jus gentium, quasi quo jure omnes gentes utuntur*," while Ulpian holds, "*Jus gentium est quo gentes humanae utuntur*..."

Here we confront a problem.   By extending the scope of the *jus naturale* to the subhuman species of the animal kingdom, a position accepted by Thomas in his treatise on law (*ST.* 1a2ae, q.95, a. 4, *ad* 1), Ulpian effectively distances the *jus gentium* from the *jus naturale* so much so that the *jus gentium* implicitly becomes aligned with positive law, viz., regulations specifically enacted by human legislatures.   It is far from clear that St. Thomas will accept this implied reduction in scope of the *jus gentium*, a matter that we will soon examine.[58]

The positions of Gaius and Ulpian can be summarized in the following propositions: (a) Both agree that the *jus gentium* is restricted to human beings; (b) Ulpian holds that the *jus naturale* is common to all members of the animal kingdom and explicitly contrasts it with the *jus gentium*; (c) Gaius does not indicate his view of the scope of the *jus naturale*, nor does he contrast it with the *jus gentium*, but makes an implied contrast between the *jus civile*, the law enacted by a specific populace or city, and the *jus gentium*, which is common to all cities and populaces; (d) Instead of using the term "natural law," Gaius will use the term *naturalis ratio* to describe the underlying basis of the *jus gentium*.

Next, we turn to the *Institutes* of Justinian. Compiled in the sixth century as an effort by Emperor Justinian to systematize the body of laws in existence at the time, the *Institutes* were largely fashioned from the extant writings of classical jurists, such as Ulpian and, in particular, Gaius. The *Digest*, a compilation of classical sources, appeared in 533 and the revised *Code* of Justinian was published a year later. Together with the *Novels*, or new legislation written mostly in Greek, these sources combined to form the *Corpus Juris Civilis*, the distillation of classsical jurisprudential wisdom for the Middle Ages.

The *Institutes* drew from both Gaius and Ulpian to canonize or codify a tripartite division of law—*jus naturale*, *jus civile*, and *jus gentium*.[59] This tripartite division was highly regarded in the Middle Ages. Its definition of the jus naturale—"what nature taught all animals"—reflects Ulpian's lasting influence, while it presents the *jus gentium* in the sense of Gaius ("*Jus autem gentium omni humano generi commune est...*").

When we note that the verbatim passages from Gaius and Ulpian are merely juxtaposed without explanation, it becomes apparent that the value of the *Institutes* does not inhere in analytical precision or rigorous classification. Its purpose was rather to provide a compendium and summary of sources.

The *Institutes* make no effort to distinguish the *jus naturale*, *jus civile* and *jus gentium* one from another. The starting point for the Roman jurists was always the *jus naturale*; the scope and meaning of the *jus civile* and *jus gentium* were examined in light of their relationship with the *jus naturale*. It is significant, in the view of Dom Odon Lottin, that the *jus gentium* is explicitly distinguished from the *jus civile*. He believes that this was done by the compiler to enhance the status of the *jus gentium* by elevating it beyond the level of positive law (i.e., *jus civile*) and thereby suggesting a comparison of it with the *jus naturale*.[60]

On the other hand, the *Institutes* omit Ulpian's statement that the *jus gentium* flows out of the natural law ("*a naturali jure recedit*"). This omission seems to place the *jus gentium* closer on the spectrum to the civil law than the natural law. In any event, the status of the *jus gentium* remains unclear. At least it will never be considered apart from the *jus naturale* and *jus civile*. Its importance is assumed, if not clearly delineated.

Another aspect of the *Institutes* which is critical to our study is its unambiguous statement that slavery, though a feature of the *jus gentium*, violates the natural law: "according to the natural law, all men were born free from the beginning." From this point on those who would justify the existence of slavery in any form are compelled to acknowledge the weight of the *Institutes* in taking the position that such an institution runs afoul of the natural law. The linkage established in the *Institutes* between slavery and captivity in war will be maintained by the Christian tradition (e.g., St. Gregory the Great in his *Moralia in Job*) which is willing to discern a benign intent in lifetime servitude following capture as a lesser penalty than death at the hands of the victor in war.

The tripartite division of laws is now firmly established, and the task of distinguishing the scope and relationship of each of these is left to subsequent commentators.

A new phase begins when St. Augustine (354-430) turns his attention to the *jus gentium* and slavery. Although Augustine did not endeavor to distinguish the three kinds of law which would be codified in the *Institutes*, a study of his writings in the light of the *Institutes* indicates that for him the *jus naturale* and *jus gentium* are equivalent. Two maxims summarize the content of the two laws: do to others as you would have done to yourself, and render to each (God, neighbor and oneself) that which is due.[61]

Noted for his elaborate etymological definitions was Isidore of Seville (c. 560-636). Clever linguistic turns did not, however, assure accurate transmission of definitions. The *jus gentium* moves from the province of the history of laws and enters the lexicon of medieval canonical and theological discussion with its appearance in the Isidore's *Etymologies*. Gilby notes that his twenty books of *Etymologies* are extremely important as "the main encyclopedia of classical learning for the Middle Ages."[62] The actual etymologies of Isidore are largely whimsical, but it is through the *Etymologies* that the classical jurists are transmitted to the currents of medieval theology. Gosselin goes so far as to say that Christianity was introduced to Roman law through the *Etymologies*.[63]

Isidore maintained the tripartite division of law found in the *Institutes* but moved away from Ulpian's notion of a *jus* common to men and animals. For Isidore there were two species of law, divine (*fas*) and human (*jus*). The former governs nature, whereas *jus*, which he terms *lex humana*, regulates human conduct.[64] Gosselin describes Isidore's differentiation as follows:

> Natural law is a law universal and instinctive, without any conventions; civil law is a law particular and conventional; the law of the peoples is a law general and conventional.[65]

Isidore follows far more closely the legacy of Gaius than Ulpian when he restricts his consideration to human law and rejects the idea of a law common to humans and beasts (*Etymologies* V, 4. PL 82, 199). However, he borrows the concept of commonality from Ulpian and applies it to the *jus naturale* in a much different meaning: "the natural law is that which is common to all *nations*." By substituting "nations" for "animals," Isidore can accentuate the universality of the natural law among rational creatures and construct a slight distinction between the natural law and the *jus gentium*: the latter is common among most, but not all peoples.

He describes the natural law as originating through inclination rather than convention, whereas the civil law stems from the conventions adopted by each city or populace. There is no clear distinction between the *jus naturale* and the *jus gentium*. The only difference cited is that the natural law is universal, existing among all peoples, while the *jus gentium* is *nearly* universal, existing among *almost* all peoples.[66]

It did not escape Thomas' notice, as we shall see, that the Archbishop of Seville abandoned Ulpian's position on the natural law, substituting "nations" for "animals" to stress at once its universality and rational character. In his first *ex professo* treatment of the *jus gentium* in the *Summa* (la2ae. q.95, a.4), Thomas will consider Isidore's division of laws and incorporate Ulpian's definition of the natural law in his reply to make the point that the *jus gentium*, the result of *naturalis ratio* (the contribution of Gaius), is proper only to humans.

There is only one other theologian before Thomas who demonstrates any real interest in the notion of the *jus gentium*, Alexander of Hales (1175-1245). His *Summa Theologiae* established a triple division of the *jus naturae—nativum, humanum, divinum*.

The *jus naturale humanum* designates that which encompasses only human actions; it is restricted to the rational creature and appears to be equivalent to the *jus gentium*. The *jus naturale nativum* designates the natural law common to humans and beasts, a legacy of Ulpian, and the *jus naturale divinum* regulates the points of contact between human nature and divine grace.[67]

Laurent Clement notes in a lengthy study of the *jus gentium* that Alexander of Hales affords a much clearer notion of the concept than did any of his predecessors. Alexander was able to reconcile the apparent divergences of the classical Roman jurists and Isidore of Seville. The close connection that he establishes between the natural law properly human and the *jus gentium* indicates that the concept has become settled in that meaning since the sixth century when Isidore of Seville wrote.[68]

The codification of the *jus gentium* will be complete in Gratian's *Decretum* (12th century). In 1141, Gratian, a Camaldolese monk, compiled a systematic classification of the extant church law of the West. This was entitled the *Decretum* or *Concordantia Discordantium Canonum*, qualifying the author as the Father of Canon Law and ushering in a new era of Christian jurisprudence.[69] The *Decretum* earned for Gratian a prestige comparable to the *Sentences* of Peter Lombard.

The opening lines of the *Decretum* are both famous and succinct:

> Mankind is ruled by two laws, nature and custom. Natural law is that contained in the Scriptures and the Gospel.[70]

Paul Van Overbeke points out that this definition, notwithstanding its fame, errs by confusing the natural law with the divine positive law.[71] By contrasting the *jus naturale* with *mores*, Gratian injects still another ambiguity into an already unclear situation.

L. Clement underscores the point that Gratian limited himself to the texts available in the *Etymologies* of Isidore of Seville. The significance of this resides in the fact that later medieval use by theologians of Roman concepts of law will be dependent upon sources and editorial judgments supplied by Isidore. Clement argues that the reader must at least accept as a distinct possibility the penetration of classical Roman law by the early scholastic mediation of canon law.[72]

We are now ready to trace chronologically the development of St. Thomas' understanding of the *jus gentium*. We begin with his *Commentary on the Sentences* (*In IV Sent*. d.33, q.1, a.1, *ad* 4). The first explicit consideration which Thomas gives to definitions of the natural law occurs in this text around 1256. Thomas does not refer explicitly to the *jus gentium* but links the natural law with divine law and specifies that "in the strictest sense" the *jus naturale* originates by way of divine law from an inherent force or motion which is common both to rational and irrational creatures.[73]

Dom Odon Lottin observes, in assessing this passage, that Thomas in no way wishes to withdraw mastery over human tendencies from the realm of reason. Rather, he intends to show that the natural law transcends, without contradicting, the dominion of human reason. Thomas is clear that law, as law, is always a work of reason. He holds that natural law, in the strictest sense, always pertains to reason. His consistent view that natural law pertains to human intelligence, rather than blind instincts, distinguishes him sharply from Ulpian, even when he cites Ulpian's famous definition.[74]

Thomas argues that if natural law is understood in its restricted meaning, it is concerned not with all matters that *naturalis ratio* grasps with reference to possible human action, but only with those matters which are common to man and other animals. But in the body of the article he insists that natural law is a *naturalis conceptio*, a reference of reason.

It seems that we can conclude two things from this passage, and indeed, from this stage of Thomas' thought: (a) very strictly speaking, those principles or premises which require the effort of human reason in order to exist can be distinguished from the natural law, which is a power ("*innata vis*"), inherent in nature, broader in scope than the operation of human reason; (b) principles or determinations which are the product of human reason, even if they do not pertain, strictly speaking, to natural law do nevertheless belong to a species of *jus* proper to the human arena. This is what might be termed a foreshadowing of Thomas' final position in his treatise *De Justitia*, viz., the *jus gentium* as that aspect of the natural law which is specific to humanity.

The next passage in the *Commentary on the Sentences* that requires our attention occurs in Book IV d. 36, q.1, a.2 (1256). We saw in the text just cited that Thomas anticipates a definition of the *jus gentium* that will draw from both Gaius and Ulpian. In this text he refers to the institution of slavery as a feature of the *jus positivum*:

> Since the *jus positivum*...proceeds from the *jus naturale*, servitude, which is of the *jus positivum*, cannot prejudice that which is of the natural law, e.g., ...the appetite to conserve the species through generation.

Later in the same commentary (*ad 2*) Thomas says that slavery is opposed to the natural law in its strictest sense (its "first intention"). We can discern from these observations of Thomas that he does not understand servitude to be a condition which affects the *servus* in all dimensions of life; it is a relative rather than an absolute state.[75]

In the sixth century, the *Institutes* of Justinian stated that slavery violated the natural law. The recognition of this contradiction perdured into the thirteenth century. Thomas ascribes the existence of slavery to the operation of the *jus positivum*, but left unexplained is the nature of the relationship between the *jus naturale* and *jus positivum* which would apparently permit such a divergence. It is clear that the *jus naturale, jus gentium* and *jus positivum* are related, each to the other, but the nature of that relationship is far from clear.

Having examined these two critical commentaries on Lombard's *Sentences*, we now turn to his later commentary on Aristotle's *Politics*, specifically *In I Politicorum, liber* I, *lectio* 4 (1268). In this text Thomas confronts the view of Aristotle that slavery is a natural condition of mankind, in which it is expedient that the more gifted have the right to control and direct the less gifted:

> 'To serve' and 'slave' can be taken in two different ways. In one sense it can be according to natural aptitude; in another sense it can mean a slave or one serving as a result of a law enacted by men. It is clear that there must be a certain promulgation of the law, as in the case of those who are victors in war, whence the vanquished are called slaves of the ones who prevailed against them. Nearly all people follow this law, whence it is called the *jus gentium*. (Emphasis added)

Paul Van Overbeke observes that this understanding of the *jus gentium* as a *promulgatio legis* seems quite different from Thomas' sense of the *jus gentium* in the *Summa* (2a2ae. q.57, a.3 ad 3), where he states that the *jus gentium* does not require any special enactment (as would a provision of *jus positivum*) since its determinations come directly from natural reason.[76] Once again the language of Gaius is used verbatim (*"jure omnes gentes utuntur."*)

Now we are prepared to consider Thomas' mature thought in the *Summa*, specifically 1a2ae. q.95, a.4 (1269-70-71). St. Thomas' first consideration of the *jus gentium* in the *Summa* occurs in his treatise *De Legibus*. In q.95, a.4, his classic considertion of the natural law, he addresses the question of whether Isidore of Seville has logically divided human laws. Thomas was intimately familiar with the fact that Isidore had juxtaposed two classifications in the *Etymologies*. On the one hand he had divided law into two categories, human and divine ("*Omnes leges aut divinae sunt aut humanae*"). In this dichotomy natural law became strongly aligned with divine law. In addition, Isidore retained the tripartite division of the *Institutes*: "*jus aut naturale aut civile aut gentium*."[77]

Thomas faces the objection which arises from Isidore's own language: how can he classify the *jus gentium* among *leges humanae* when the definitions he has furnished of the *jus gentium* ("*quo omnes fere gentes utuntur*") and the *jus naturale* ("*quod commune est omnium gentium*"), which is so closely aligned to divine law, are practically identical? We shall see that in his later *Commentary on the Nicomachean Ethics*, Thomas will closely connect the *jus gentium* with the *jus naturae*.

Lottin writes that Thomas faces the question "resolutely...in order to maintain the prestige of a received authority." The "*sed contra*" given by Thomas is pointedly concise: "*auctoritas Isidori sufficiat*."[78]

Thomas has already laid the groundwork for his resolution of this thorny problem in article 2. He distinguished there between a "conclusion" which is derived from premises, and a "determination" which is more remote from a premise or a precept than is a conclusion. Gilby believes this understanding of "determination" to be crucial:

A *determinatio* here is a form defined rather by choice than intellectual necessity. This is a key-passage in the history of State theory, and an early recognition by a social philosopher that pure legality and politics have their own proper interests which cannot be explicated in terms of individual and social morality.[79]

"Determinations" are thus choices made by legislators to implement premises which flow from the natural law. These determinations or choices are not necessary inferences, as would be conclusions drawn from the principles of natural law. Reasonable people can disagree on the choices to be made.

Thomas applies his distinction of q.95, a.2 to a concrete example:

> To apply: some commands are drawn like conclusions from natural law, for instance, 'You must not commit murder' can be inferred from 'You must do harm to nobody.' Others, however, are based like constructions (*'per modum determinationis'*) on natural law, which, for instance, pronounces that crime has to be punished without deciding whether this or that should be the penalty; the punishment settled is like a determinate form given to natural law.

It is thus the province of a legislature to choose the kind of punishment best suited to a crime. Such a choice amounts to a "construction" or "determination," upon which there can be real disagreement. This kind of decision stands in contrast to the proposition that criminal behavior ought to be punished, a conclusion from the first principles of the natural law and a necessary inference from the governing premise (viz., "evil should be avoided").

There is no doubt that the *jus positivum* controls the "determinations" or "constructions" illustrated above. But the question remains, does the *jus gentium* fit in this second category (determinations by legislative bodies... i.e. positive law), or does it belong in the first category with the "conclusions," i.e., necessary inferences of the natural law?

Thomas answers this question in q.95, a.4, placing the *jus gentium* as a concept with the natural law, but he implicitly classifies it with positive law. He is at least conceptually consistent with his earlier alignment of the *jus gentium* with the natural law in his commentary on Aristotle's *Ethics*:

> First of all, to depend on natural law is of the essence of human law, as has appeared; on this account positive law and justice are divided into the *jus gentium* and the civil law, and according to the two processes of derivation from natural law explained in [article 2]. Those precepts belong to the *jus gentium* which are drawn like conclusions from the premises of natural law, such as those requiring justice in buying and selling and so forth, without which men cannot live sociably together; this last is a condition of natural law, since, as is shown in the *Politics*, man is by nature a sociable animal. Constructions, however, put upon natural law are proper to civil law, and here each political community decides for itself what is fitting.

By showing that all human laws are derived from the natural law through these "two processes of derivation," Thomas has established the line of demarcation between a logical conclusion derived from the natural law—category I, one might say—and determinations or constructions not logically inferred but rather prudentially chosen by lawmakers to implement principles of the natural law—category II, as it were, or positive law.

Now in *ad* 1 Thomas makes a further distinction. He states that features of the *jus gentium* are derived from the natural law "by means of a conclusion which is not very remote from the principles" (of the natural law):

> The *jus gentium* is indeed in a certain manner natural to man, insofar as he is rational and insofar as it is derived from the natural law by a sort of conclusion, which is not very remote from precepts, whence men may readily agree on it...

By writing "*per modum conclusionis*," Thomas appears to qualify the nature of the provision of the *jus gentium*. It is not a conclusion per se, nor a direct deduction. Rather, a provision of the *jus gentium* is "like" a conclusion or "in the manner" of a conclusion.

L. Clement points out that this nuance appears in every discussion by Thomas of the *jus gentium*. Wherever he analyzes the provisions of the *jus gentium*, Thomas is careful not to reduce them to the level of "determinations" of the positive law but is equally careful to qualify the nature of the conclusion by showing that the process of derivation leads only to a "quasi-conclusion." Thomas' language bears out this nuance discerned by Clement: *"quasi* conclusio..." (*In Ethic.* V lect. 12, n. 1023), *"sicut* conclusiones ex principiis..."(q.95, a.4), *"per modum* conclusionis..."(95.4 ad 1).[80]

Clement also points out in this section that for Thomas the provisions of the *jus gentium* were proximate to the natural law because they were implicitly contained in the natural law. But these provisions could only be "quasi-conclusions" because the content of the major and minor premise of the relevant syllogism (or, perhaps more accurately, enthymeme) are different. The content of the major premise is the natural law (e.g., good is to be pursued) but the content of the minor premise is the social condition of the time (e.g., contracts are to be honored; however, the social milieu provides the specific meaning and context of a contract).

As quasi-conclusions, the provisions of the *jus gentium* would have only a relative value and constitute a moral but not ontological necessity. Subject to the exceptions and concrete modifications called for by a plurality of people and circumstances, the force and weight of these quasi-conclusions of the *jus gentium* would be limited by the social contingencies in which they occurred. Thomas clearly recognized this in article 2, *ad* 3 of question 95:

> Owing to the great variety of human affairs the common principles of natural law do not apply stiffly to every case.

We can conclude that provisions or features of the *jus gentium*, though weightier than positive law, apply only *ut in pluribus*.

In his usual style St. Thomas modifies the views of predecessors by scrupulously identifying their positions prior to reformulating the issues in a manner that allows him to accentuate the point that to him matters most. Dom Odon Lottin remarks that the *Commentary on the Nicomachean Ethics* (namely, *In V Ethicorum, lect.* 12, written around 1271-1272) furnished Thomas with the opportunity of comparing the tripartite classification of Roman law enshrined in the *Institutes* (viz., *jus naturale, jus gentium* and *jus civile*) with the classification used by Aristotle.[81] Aristotle held in Book V of the *Nicomachean Ethics* that there are two classes of law which govern citizens, the *jus naturale* and the *jus legale*. In his commentary (Edition Pirotta, n. 1019) Thomas will make it clear that in the classification of Aristotle the *jus gentium* belongs to the *jus naturale*, not the *jus civile* (i.e. civil or positive):

> It must however be considered that *jus naturale* is that to which a man is inclined by nature... The jurists however call only that *jus naturale* which is consequent on an inclination of nature common to men and to other animals, as the conjunction of man and woman, the education of children, and other things of this sort. That *jus* however which is consequent upon an inclination proper to human nature, insofar as man is a rational animal, the jurists call *jus gentium*, since all nations use it, e.g. *pacta sint servanda*, and that ambassadors are safe between enemies, and other things of this sort. *Both of which however are comprehended under the jus naturale, as the term is used by the Philosopher*. (Emphasis added)

In his exhaustive study of Thomas' understanding of the natural law, Lottin traces the argument which Thomas employs to link the *jus gentium* with the *jus naturale*, in accord with Aristotle. I shall paraphrase Lottin's study.

First, one must distinguish the *jus naturale* from the *jus civile*. This can be done by analyzing the order of theoretical knowledge. We can identify two species of judgment: (a) those known naturally—first principles and immediate corollaries; (b) determinations reached through reasoning—conclusions more or less remote from first principles. The same division applies to our practical knowledge: the ordinary grasp of fundamental certainty is different from a reflective analysis of its elements.

An example of the first species of judgment, viz., first principles naturally known, is the precept "it is necessary to avoid evil." An immediate corollary of this first principle or primary precept is "it is necessary to avoid stealing." These principles belong in the realm of the natural law.

Examples of the second species of judgment, viz., determinations arrived at through sound human reasoning, are provided by rules of conduct elaborated by legislators. Illustrations cited by Thomas are fidelity to contracts and the safety of ambassadors from belligerent countries. Thomas thus concludes that the *justum legale* of Aristotle is identical to the *jus civile* of the Roman jurists.

To ascertain whether the *jus gentium* of the Romans is attached to the *justum naturale* or the *justum legale*, Thomas argues as follows (in Lottin's summary):

Man...has a double nature: one which is common to him and the animals; the other which is proper to him as a rational being. The jurists reserve the name of *jus naturae* to that which regulates the tendencies which man shares with the animal kingdom, e.g. the union of the sexes and the education of offspring. To designate that which regulates the specifically rational life of man, these same jurists employ the term *jus gentium*, since these norms of action are the property of the human species, such as fidelity to contracts and the respect due to ambassadors from belligerent nations. The double law of the Roman jurists, *jus naturae* and the *jus gentium*, the Angelic Doctor continues, is contained within the *iustum naturale* of Aristotle.[82]

Overbeke concludes from his study of this passage that the *jus gentium* can be taken, according to Thomas, in both a broad sense and a restrictive sense. Considered in the broad sense, i.e., from the standpoint that its prescriptions are *uniquely* the result of natural reasoning, the *jus gentium* is part of the natural law. Considered in the strict sense, i.e., viewed as a body of humanly prescribed laws, the *jus gentium* can be understood as positive law.[83]

In referring to the "Roman jurists" in the cited passage from his *Commentary on the Nicomachean Ethics*, Thomas obviously alludes to Ulpian as the source of the view that the natural law is that which is common to man and other animals. He is careful, as Lottin emphasizes, not to attribute this position to Isidore who, as we saw, ignored in effect Ulpian's formulation in the *Etymologies*. Nevertheless, the two illustrations provided by Thomas of the jus gentium—fidelity to contracts and the safety of ambassadors from belligerent countries—come directly from the *Etymologies* of Isidore.

Lottin further remarks that while the favor accorded the Roman jurists by Thomas in general is apparent, his willingness to grant the *jus gentium* a prominence above mere positive law is due in particular to his acceptance of the view of the *Institutes*. Lottin construes the specific reference to the *jus gentium* in the *Institutes*, in contradistinction both to the *jus naturale* and the *jus civile* to indicate that the intent of the redactor of the *Institutes* was to highlight the importance of the *jus gentium*. He accomplished this, Lottin theorizes, by distinguishing it from the *jus civile*, which corresponds roughly with positive law, and thereby elevating it to an implicit comparison with natural law, the premier instance of *jus humanum*. Lottin believes that Thomas correctly drew this inference and acted on the implied suggestion by linking the *jus gentium* in explicit terms with the natural law.

The language of Thomas later in the same commentary bears out the interpretation of Lottin that Thomas is inclined to link the *jus gentium* with the *jus naturale* and thereby enhance its status as a product of human reason and not merely as a body of laws. In his *Commentary* (Edition Pirotta, n. 1023) Thomas definitively connects the *jus gentium* with the *jus naturale* when he holds that a quasi-conclusion of the *jus gentium* is as well a precept of the natural law: "*Necesse est quod,*

quidquid ex justo naturali sequitur quasi conclusio, sit justum naturale."
The phrase *"quasi conclusio"* will reappear in Thomas' first
consideration of the *jus gentium* in the *Summa* (1a2ae. q.95, a.4). It will
further strengthen the position of Lottin, Overbeke, Clement, et al., that
Thomas wishes to grant the *jus gentium* a prominence not accorded
positive law per se.

Our final analysis brings us to the classic consideration of law in the
Summa, 2a2ae. q.57, a.3, most likely written around the same time as
Thomas' *Commentary* on Book V of the *Nicomachean Ethics*, 1271-72.
In his treatise *De Justitia*, Thomas returns to the question of *ST*. la2ae.
q.95, a. 4: should the *jus gentium* be considered as identical with the *jus
naturale*? If the *jus gentium* is common to all men, in the words of
Ulpian, would it not embody the universality of the natural law?
Moreover, in view of the fact that representatives of all of the nations did
not meet to ratify what is generally considered the *jus gentium*, it could
not be considered as positive law; it must therefore be of the natural law.

Thomas responds by observing that an institution can be considered
part of the natural law in two different ways. Since *jus* always entails an
adaptation or "adjustment" to something else, whatever is of the natural
law entails an adjustment to another thing. This "ad-*jus*tment"
necessarily entails a modality. Thomas observes that something can be
considered abstractly or absolutely in itself. This is the primary mode
of the natural law, common to men and animals. Thomas again cites
Ulpian as the authority for and proponent of the commonality of natural
law among rational and irrational creatures.

But he goes on to cite Gaius also, to the effect that the function of
natural reason among all peoples constitutes the *jus gentium*, which
corresponds to a secondary mode of the natural law. From the
standpoint of this secondary mode, something is considered not abstractly
or absolutely in its own terms, but rather according to the consequences
or relative conditions involved, such as the good pursued or the end
desired.

Thomas then furnishes an example of the two modes of natural law in operation. A study of the primary mode of the natural law discloses that a union of the sexes for the preservation of the species is common to all creatures, rational and irrational. A study of the secondary mode of the natural law, which requires the application of reason to a problem, indicates that private property is a legitimate and potentially beneficial arrangement for the use of goods. But private property is not relevant to the relation of irrational creatures and goods because they cannot bring to bear the component of reason which dictates that a particular field belongs to one and not another.

By weaving together the perspectives of the jurisconsults Ulpian and Gaius, Thomas is able to confirm the opinion of Isidore that the *jus gentium* is to be distinguished from the *jus naturale*. His answer is that the *jus gentium* is distinct from the primary mode of the *jus naturale*. But he is also consistent with his own position expressed in his commentary on the *Ethics* that the *jus gentium*, understood in a broad sense, is identifiable with the *jus naturale*, viz., in its secondary mode of adaptation. His citation of Gaius on *ratio naturalis* enables him essentially to designate the *jus gentium* as the natural law specifically human.

Dom Odon Lottin expresses a profound admiration for the manner in which Thomas can defend the opinion of Isidore, whose *Etymologies* were highly regarded in the contemporary setting, and yet subtly indicate a preference for the clarity of the Roman jurists:

Have we seen the skillful escape which is hidden under this last path of the saintly doctor? He acted to save the authority of Isidore; it has become normal to interpret Isidore through him. He tried moreover to defend Isidore against himself, for there were texts of the same author which he had failed to reconcile. It is to a notion outside of Isidore, to the definition of the Roman Ulpian, which St. Thomas resorts to when he must, in order to save Isidore, by finding a difference between the *jus naturale* and the *jus gentium*. But this same facility will lay the foundation for the thought of Thomas, namely, his secret sympathies for the formulas of the Roman law. He did not find in the explanation of Isidore the requisite clarity to remove the obscurity which the same text of the author had created. The lapidary definitions of the Roman jurisconsults furnished him with the desired response.[84]

Lottin observes that ST. 1a2ae. q.95, a.4 is "clearly apologetic," for "desiring to defend the classification of Isidore, Thomas orients his argument toward the isidorean conclusion: the *jus gentium* becomes part of the *jus humanum* and is distinct from the *jus naturae*." In contrast, the approach of 2a2ae. q.57, a.3 is relatively "unencumbered."

In a judgment very much compatible with Lottin's view, Louis Clement concludes his study of the *jus gentium* by holding that the *jus gentium* is a species of law which participates in the nature of both natural and positive law. As a "quasi-deduction of evident principles of synderesis," the *jus gentium* participates both in the natural law and the positive law. It is smaller in scope than the natural law for it requires the application of the discursive activity of human intelligence to a particular social context. Unlike positive law, the *jus gentium* results neither from private agreements nor from the authority of a human legislator.[85]

But the *jus gentium* unites quasi-syllogisms, which derive ultimately from the natural law, with the initiative of human reason operating in a social context. It can claim neither the universality nor immutability associated with the natural law, a limitation evidenced by the issue of slavery. Changing social patterns require a re-examination of the "quasi-deductions" arrived at in an earlier period. The bringing to bear of the *ratio naturalis*, posited by Gaius and underscored by Aquinas, upon social problems is indispensable in Thomas' understanding of the *jus gentium*. Nor does natural reason operate independent of the virtues. On the contrary, as Thomas notes in his very last statement on the meaning of the *jus gentium*, its precepts are dictated by the close interaction and combination of natural reason and equity (*ad* 3 of q.57, a.3). It remains to be seen whether considerations of equity receive due weight in subsequent readings of the *jus gentium* on the subject of slavery.

3. Repugnance of Slavery to the Natural Law

Even though St. Thomas was unacquainted with the harsh slavery of the New World which confronted Vitoria and Soto in the sixteenth century, there is ample evidence that he was disposed to point out the inherent or inchoate opposition between the natural law and *servitus*, whether the relatively benign, medieval form akin to serfdom, or the virulent embodiment of it based on race. An examination of several texts from the *Summa* readily demonstrates this.

First, let us consider 1a. q.96, a. 4. While the next section will consider in depth Thomas' understanding of dominion, we can simply note here, in his threshold consideration of human dominion in the *Summa*, that Thomas identifies two kinds of dominion, one designed to advance the interest of the master, the other a general rule over subordinates. This distinction builds upon his *Commentary on the Sentences* (d.44, q.1 and 3), where Thomas has already characterized these two classes of dominion as despotic (*ad dominandum*) and for the sake of government (*ad regimen ordinatus*). Because the subject of the first kind of dominion, which Thomas has already called "despotic," must surrender to the master the good that is naturally and of right his own, this kind of relationship is inherently grievous and punitive (*contristabile...poena*).[86]

Second, we turn to 1a2ae. q.2, a.4, *ad* 3. At the beginning of his treatise on the return of the rational creature to God, even before he begins his consideration of human acts, Thomas inquires about the ultimate happiness of man. In asking whether it consists in power, in view of the fact that men naturally flee servitude, the antithesis of power, he answers that servitude is opposed to the good use of power, for which reason it is naturally to be avoided. Thomas notes that the highest good is not to be found in human power, pointedly contradicting any putative analogy between divine power and the power of a ruler or master.

Third, we examine *ST*. 1a2ae. q.94, a. 5, *ad* 3, the *locus classicus* of Thomas' natural law approach. In his consideration of the natural law, Thomas links slavery with private property as a product or "contrivance" of human reason designed to effect a greater utility in social relationships, and not a consequence of the natural law. *Servitus* represents an "addition" to the natural law rather than a violation. Despite the suggestion of this text of an apparent indifference between the precepts of the natural law and slavery, the overall topic of *ad* 3 is the scope of imperatives enjoined by the natural law. Two such imperatives cited in the objection are that injury must not be done to another and that universal liberty is of the natural law. The "addition" of servitude would only make sense if it could be shown to eschew injury, allow for universal liberty and increase general patterns of well-being among all involved. The hypothesis thus constructed is clearly at odds with the reality of slavery after Columbus' voyage to the New World.

Fourth, we turn again to *ST*. 2a2ae. q.57, a. 3, *ad* 3. In his last consideration of the *jus gentium*, unencumbered by the need to defend statements by Isidore of Seville on the relatonship between the *jus gentium* and the *jus naturale*, Thomas asserts that servitude is not natural according to the primary mode of operation of the natural law. He also observes that there is no natural justification for one man rather than another being a subject, thus removing any possible justification for slavery based on race or religion. Moreover, it must be predicated on a usefulness to the subject, insofar as he is aided by the addition of wiser counsel from another. This sharpens the focus on human well-being sketched in the earlier text (*ST*. 1a2ae. q.94, a. 5, ad 3).

Fifth, we turn to ST. 2a2ae. q.104, a. 5, where Thomas quotes from the *De Beneficiis* of Seneca, while probing the scope of obedience, to the effect that servitude does not entail a total subjection to the master: the mind of the slave is exempt from the coercive power of slavery. Thomas amplifies Seneca's observation by holding that in all matters which pertain to the integrity of the human will, the subject is obligated only to obey God, not human beings. In matters which pertain to the nature of the body (e.g., physical health and the generation of children), all people are equal. A subject is not obligated to obey a human superior in any matter where these goods would be violated by the command of the superior.

Further, in external actions where the obedience of the subject is justly expected, the standard of judgment is right reason, not authority or power. The subject is compared to a soldier obeying an officer and a child obeying a parent.

The implicit comparison of a *dominus—servus* relation with a *pater—filius* and *dux—miles* relationship indicates that Thomas does not view a *servus* as a pariah but one whose relations and rights are constituted within an overall social fabric.

The context of *servitus* is clarified by the implicit analogy of proper proportionality which is rendered by the relationships of *pater—filius* and *dux-miles*: master: slave :: father: son :: leader: soldier. These analogous relationships are governed by the exercise of *naturalis ratio*, viz., human understanding of and participation in the *lex aeterna*.

4. *Dominium* and Slavery in St. Thomas

In question 7, article 10, ad 4, of his *De Potentia Dei*, St. Thomas inquires whether there is a real relation between God and His creatures from the standpoint of God, i.e., whether God is really related to creation. He begins by examining the argument that since God is *Dominus* of creation, He must be really related to creatures:

Terms that are predicated of God properly and not metaphorically indicate the thing signified as being in God; and among terms of this kind Dionysius (*Div. Nom.* i) reckons *Dominus*. Wherefore the thing signified by this word *Dominus* is really in God. But it is a relation to the creature. Therefore...the Creator is really related to the creature.[87]

In his response to the argument that he has constructed, Thomas indicates that God is truly Lord or *Dominus* of all creation but, unlike other *dominii*, does not have a real relation with His subjects:

The denomination *dominus* comprises three things in signification: namely, first, power to compel subjects; secondly, arising from that power, relation to those subjects; thirdly, a relation in those subjects to their lord, since one relative implies the other. Accordingly the term *dominus* retains its meaning in God as regards the first and third, but not the second. Hence Ambrose (*De Fide* i, I) says that this name *dominus* is a name of power, and Boethius says that dominion is the power of compelling slaves.[88]

In an earlier question in the *De Potentia*, Thomas provides his reasoning for the view that God cannot have a real relation with creatures. Thomas argues in article 7 of question 7 that the relation of God, Uncreated Being, to being precludes a real relation with creatures, created beings:

God's relation to being is different from that of any creatures; for he is his own being, which cannot be said of any creature. Therefore being cannot be predicated univocally of God and a creature. Therefore neither can any of the other predicables be predicated univocally of God and a creature, even the first of the predicables, *Esse*.

In the next article at *ad* 6, Thomas underscores the sovereignty of God by comparing His relation to creatures to that of a builder vis-à-vis a house:

God's existence does not depend on creatures as neither does the builder's existence depend on the house: wherefore just as it is accidental to the builder that the house exists, so it is accidental to God that the creature exists...Anything without which a thing can exist is accidental to it.

Nevertheless, he continues, the simplicity of God gives rise to an infinite number of relations in a pattern of extensive causality:

The more simple a thing is, the greater the number of its concomitant relations: since its power is so much the less limited and consequently its causality so much the more extended...From God's supreme simplicity there results an infinite number of respects or relations between creatures and Him, inasmuch as He produced creatures distinct from Himself and yet somewhat like Him.

The fact that God is not in the same genus as the creature does not preclude a real relation between the creature and God. This real relation is, however, analogical rather than univocal as he notes in the *ad 2* of article 8:

Although God is not in the same genus as the creature as a thing contained in a genus, He is nevertheless in every genus as the principle of the genus: and for this reason there can be relation between the creature and God as between effect and principle.

Thomas summarizes his views expressed in *De Potentia* on the relations between God and His creatures in q.7, a.10:

Relations whereby we refer God to creatures are not really in God. Since a real relation consists in the order of one thing to another, a real relation is mutual in those things alone wherein on either side there is the same reason for mutual order...The action of God is His substance and is wholly outside the genus of created being whereby the creature is related to Him. There is no real relation in God to creatures, although creatures are really related to Him as effects to their cause.[89]

When we turn to his later texts, such as question 13, art. 7 of the *Prima Pars*, Thomas again links the dominion of God with the category of relation:

Some relative words signify simply a relationship, others signify that on account of which there is a relationship. Thus 'lord' says nothing more about a lord except that he stands in some relationship. To be a lord precisely is to be related to a servant--the same is true of words like 'father' and 'son' and so forth. Other relative words, however, such as 'motor' and 'moved,' 'head' and 'being headed,' signify something on account of which there is a relationship. Some of the words we use of God are of the first kind and some of the second. 'Lord' for instance signifies nothing but a relation to creatures, though it presupposes something about what He is, for He could not be lord without his power which is his essence.

Consistent with his position in the *De Potentia*, Thomas holds further in article 7 that there is a relation between God and his creatures, and that the relation of God as *dominus* to his creatures is logical rather than real:

God is related to creatures insofar as creatures are related to him. Since the relation of subjection to God is really in the creature, God is really Lord. It is the relationship of lordship in him that is supplied by our minds, not the fact of his being the Lord.

In God the only relations that are real are those that constitute the Persons of the Trinity. He reiterates this position later in the *Prima Pars* in q.28, a. 1.

It is clear that the creature's relation as a subject is one of total dependency upon the power of God, which is identical to His being, and antecedent to His relationality with creation. God has plenary and principal dominion in respect to every creature. All creatures are subject totally to the power of God (ST. 2a2ae. q.103, a. 3).

The question now arises, do creatures share in the supreme and plenary dominion of God, and if so, in what manner? Thomas answers in the *De Potentia* that rational creatures do exercise dominion over their acts; this means that both angels and humans have this capacity. His position is consistently expressed in his various works that only rational creatures have the capacity to exercise dominion (*De Potentia Dei*, q.9, a. 1 *ad* 3; III *Summa Contra Gentiles* 111; *ST*. 1a1ae. q.1, a. 1, *ad* 2). The importance of the concept of dominion to Thomas is shown by its inclusion in the first article of the first question of the *Summa*.

At the very beginning of his treatise on human acts (*ST*. 1a2ae. q.1, a.1), Thomas states that creatures exercise a sovereignty or dominion over their actions through the power of intellect and will. A little later in his consideration on human acts (*ST*. 1a2ae. q.109, a. 2 *ad* 1), he underscores the dependency of the creature upon the causality of God even in the exercise of this dominion in his treatise on grace:

> Man is master [*dominus*] of his acts and of his willing or not willing, because of his deliberate reason, which can be bent to one side or another. And although he is master of his deliberating or not deliberating, yet this can only be by a previous deliberation; and since it cannot go on to infinity, we must come at length to this, that man's free will is moved by an extrinsic principle, which is above the human mind, to wit by God...Hence the mind of man still unweakened is not so much master of its act that it does not need to be moved by God, and much more the free will of man weakened by sin, whereby it is hindered from good by the corruption of the nature.

That this exercise of rational creatures is a participation in the divine sovereignty is made explicit in Thomas' analysis of the names attributed to the orders of angels in his treatise on the divine government. He considers the three meanings of "domination" proposed by Boethius as attributes of God: (1) a freedom from servile conditions; (2) a rigid supremacy which does not accede to servile acts; (3) a desire for and participation in the true dominion which belongs to God. In q.108, a. 5 *ad* 2, Thomas uses this third meaning of Boethius to underscore the themes of divine efficient causality and human participation in divine life as exemplars of the authentic existence and exercise of dominion:

> Similarly the name of each order signifies the participation in what belongs to God, as the name "Virtues" signifies the participation in the Divine virtue.

Because the meaning of human dominion is contingent upon God as its ultimate exemplary cause, divine efficient causality is necessarily entailed in the participation of human dominion in the perfection of divine dominion. The resemblance of human dominion to divine dominion depends upon the efficient action of the Creator, Who, as agent, produces effects which resemble, though deficiently, Himself and His dominion.[90]

Thomas expands upon the resemblance of the creature to God and creaturely participation in the divine perfection in question 7 of *De Potentia*. In article 7, *ad* 2, he explains why the participation must be analogical, i.e., why the divine perfection is the analogical (exemplary and efficient) cause of the creaturely exercise of the quality or relation:

> The likeness of the creature to God falls short of univocal likeness in two respects. First it does not arise from the participation of one form, as two hot things are alike by participation in one heat: because what is affirmed of God and creatures is predicated of him essentially, but of creatures, by participation. A creature's likeness to God is as that of a hot thing to heat, not of a hot thing to one that is hotter. Second, because of the form in which the creature participates falls short of the thing which is God, just as the heat of fire falls short of the nature of the sun's power whereby it produces heat.

In a comprehensive study of Thomas' use of analogy, George Klubertanz has identified the texts of the thomistic corpus which pertain to the analogy of participation between God and creatures. Klubertanz notes that this species of participation always entails causal participation, i.e., effects participate in the perfection of the Creator.[91]

The study of Klubertanz indicates that the thomistic texts which deal with analogical participation fall into three different categories. The first category, comprising early texts, rejects as unsuitable any participation between God and creatures which is not analogical. The second category simply speaks of the relationship between God and creatures as one of participation without elaborating on the kind of participation involved or the specific meaning of the term. This second category is not, Klubertanz notes, very helpful in determining the nature of thomistic participation. The third category of texts, coming from the middle and late periods, describes the analogy of participation "between God and creatures as centering around an analogous perfection which God possesses by his essence (or, substance) and which creatures possess by participation."[92]

Because the concept of human dominion will loom very large in the justifications for slavery considered by both Vitoria and Soto, we will now cite representative texts from the three categories described by Klubertanz so that the analogical character of dominion in Thomas might be placed in sharp relief.

The early texts which comprise the first category reject any logical or univocal participation in the divine perfection:

The Creator and his creature are reducible to a community not of univocation but of analogy. Such a community may be of two types. Either some things participate in some one perfection according to a relation of priority and posteriority (as do potency and act in the intelligibility of being, and substance and accident in like manner), or *one thing receives its being and intelligibility from the other. The analogy of the creature to its Creator is of this latter type.*[93] (Emphasis added)

The participation of the creature in the divine perfection of *dominium* is a participation not in any perfection independent of God but ultimately in the divine being:

> Agreement can be of two kinds. Two things may participate in some one perfection; this type of agreement *cannot* obtain between the Creator and his creature...Or one thing may exist simply and another participate in that thing's likeness as far as it can...Such is the agreement of the creature with God.[94] (Emphasis added)

Finally Thomas rejects explicitly the notion that God somehow resembles the creature by a common sharing in a perfection independent of the divine goodness:

> The creature is not said to be similar to God as though God participated in the same form which the creature shared. Rather, the reason is that God is the very form substantially, while the creature participates in this form through a kind of imitation.[95]

The second category of texts does not elaborate on the kind of participation present. In view of the fact that most of these texts come from Thomas' later writings, one can plausibly infer that such elaboration is not present because it has already occurred in the earlier writings. Klubertanz cites q.23 of the *Secunda Secundae* as representative of this second category. It is valuable in our study for making the point that human dominion, like human goodness or virtue, is nothing other than a participation in the divine perfection, so that its proper exercise must be analogous to the exercise of divine dominion:

The goodness by which we are formally good is a certain participation of the divine goodness, and the wisdom by which we are formally wise is a certain participation of the divine wisdom.[96]

In the third category of texts grouped by Klubertanz, the analogy of participation revolves around perfections possessed by God essentially and by the creatures through participation:

Because that which exists in God is perfect but is found in other things through a certain deficient participation, the participation which grounds the similitude belongs to God simply, not to the creature.[97]

Klubertanz concludes this section of his study as follows:

The texts in this third group come closest to summarizing the thomistic analogy of participation between God and creatures; God, the first efficient and exemplary cause of all creatures and their ultimate goal, possesses being, goodness, and similar perfections by His very essence, in a most perfect manner, as identical with that essence and with each other; creatures, the effects of God's causality, participate or share in an imperfect manner in such analogous perfections, and so that these perfections are distinct from each other, because they are received in the creatures' potencies.[98]

5. Authentic Dominion Excludes Slavery:

From his earliest writings, Thomas distinguished two classes of dominion.[99] In his *Commentary* on Book II of the *Sentences* (d.44, q.1), Thomas inquires whether there was dominion (*praelatio, seu dominium*) in the state of innocence. He begins his discussion by citing a passage from the *Moralia* of Gregory the Great which was well-known in the medieval era for its forthright affirmation of the equality of all rational creatures.[100] In addition to Gregory's passage on equality, he cites

Augustine's *City of God* on the proposition that all human beings are created in God's image and therefore equal.[101] He also cites the *Ethics* of Aristotle to the effect that a need exists in a society for rulers and leaders and laws to direct the community toward virtuous behavior.

In his solution, Thomas begins by distinguishing two modes of rule: one is for the sake of government (*ad regimen ordinatus*), whereas the other is for the sake of domination (*ad dominandum*). Citing the *Ethics* of Aristotle as his authority, Thomas asserts that a tyrant differs from a king in that the tyrant exercises dominion for his own purpose (*ad utilitatem propriam*), while a king governs for the good of his people.

Thomas then (d. 44, q.1, *ad* 3) draws the obvious analogy. The first mode of dominion (*ad regimen ordinatus*) corresponds with the rule of the king, whose primary intention is the good of his subjects. The second mode of dominion (*ad dominandum*) corresponds with the rule of a tyrant, whose primary concern is his own advantage (*proprium bonum*).

Thomas next asserts that a rational creature cannot be subordinated to another man in such a way that the creature becomes merely a means to the other creature considered as an end:

Insofar as he is a truly integral being (*de se*), the rational creature is not ordained to another as an end. But if this should occur, it will only exist insofar as man is similar to irrational creatures on account of sin.

Thomas concludes that there could not have been the tyrannical domination of one man over another in creation before sin. Following the introduction of sin in creation, man could be subordinated to another man's purpose in the manner of an irrational creature made to serve the needs of a master. The comparison of a subject (*servus*) to an irrational creature, cited above, is qualified, however, by the imagery of a servant as a "living organ," a phrase he takes from Aristotle's *Ethics*. The growth of the creature, weakened by the presence of sin, is to be facilitated by a rational ordination to a human end.

Thomas' view on the two modes of dominion or authority has been summarized as follows:

> The authority of domination could therefore exist in the state of innocence only over creatures made to subserve human purposes, not over other men; for men are not made to serve human ends. This subjection comes about only in so far as their condition is assimilated, as a consequence of sin, to that of irrational creatures. Only the authority of ruling men in their own interests could have belonged to man in his creational integrity.[102]

Having distinguished the two modes of *dominium*, Thomas then identifies three functions (*usus*) of the only kind of dominion, the one "ordained for the sake of government," which could have existed in creation in the state of natural integrity. The first function is the direction of subjects in whatever actions need to be done. The second is the supplying of certain needs, such as defense of a people against foes, while the third function is the correction of morals, "so that the wicked may be coerced to perform the actions of virtue" by the threat of punishment.

Thomas responds to the objections posited at the beginning by saying that although all men were created equal, this equality did not extend to natural perfections, in which they differ, but only to their freedom, insofar as each creature is *sui causa*.

The conclusion of question 3, article 3 is a clear statement that a subject cannot be related to a master as a means to an end:

> One man is not by nature ordained to another man as to an end. Therefore there was not (in the state of original justice) the second manner of dominion which removed the liberty of subjects. But there could have been the first manner of dominion, which does not grant privilege to the free since the subordinate are not ordered to the good of the greater, but, on the contrary, the rule of the greater is ordered

to the good of the subordinate. Hence they appropriately call them
servos.

In summary, the kind of dominion exercised by a legitimate ruler is
ordained to the good of the subjects. The meaning of *servus* includes the
notion of being "preserved" as well as being subordinate. The good of
the *servus* is always a consideration.

Just as there are two kinds of dominion, so there are two kinds of
subjection, as our examination of the *Summa*, la. q.92, a. 1, *ad* 2 will
make plain.

St. Thomas enunciates an important distinction in regard to the kinds
of *subjectio* which exist in creation in q.92, a.1. He distinguishes in
article 2 between servile subjection or slavery, on the one hand, and
"economic" (translated in the Blackfriars' edition as "domestic") or civil
subjection, on the other hand:

> Subjection is of two kinds; one is that of slavery, in which the ruler
> manages the subject for his own advantage, and this sort of subjection
> came in after sin. But the other kind of subjection is domestic or civil,
> in which the ruler manages his subjects for *their* advantage and benefit.
> And this sort of subjection would have obtained even before sin. For
> the human group would have lacked the benefit of order had some of
> its members not been governed by others who were wiser. Such is the
> subjection in which woman is by nature subordinate to man, because the
> power of rational discernment is stronger in man. Nor is inequality
> among men incompatible with the state of innocence, as we shall see
> later on. (Emphasis added)

In distinguishing servile subjection from civil or economic subjection,
it appears that St. Thomas continues to weave together two strands of
thought, namely, Augustine's view that slavery is a consequence of sin
(*propter peccatum; poena peccati*), on the one hand, and Aristotle's
view, on the other hand, that slavery is a natural device for the strong

and the wise to direct the weak and the dull in the fulfillment of social harmony.

The key to the distinction is Thomas' approach to the consequences of sin upon creation. The condition of inequality which existed in the state of innocence pertained to differences in regard to sex, age, mental, moral and physical qualities (*ST*. 1a. q.96, a.3). Some creatures were more intelligent, more attractive and more just than others. These differences were not caused by sin and, as we saw above in *In II Sent.* d.44, q.1, Thomas notes that Augustine did not understand the creation of all individuals in the image of God to mean that all had equal perfections. The onset of sin, distinguishing the integrity of original justice from the vulnerability of infralapsarian man, is the critical fulcrum in the understanding of both dominion and subjection for Thomas as well as Augustine, whose influence he clearly demonstrates.

Thomas became familiar with the thought of Aristotle in regard to the natural inequality of creatures and his concomitant view that slavery is a natural institution in which the more intelligent direct the less intelligent in his commentaries on the *Ethics* and the *Politics*.

Thomas reveals clearly both his familiarity and agreement with the thought of Augustine in Book Nineteen of Augustine's *De Civitate Dei*. The strong similarity in views on modes of dominion between St. Augustine and St. Thomas makes it clear that Thomas' thought at this point was primarily influenced by Augustine's *City of God*, Book XIX, dealing with the introduction of slavery into creation as a consequence of sin, along with suffering, pain and death. The structure of this section of the *Prima Pars* bears out the confluence of Aristotelian and Augustinian thought, as R.A. Markus demonstrates in his earlier cited work. The focus is on the difference between the condition of supralapsarian man, the state of innocence, and infralapsarian man, the human condition after original sin.

Such a focal point would flow more strongly from Augustine's reflections on slavery in Book XIX of the *Civitas Dei—servitus propter peccatum*—rather than Book I of Aristotle's *Politics*, in which no comparable discussion of sin is found, but where the focus is on the relation of the wiser to the slower.

When we turn to q.96, a. 4 of the *Prima Pars* of the *Summa*, we see the influence of Augustine. Referring his reader to q.96, a.3 for his earlier discussion of the differences in physical, moral and intellectual qualities present in creatures before the fall (q.92, a.1), Thomas cites Book XIX of the *City of God* at the beginning and end of this article, the first comprehensive treatment of human dominion in the *Summa*. In considering whether men would have dominated other men in the state of innocence, Thomas begins by citing Augustine on the proposition that rational creatures, created in God's image, were intended only to dominate irrational creatures. Thomas responds to this point by arguing that it applies only to dominion understood as domination of another for personal advantage (the *ad dominandum* of *In II Sent*. d.44, q.1) rather than dominion for the sake of government (the *ad regimen ordinatus* of *In II Sent*. d.44, q.l).[103]

Because of its importance in setting forth the mature thought of Thomas on human dominion in respect to slavery, we shall present nearly all of the reply of q.96, a.4:

Dominion can be taken in two ways; first, as opposed to servitude, and in this sense we call someone a lord who has someone else subjected to him as a slave. Secondly dominion can be taken as relative to any sort of subjection in general, and in this sense even the man who has the office of governing and directing free men can be called a lord. If it is taken then in the first way, man did not dominate other men in the state of innocence. But if it is meant in the second sense, he could have done so.

Here is the reason; the difference between a slave and a free man is that "a free man is because of himself," as it says at the beginning of the *Metaphysics*; whereas a slave is geared to the benefit of another. So someone dominates another as a slave when he simply uses him for his own, that is, the lord's, purposes. And because everyone naturally values his own good, and consequently finds it grievous to surrender entirely to another the good that ought to be his own, it follows that dominion of this kind cannot but be punitive to those subjected to it. For this reason man cannot have dominated other men in the state of innocence in that sort of way.

But someone dominates another as a free man when he is directing him to his own, the free man's, proper good, or to the common good. And such domination of one man by another would have existed in the state of innocence for two reasons. First, because man is naturally a social animal, and so men in the state of innocence would have lived in social groups. But many people cannot live a social life together unless someone is in charge to look after the common good. For many, left to themselves, are concerned with many things, one with only one...Second, because if one man greatly surpassed another in knowledge and justice, it would be all wrong if he did not perform this function (of being principal or director) for the benefit of others.[104]

It is clear that Thomas has built upon the foundation established in *In II Sent*. d.44, qq.1 and 3 in distinguishing two kinds of dominion and in concluding that despotic dominion, ordered solely toward the personal good of the master, could not have existed in the state of original justice. The second kind of dominion, ordered toward the common good, does not have the "punitive" character of despotic dominion; on the contrary, its purpose is greater social utility for the particular benefit of creatures lacking in mental and physical perfections.

We can now with Thomas recognize the connection between authentic dominion and natural law in the classic text of the *Summa*, 2a2ae. q.10, a. 10. This text is not only important for an understanding of Thomas' thought; it was often cited by antagonists of slavery in the Spanish debates of the sixteenth century. Thomas addresses the question of whether infidels may have "authority or dominion" (*praelationem seu dominium*) over the faithful.

In his response Thomas distinguishes between dominion established as a new condition, that is, for the first time, over believers, and the dominion of unbelievers which already exists in the social order. The former, he holds, is a stumbling block to the free practice of the faith and should not on that account be permitted.

But his conclusion is different when the dominion in question is a pre-existing authority of unbelievers over believers. He classifies this sort of dominion as an institution of human, not divine law:

> Secondly, we may consider dominion or authority when it is already an established fact. Then we should bear in mind that it is an institution of human law, whereas the distinction between the faithful and infidels is by divine law. Now divine law, which is from grace, does not do away with human law, which is from natural reason. *Consequently the distinction between the faithful and infidels, considered in itself, does not cancel the dominion or authority of infidels over the faithful.* (Emphasis added)

Thomas goes on to state that the church has the authority under some circumstances to take this right away from unbelievers, e.g., in cases where the rights of believers to worship God are abused or abridged.

When the question arose in the sixteenth century about the propriety or legitimacy ("title") of the Indians of the New World exercising authority and ownership within their community, the text of *ST*. 2a2ae. q.10, a. 10 became the foundation of those such as Las Casas who found Spanish slavery to be reprehensible and intolerable: *Jus autem divinum, quod est ex gratia, non tollit jus humanum, quod est ex naturali ratione*.[105]

Thus it is Thomas' position that dominion can be exercised by all rational creatures, and not merely believers. Considered as a political institution, dominion is the product of natural reason and human law. It is neither a consequence of grace nor an imperative of divine law. The *norma normans* which Thomas held out to measure the validity or appropriateness of dominion as a political institution is natural reason, the identical norm, along with equity, proposed for implementing the *jus gentium* in the *ST*. 2a2ae. q.57 a.3, *ad* 3.

The role played by 2a2ae. q.10, a. 10 in the Spanish debate on slavery in the *siglo de oro* was supplemented by a cross-reference to another text from the *Summa* which sheds light on Thomas' position on the effects of sin upon man's natural powers. In considering whether generation of the species in the state of innocence would have been by copulation or other means in *ST*. 1a. q.98, a. 2, Thomas holds that "everything that is natural to man is neither withdrawn from nor given to him by sin."

This text, and the argumentation underlying it, was used to rebut the argument that the the Indians of the New World lost their right to dominion through actions of fornication and homosexuality, a claim raised by proponents of unchecked Spanish imperialism.

These considerations impel us to recognize that for Thomas authentic dominion is over the *use* of things, not their *nature*. Question 66, a. 1 of 2a2ae of the *Summa* establishes this point with lucidity and authority, for here Thomas limits the natural dominion of man to external things. Its origin resides in the identity of human beings as *imago Dei*. Having just considered Thomas' view that political dominion is only from human law and a product only of human reason, we are alerted to the key distinction that Thomas makes in this text: the dominion in question extends only to the rational use of things. It is not an authority over the nature of other creatures:

> We can consider external things in two ways. Looked at first of all from the point of view of their nature, this is not subject to man's power, but only to God's sovereign power. Alternatively, they can be looked at from the point of view of their use and management, and in this regard man has a natural dominion over external things, for he has a mind and a will with which to turn them to his own account. They

seem to be made for him in so far as imperfect things are for the sake of the more perfect...

Hence: I. God has pre-eminent dominion over all things, and in his providence he ordered certain things for men's material support. This is why it is natural for man to have dominion over things in the sense of having the power to use them.

Thomas is entirely consistent with his consideration of the metaphysical background of dominion in *De Potentia*. He describes human dominion as the power to use external goods in order to promote social harmony.[106] This power is found only in rational creatures.[107] The consistency is maintained on the subject most important in understanding Thomas' thought on slavery: this power held by rational creatures does not include the authority to subject another to a status whereby the subject becomes merely a means for the attainment of the master's good, as his *Commentary on the Sentences*, III, d. 44, q.1, a. 3 *ad 3* succinctly states:

One man is not by nature ordained to another as though toward an end.

This crucial distinction between the authority to use external goods, deemed by Thomas to flow from man's inherent identity as a creature made in God's image, and the power of compelling another man to serve one's needs, deemed permissible by Thomas in a relative (i.e., external) but not absolute (i.e. *ex natura*) context, has its foundation in Thomas' understanding of dominion as a transcendental relation and not merely a power.

It can be demonstrated readily that Thomas understands dominion as a relation and not merely a power. First, in his consideration of dominion in the *De Potentia* considered earlier, Thomas indicates a subtle but significant difference in his position from that of Boethius. Boethius had defined dominion as a power; Thomas, in contrast, states that dominion presupposes a power or force (*potentia sive virtus*), but does not equate dominion with power.[108]   Second, Thomas will state explicitly in the *Tertia Pars* that servitude is based on the relation of action and passion.[109]   These categories, borrowed from Aristotle, are employed in the context of *ST*. 2a2ae. q.66, a.1 *ad* 1 to establish a reciprocal rapport between the pre-eminent dominion of God over all creatures and the natural dominion of man in the use of external goods.

Human dominion is thus based on the categories of action and passivity and occurs in an imitative or providential context: human dominion imitates (through participation) the supreme dominion of God. The relation of God to his creatures is the primary analogue for the relation of a master to his subject.   This relation of dominion between man, other creatures and created goods is nothing less than a participation in the goodness of God the Creator, a goodness which can never be univocal and must always be participative in the being of God.[110]

Now we can say what dominion *is* and not merely what it is *not*. *ST*. 2a2ae. q.103, a.3 connects human dominion with divine dominion through the reality of creaturely *participation*.   We have seen that Thomas' understanding of dominion departs from that of Boethius in considering it not merely as a power (*potestas*) but as a transcendental relation.   We have also seen that the human exercise of dominion is analogous to the exercise of God's supreme dominion over creation. Thomas links these ideas together in his treatise on the social virtues. He renders explicit the participatory nature of human dominion in the dominion of God:

> Servitude is due to God and to man under different aspects: even as dominion is suitable to God and to man under different aspects.   For God has absolute and paramount dominion over the creature wholly and singly, which is entirely subject to His power, whereas man participates in a certain likeness to the divine lordship, insofar as he exercises a particular power over some man or creature.[111]

This understanding of dominion—a participatory sharing in the divine goodness—is virtually identical to the understanding of dominion which Thomas sketched in the *De Potentia*.

The transcendental relation of servant to master presupposes and requires that the actions of the *dominus* be ordained toward the attainment of the common good. The common good constitutes a *norma normans* in regard to the activity of the *dominus* toward his *servus*. His powers are justifiable only to the extent that they promote the common good, which includes of course the good of the *servus*.

The consistency of thought does not of course preclude the growth of Thomas' thought. Having established the metaphysical basis for dominion in the *De Potentia*, he was able to examine the concept in its application to various social settings, e.g. parent and child, ruler and people governed, and, most urgently, master and subject. The development of Thomas' thought underscores the importance of dominion as a concept in the schema of the *Summa*. Properly understood in its metaphysical breadth, it is seen to flow immediately from the very identity of human beings as *imago Dei* (*ST*. 2a2ae. q.66, a.1 *ad* 1). When the term *dominium* is applied to a political or social context, however, it can be considered a matter of human law only, subject to the norm of reason (*ST*. 2a2ae. q.10, a.10). Ceslaus Spicq concludes in a classic and comprehensive study that Thomas will use the term *potestas*, not *dominium*, when he intends a univocal or subjective right.[112]

Finally, we consider *ST*. 2a2ae q.122, a.1, which insists that all considerations of human dominion are to be compatible with and subject to the understanding of justice sketched so thoroughly by Thomas in the *Summa*. This final look at dominion takes us to the end of his treatise on the social virtues. He observes that in some matters man is truly autonomous, but in anything that involves another human being his dominion is restricted; he must render to the other whatever is due him:

> In matters of self-concern, it seems, at least on the face of it, that a man is autonomous and can do what he likes; but in matters involving

other people it is evident that he is under obligation to render to them whatever he owes them.

Here we find the confluence of the two concepts examined in this chapter, *dominium* and *jus*. Thomas circumscribes the scope of human dominion by the *debitum* owed to another. Dominion is not unlimited; it is fundamentally *ad alterum*, the definition of justice considered earlier.

We conclude by saying that dominion is a human participation in the goodness of God in such a way that man's relation to other creatures is analogous to the providential concern of God for his creatures. It is fundamentally inconsistent with any sort of servitude that treats the subject *ex natura* merely as a means to an end. Its application in a social setting is permissible only where the precepts of justice are equitably observed.

Although Thomas held that a master could exercise a *jus dominativum* over a slave, the exercise of that *jus* was necessarily restricted by the precepts of justice dictated by *naturalis ratio*, the foundation for human understanding of the *lex aeterna* and the basis of the *jus gentium* in Thomas' approach. Since St. Thomas deemed the kind of slavery known to him (medieval serfdom) to be repugnant to *naturalis ratio*, he could not have failed to categorize the far more perncious species of slavery based on race in the New World as *a fortiori* repugnant to *naturalis ratio* and therefore by definition to his understanding of the *jus gentium*.

Notes for Chapter One

1. Saint Thomas Aquinas, *Summa Theologiae* (hereafter *ST*), 2a2ae. q. 57, a.1. Unless otherwise indicated, the translation of the *Summa* will come from T. Gilby and T.C. O'Brien, ed. *Summa Theologiae* Blackfriars, New York, 1964-, McGraw-Hill Book Co. (Latin text and

English translation), sixty volumes.

2. Jean Tonneau, OP, "Justice," in *The Virtues and States of Life*, vol. 1, ed. A.M. Henry, OP (Chicago, IL: Fides, 1957), p. 264.

3. *Ibid.*, p. 270.

4. *Ibid.*: "The end is not altogether extrinsic to the act, because it is related to the act as principle and terminus; and it is just this that is essential to an act, namely, that it proceeds from something, considered as an action, and that it proceed toward something, considered as a passion." The relation of the end of the agent and the moral quality of the act is a transcendental one, identified with the very essence of the act. We shall see that the relation of the just person and the other to whom he acts justly is likewise a real, transcendental relation.

5. See *Commentum in libro I Sententiarum*, (hereafter *Sent.*) I, d. 26, q.2, a.1; *Quaestiones Quodlibitales*, IX, q.2, a.4; *Summa Contra Gentiles*, (hereafter *Cont. Gent*) c.14.

6. We see this in *De Potentia*, q.7, a.9; *In Metaphysicam Aristotelis Commentaria*, ed. R. Cathala (Turin: Marietti, 1935), *lect.* XVII, n. 1004. See Norbert D. Ginsburg, "Metaphysical Relations and St. Thomas Aquinas," *New Scholasticism* 15 (1941), p. 243.

7. *De Potentia*, q. 7, a.9.

8. The parallel identified between the father-son relationship, on the one hand, and the master-slave relationship, on the other hand, illustrates the mindset of Thomas which contemplates under the term of "master" a guardian rather than an oppressor, illustrated by *In Meta.*, lect. IV, n. 2457: "Ea quae sunt ad aliquid, remotiora videntur esse a substantia quam alia genera, ex eo quod sunt debilioris esse. Unde et substantiae inhaerent mediantibus aliis generibus, sicut...pater et filius, *dominus et servus*, mediante actione et passione." (Emphasis added)

9. P. Coffey, *Ontology or the Theory of Being: An Introduction to General Metaphysics* (NY: Peter Smith, 1938), p. 345.

10. Laurent Clement, "Le *'jus gentium,'"* *Revue de l'Université d'Ottawa* 10 (1940), p. 104.

11. *ST.*, 2a2ae. q.80, a. 1. Equality and that which is due are integrally related: "Ad justitiam videtur pertinere ut quis debitum reddet." *ST.* 1a2ae. q. 60. a.3; *Cont. Gent.* II, c. 28.

12. A. Folgado, "Los Tratados 'De Legibus y De Iustitia et Iure' en los autores españoles del siglo XVI y primera mitad del XVII," *Ciudad de Dios* 172 (1959), p 276f.

13. M. Arbus, "Humanisme et sagesse dans les sciences du droit," *Revue Thomiste* 50 (1950) 611, holds right and law to be interchangeable: "...saint Thomas, pour qui droit et loi, [jus et lex], [praeceptum et debitum] s'equivalent." Arbus conceded subsequently (vol. 57, n.2, p. 330) that the context qualifies this identity.

14. L. Clement, *art. cit.*, at 101.

15. J. T. Delos, OP, *Somme théologique de saint Thomas d'Aquin,* ed. de la Revue des Jeunes, *La Justice*, vol. I, Appendice II, p. 227.

16. *Ibid.*

17. Tonneau, *art.cit.*, p. 271.

18. E.g., Cathrein, *Philosophia Moralis*, n. 284: "Jus sensu stricto acceptum recte definitur 'potestas moralis in rem suam.'"; A. Liguori, *Theologia Moralis*, ed. A. Konings, C.SS.R., 7th. ed., n. 584: "Jus...definitur: 'Legitima moralis facultas, qua quis aliquid facere vel habere ita potest, ut nemini absque aliqua injuria illam violare liceat.'"

19. See L. Clement, *op.cit.*, p. 111; cf. *Sent.* III, d.37, q.1, a.4; *ST.* 2a2ae. q. 64, a.7; q. 66, a.1 and a. 2.

20. *ST.* 2a2ae. q.57, a.1 ad 2; 1a. q. 21, a.2; see also 2a2ae. q. 80, a.1.

21. L. Clement, *art. cit.* , p. 111.

22. Jean Tonneau, *art. cit.*, p. 273.

23. Delos, *art. cit.*, p. 226. We have seen *supra* that the relation of a master and slave is based on the predicament of *actio-passio* in the aristotelian system.

24. See A. Ernout-A. Meillet, *Dictionnaire etymologique de la langue latine* (Paris: Librairie C. Klincksieck, 1932) *ad verbum*.

25. For instance, St. Alphonsus Liguori, *Theologia Moralis*, ed. A. Konings, CSSR, 3rd ed. vol. I (London: Burns & Oates, 1877), tr. "De Jure et Justitia," cap. I, art. II, p. 256; A. Ballerini, *Opus Theologicum Morale in Busembaum Medullam*, ed. D. Palmiere, 3rd ed. vol. III, Prati (1899), tr. VIII, par. I, cap. 1, n. 7.

26. *ST*. 2a2ae. q. 58, a. 10 *corp*. and *ad* 1.

27. See Thomas Gilby, OP., ed., *Summa Theologiae* (NY: McGraw-Hill Book Co., Blackfriars, 1975), vol. 37, p. 45.

28. See J. D. Brokhage, *Francis Patrick Kenrick's Opinion on Slavery*. C.U.A. Studies in Sacred Theology. Ser. 2, n. 85. Washington, DC (1955). Kenrick's views on slavery were accomodated to prevailing political sentiments.

29. *ST*. 2a2ae. q. 57, a.1.

30. See J.A. Weisheipl, OP, *Friar Thomas D'Aquino: His Life, Thought and Works* (Garden City, NY: Doubleday, 1974), p. 380.

31. W.D. Hughes, OP, ed. *Summa Theologiae*, vol. 23 (London: Eyre and Spottiswoode Limited, Blackfriars 1969), p. 249.

32. *In V Eth.*, c. 3, lect. 4, n. 934.

33. L. Clement, *op.cit.*, p. 107.

34. See Stefan Swiezawski, "Quelques déformations de la pensée de St. Thomas dans la tradition thomiste," in *Aquinas and the Problems of His Time,* ed. M. Verbeke and D. Verhelst. (The Hague: Leuven Univ.

Press, 1976), p. 38ff.

35. J. Tonneau, *op.cit.*, p. 259.

36. "[...] *Amicitia consistit in adaequatione quantum ad affectum; sed justitia in adaequatione rerum"* III *Sent.*, d. 28, q.1, a.6, *ad* 4.

37. *ST.* 2a2ae. q. 57, a.4. Thomas Gilby provides a helpful note in the Blackfriars edition of the *Summa Theologiae* (New York: McGraw-Hill Book Co., 1975), vol. 37, p. 14: "Slave and slavery (from late Latin *sclavus*, a tribal name for a Slav) have not the same ring as *servus* and *servitus*, the condition of not being one's own master, *dominus*, or of not having *dominium*, a condition which allows for differences of degree[...] *Servus*, it seems, is best translated 'servant' and sometimes 'bondservant.'"

38. "Il n'en faudrait pas concluire que l'esclave n'a pas de droits et qu'à son egard on ne commet pas d'injustice. Thomas l'explique à l'1 *ad* 2. L'esclave est un homme, et à ce titre il est par nature un subject de droit; il a la dignité defin en soi." J. T. Delos, OP, *op.cit.*, Appendice I, pp. 191-192.

39. The etymology of the Latin *alter* suggests a reciprocal relationship between two parties. The first syllable "al," of Greek origin, comes from *alius*, meaning the distinction or opposition of certain realities, without anything else being specified. The second syllable "ter" is also of Greek origin, suggesting a comparison. This suffix has the force of making a comparison with a second term whereby the second is in opposition and not merely unspecified. *Unus et alius* is vague and unspecific, with no inherent comparison. *Unus et alter* contains a specific comparison. See A. Ernout—A. Meillet, *op.cit., ad v.* The absence of a strict *ad alterum* relationship does not mean that father—son or master—slave are thereby *unus—alius* (vague and unspecified) but rather that their relationship is much closer to an identity, namely, *unus—unus*.

40. *Nicomachean Ethics* V, c.3, n. 1131a. 12-21.

41. *In Ethic.*, lect. 1 and lect. 4, ed. Pirotta-Gillet, n. 896, p. 297 and n. 933, p. 310.

42. *"Cum ergo justum sit et medium et aequale, oportet quidem quod inquantum...est aequale sit in quibusdam rebus, secundum quas scilicet attenditur aequalitas inter duas personas."* *In V Eth.*, lect. 4, n. 934.

43. L. Lachance, OP, *Le Concept de droit selon Aristotle et Saint Thomas* (Montreal: Levesque, 1933), p. 274ff.

44. L. Lachance, *op.cit.*, p. 281.

45. *"Idem est unum in substantia, simile unum in qualitate, aequale vero unum in quantitate."* *Commentary on the Metaphysics*, Book X, n. 1999 (Cathala).

46. P.N. Zammit, OP, "The Concept of Rights according to Aristotle and St. Thomas," *Angelicum*, 16 (1939), p. 249.

47. L. Lachance, *op.cit.*, pp. 31-32.

48. Zammit, *op.cit.*, p. 265.

49. *Ibid.*, p. 263.

50. P.D. Dognin, OP, "La justice particuliere comporte-t-elle deux especes?" *Revue Thomiste* 65 (1965) 3, 401ff.

51. P. Van Overbeke, OP refuses to consider the relation as predicamental for the simple reason that St. Thomas did not so consider it. Thomas does however seem to regard it, in later terminology, as a transcendental relation. See Overbeke, "St. Thomas et le droit," *Revue Thomiste*, 55 (1955), 519-565. Others simply describe *jus* as a relation of equality without specifying the kind of relation entailed (e.g. L. Lachance, OP, P. Zammit, OP).

52. J. Delos, OP, *La Justice*, vol. I: St. Thomas Aquinas, *Somme théologique de saint Thomas d'Aquin*, ed. de la Revue des Jeunes, Appendice II, p. 211n.

53. G. Del Vecchio, *Leçons de Philosophie du Droit*, Paris, 1936, pp. 42-43.

54. *Ibid.*

55. "Omnes populi qui legibus et moribus reguntur, partim suo proprio, partim communi omnium hominum jure utuntur. Nam quod quisque populus ipse sibi jus constituit, id ipsius proprium civitatis est; vocaturque jus civile, quasi jus proprium ipsius civitatis. Quod vero *naturalis ratio* inter omnes homines constituit, id apud omnes peraeque custoditur, vocaturque *jus gentium*, quasi quo jure omnes gentes utuntur." *Digest* I, 1, 1, 9. (Emphasis added)

56. "Jus naturale est quod natura omnia animalia docuit. Nam jus istud non humani generis proprium, sed omnium animalium quae in terra, quae in mari nascuntur, avium quoque commune est. Hinc descendit maris atque feminae conjunctio quam nos matrimonium appellamus; hinc liberorum procreatio, hinc educatio: videmus etenim coetera quoque animalia, feras etiam, istius juris peritia conseri. *Jus gentium est quo gentes humanae utuntur: quod a naturali recedere facile intelligere licet; quia illud omnibus animalibus hoc solis hominibus inter se commune sit...Jus civile est, quod neque in totum a naturali vel gentium recedit nec per omnia ei servit: itaque cum aliquid addimus vel detrahimus juri communi, jus proprium id est civile efficimus.* "*Digest*, I, 1, 1 and 6. (Emphasis added)

57. *ST.* (London and New York: McGraw-Hill, 1975) Blackfriars ed., Thomas Gilby, OP, vol. 28, p. 111n.

58. "The Low Latin term *'positivus'* signified what was accidental and imposed, not essential and inherent. So positive laws, though they should not contradict, are not prolongations of inherently moral precepts. Legislators and statesmen are artists, not social moralists; *In Ethic.* V, *lect.* 12; VI, *lect.* 7; *ST.* 2a2ae. q. 57, a.2 & a.3." Gilby, *op.cit.*, p. 107n.

59. Despite its length, a statement of this definition for the record is in order. "Jus naturale est quod natura omnia animalia docuit: nam jus istud non humani generis proprium est, sed omnium animalium quae in coelo, quae in terra, quae in mari nascuntur. Hinc descindit maris atque feminae conjunctio, quam nos matrimonium appellamus, hinc liberorum procreatio, hinc educatio. Videmus etenim cetera quoque animalia istius juris peritia censeri. *Jus autem civile vel gentium* ita dividitur. Omnes

populi qui legibus et moribus reguntur, partim suo proprio, partim communi omnium hominum jure utuntur; nam quod quisque populus ipse sibi jus constituit, id ipsius civitatis, proprium est, vocaturque jus civile, quasi jus proprium ipsius civitatis. Quod vero naturalis ratio inter omnes homines constituit, id apud omnes peraeque custoditur, vocaturque jus gentium, quasi quo jure omnes gentes utuntur...Jus autem gentium omni humano generi commune est: nam usu exigente et humanis necessitatibus, gentes humanae quaedam sibi constituerunt. Bella etenim orta sunt, et captivitates secutae et servitutes, quae sunt naturali juri contrariae. Jure enim naturali omnes homines ab initio liberi nascebantur. Et ex hoc jure gentium omnes pene contractus introducti sunt, ut emptio, venditio, locatio, conductio, societas, depositum, mutuum et alii innumerabiles." *Institutes*, 1, II, 1 and 2. (Emphasis added)

60. Dom Odon Lottin, OSB, *Le Droit naturel chez S. Thomas d'Aquin et ses prédécesseurs*, 2d. ed. (Bruges: Beyaert,1931), pp. 63ff.

61. B. Roland Gosselin, *La Doctrine politique de S. Thomas d'Aquin* (Paris: Riviere, 1928), pp. 27-28. Gosselin, a professor at the Institut Catholique de Paris in the first half of this century, concludes that in Augustine's schema there would not have been war, slavery or private property in the absence of original sin: "C'est ainsi que la domination par contrainte et tout ce qui l'accompagne, le glaive, la guerre, la propriété privée, l'esclavage, ressortissent au droit naturel secondaire, ce qui veut dire que ces choses sont la juste peine du péché et la meilleure sauvegard de l'ordre naturel après le péché." *ibid.* These features are essential to retain the natural order which is powerless, however, without the law of grace. We shall see in greater detail how this *propter peccatum* thesis on the origin of slavery will influence Thomas' concept of *dominium*.

62. *ST*. Blackfriars ed., vol. 28, Gilby, p. 9n.

63. Gosselin, *op.cit.*, p. 33.

64. "Jus aut naturale est aut civile aut gentium." *Etymol.* V.4, PL 82, 199 (the identical tripartite division of the *Institutes*); "Jus lex humana est." V.2. PL 82.198.

65. Gosselin, *op.cit.*, pp. 34-35.

66. "Jus gentium est sedum occupatio, aedificatio, munitio, bella, captivitates, servitutes, postliminia, foedera pacis, induciae, legatorum non violandorum religio, connubia inter alienigenas prohibita; et inde jus gentium, quo eo jure omnes *fere* gentes utuntur." *Etymol.* V, 6. (Emphasis added) It can be noted that "*fere*" is the only difference in range cited between the natural law and the *jus gentium*. Dom Odon Lottin speculates that Isidore had in mind tribes of the seventh century not deemed civilized by contemporary standards. Lottin, *op.cit.*, pp. 10-11.

67. "Est jus naturale triplex: scilicet nativum, humanum, divinum. Jus nativum dicitur communiter, quia est illud debitum quod innascitur; et est commune non solum ratione naturae singularis, sed etiam ratione salutis speciei, et secundum hoc jus naturae se extendit ad omnia animantia, sicut dicit Ulpianusquod lex naturae est quod natura docuit omnia animalia. Jus autem humanum solum respicit ordinationem naturae singularis; unde hoc mode appellatur jus humanum, secundum quod dicitur jus gentium, quia jus gentium est quo gentes humanae utuntur; sed hoc solum pertinet ad rationalem creaturam. Jus autem divinum dicitur quo ordinatur rationalis creatura ad gratiam." *Summa Theologiae*, part III, q. 27, membro 4, art. 1, ed. 1575.

68. L. Clement, *op.cit.*, p. 181.

69. Together with the *Decretals* of Gregory IX, edited by St. Raymond of Peñafort, the *Decretum* inaugurated the era of the *Jus Novum*. Thomas refers to Gratian 193 times in the *Summa* and *Contra Gentiles* while there are only 155 references to the *Corpus Juris Civilis*. Despite the impressive number of citations, most of them are on minor matters and the appeal to authority does not carry much weight in Thomas' argumentation. Gilby, *ibid.*, pp. xxv, 13n.

70. "Humanum genus duobus regitur, naturali videlicet jure et moribus. Jus naturale est, quod in Lege et Evangelio continetur, quo quisque jubetur alii facere quod sibi vult fieri, et prohibetur alii inferre, quod sibi nolit fieri." *Decretum*, I, 1 preface.

71. P. Van Overbeke, *op.cit.* in note 63, pp. 555-556.

72. L. Clement, *op.cit.*, pp. 180-181.

73. *In IV Sent.*, d.33, q.1, a.1, ad 4: "Jus naturale multipliciter accipitur. Primo enim jus aliquod dicitur naturale ex principio, quia a natura est inditum, et sic definit Tullius in *II Rhetoricorum*, dicens: 'Jus naturae est quod non opinio genuit, sed quaedam innata vis inseruit.' Et quia etiam in rebus naturalibus dicuntur aliqui motus naturales, non quia sint ex principio intrinseco, sed quia sunt a principio superiore movente...ideo ea quae sunt de jure divino, dicuntur esse de jure naturali, cum sint ex impressione et infusione superioris principii, scilicet Dei; et sic accipitur a Gratiano, qui dicit quod jus naturale est quod in Lege et Evangelio continetur. Tertio dicitur jus naturale non solum a principio, sed a natura, quia de naturalibus est. Et quia natura contra rationem dividitur, a qua homo est homo, ideo strictissimoaccipiendo jus naturale, illa quae ad homines tantum pertinent, etsi sint de dictamine rationis naturalis, non dicuntur esse de jure naturali; sed illa tantum quae naturalis ratio dictat de his quae sunt homini aliisque communia; et sic datur definitio: Jus naturale est quod natura omnia animalia docuit." Thomas' hasty deference to Gratian's definition of the natural law as that which is contained in the Law and the Gospel ("impression...infusion") suggests his unhappiness with this elastic "definition."

74. See Wiliiam E. May, "The Meaning and Nature of the Natural Law in Thomas Aquinas," *American Journal of Jurisprudence* 22 (1977), 168-189.

75. I will use the Latin *servus* instead of the English "slave" because it becomes evident from the serious restrictions that Thomas attaches to *servitus* (e.g. it in no way circumscribes the right to procreate and marry) that he is describing a condition much different from that commonly denotated by the term "slavery." T. Gilby's suggestion that "bondservant" comes closest to Thomas' understanding of *servus* is most relevant here.

76. P. van Overbeke, OP, *op.cit.*, p. 558.

77. "Divinae natura, humanae moribus constant." *Etymologies* V. 4, PL 92, 199; V. 2, PL 82, 198.

78. Lottin, *op.cit.*, p. 64.

79. *ST.* Blackfriars ed., vol. 28, p. 105n.

80. L. Clement, *op.cit.*, pp. 184-85.

81. Lottin, *op.cit.*, p. 62.

82. Lottin, *op.cit.*, pp. 63-64.

83. Overbeke, *op.cit.*, p. 559.

84. Lottin, *op.cit.*, pp. 65-66.

85. L. Clement, *op.cit.*, pp. 194-5.

86. Since Thomas constructs his moral methodology around the reality of beatitude, namely, the natural quest for happiness which can only be fulfilled through union with God. It is noteworthy that in his commentary on the *Sentences* (III, d. 44, q. 1) Thomas identifies in the sorrow of servitude as the surrender to another of the appetite for the good that is distinctive of each human being: *Et quia unicuique est appetibile proprium bonum, et per consequens contristabile est unicuique quod illud bonum quod deberet esse suum cedat alteri tantum; ideo tale dominium non potest esse sine poena subjectorum.*

87. *De Potentia Dei*, translated by the English Dominicans (Westminster, MD: Newman Press, 1952), pp. 55ff.

88. *Ibid.*, p. 61.

89. *Ibid.*, q.7, a.10. Catherine LaCugna has examined the caricature of a "one-sided, self-sufficient and not 'really related'" God that can result from an oversimplification of Aquinas' views. She argues that the Thomistic framework of the ontology of divine relationality is designed to preserve the point that "God freely relates to what God creates." She notes that this "relating is a thoroughly intentional activity, in which God bestows a participation in divine being to what otherwise would not even be at all (*ST.* 1a, q. 45)...The radical contingency of our being is the other face of the intentionality of God's act of creating." (p.660ff.) LaCugna considers the structure of the *Summa* as well as its theology to demonstrate Thomas' concern that creation be viewed as a gift from a

loving Creator. See Catherine LaCugna, "The Relational God: Aquinas and Beyond," *Theological Studies* 46 (1985), pp. 647-663.

90. Robert J. Henle, SJ, *St. Thomas and Platonism* (The Hague: Nijhoff, 1956), pp. 378-79.

91. George Klubertanz, SJ, *St Thomas Aquinas on Analogy*, Jesuit Studies (Chicago, IL: Loyola Univ. Press, 1960), p. 56.

92. *Ibid.*, p. 59.

93. *In I Sententiarum*, prol., q.1, a.2, ad 2.

94. *In II Sententiarum*, d.16, q.1, a.1, ad 3.

95. *De Potentia*, q. 7, a. 7, *ad* 3.

96. *ST*. 2a2ae. q. 23, a.2 *ad* 1. This corresponds exactly with the view expressed in the *Quaestiones quodlibetales*, group II, I, (q.10) a.22 ad 1: "God is said to be good essentially because He is goodness itself; creatures however are said to be good through participation, because they have goodness." We might paraphrase this as follows: God is said to be a lord essentially because He is dominion itself; creatures however are said to be masters through their participation (in God's dominion), because they have (human) dominion.

97. *I Summa Contra Gentiles* 29.

98. Klubertanz, *op.cit.*, p. 63.

99. The chronology of Thomas' works is taken from James Weisheipl, OP, *Friar Thomas D'Aquino: His Life, Thought and Works* (Garden City, NY: Doubleday, 1974), pp. 355-405.

100. St. Gregory the Great, *Moralia in Job*, XXI, 22: "Natura omnes homines aequales fecit; sed pro meritis alios aliis occulta, sed justa Dei dispensatio subjecit."

101. *City of God*, 15, col. 643, t.7.

102. See R.A. Markus, "Two Conceptions of Political Authority: Augustine, *'De Civitate Dei,'* xix. 14-15, and some Thirteenth-century Interpretations," *Journal of Theological Studies* 16 (April 1965), p. 89.

103. St. Augustine, *City of God*, XIX, 15. PL 41, 643: "Hominem rationalem ad imaginem suam factum non voluit Deus nisi irrationabilius dominari; non homini, sed hominem pecori."

104. The Blackfriars edition of the *Summa* (London: Eyre and Spottiswoode, 1966), vol 13, translates *dominium* as "lording it," and *servitus* as "slaving it." Because these renderings appear to me to be idiomatic, if not idiosyncratic, *dominium* and *servitus* will be rendered as dominion and servitude. Earlier linguistic notes on these terms are of course applicable again.

105. See Enrique R. Maldonado, *"Tomas de Aquino, Bartolomé de las Casas y la controversia de Indias,"* Studium 14 (1974): 519-542.

106. *De Potentia* 7, 10, *ad* 4: "Non est dominium ubi non potentia sive virtus...nomen dominus in suo intellectu includitur potentiam coercendi subditos, et ordinem ad subditos, qui consequitur talem potestatem et terminationem ordinis subditorum ad dominum."

107. *Ibid.* 9, 1 ad 3: "Nam solae substantiae rationales habent dominium sui actus, ita quod in eis est agere et non agere; aliae vero substantiae magis aguntur quam agunt." Also, see the Prologue to 1a2ae of the *Summa*.

108. The definition of Boethius was "*dominium est potestas quaedam qua servus coercetur,*" and is cited in *De Potentia* 7, 10, ad 4.

109. *ST.* 3a. q. 20, a.1 ad 2; "potentia activa...est principum actionis...illud quod recipit actionem agentis...est potentia passiva." *In I Sent.*, 42, 1, 1.

110. *ST.* 1a. q. 5, a.6 ad 3: "Bonum non dividitur sicut univocum...sed sicut analogum"; "bonum universale, quod non invenitur in aliquo creato, sed solum in Deo: quia omnis creatura habet bonitatem participatum." *ST.* 1a2ae. q. 2, a.8. See E. Kaczynski, OP, "Il 'naturale dominium' della IIa IIae, 66.1," *Angelicum* 53 (1976), pp. 456-60.

111. I have departed from the Gilby translation and will present the Latin text here: "Alia autem ratione debetur servitus Deo, et homini: sicut alia ratione dominum esse competit Deo, et homini. Nam Deus plenarium et principale dominium habet respectu totius et cuiuslibet creaturae, quae totaliter eius subiicitur potestati: *homo autem participat quandam similitudinem divini dominii, secundum quod habet particularem potestatem super aliquem hominem vel super aliquam creaturam.*" *ST.* 2a2ae. q. 103, a.3 (Emphasis added)

112. C. Spicq, "La notion analogique de dominium et le droit de propriété," *Revue des Sciences Philosophiques et Théologique* 20 (1931) 52-76.

CHAPTER TWO
Francisco de Vitoria and Slavery

According to Luis Getino, OP, a biographer of Vitoria as well as archivist of the University of Salamanca and secretary of the "Association of Francisco de Vitoria" for many years, Vitoria was born in approximately 1480. Vitoria received his surname from the chief town of the province of Alava, where he was born. The custom of taking one's surname from one's birthplace was common in the Dominican community: Alberto de Colonia, Pedro de Verona, Juan de Torquemada, Alonso de Burgos, Luis de Granada, Pablo de Leon, Bartolomé de Medina and, of course, Thomas d'Aquino.[1]

Francisco's parents moved to Burgos when he was still a child and he attended school there as a young man. It was in the Dominican convent of St. Paul's at Burgos where he professed his religious vows. Burgos was famous as the capital of Castile and the residence of the Catholic kings of Spain.

Burgos was also destined to play an important historical role in the relationship of the Spanish empire to the Indians of the New World. In 1512, when Vitoria was studying theology at the University of Paris, an assembly was held at Burgos among councilors of the King for the purpose of considering the denunciations of Spanish treatment of the Indians that had been received by the Crown. Many of these complaints were made through the concern of missionaries who accompanied the *encomenderos*, the merchants and opportunists chiefly responsible for the exploration, if not exploitation, of the natural resources discovered by Columbus on his first and subsequent journeys. These deliberations became known as the *Consejo de Indias*, the Council of the Indies. Their resolutions became the basis for the *Leyes de Indias*, the "Laws" designed to protect the Indians from abuse. The occurrence of the *Consejo de Indias* in the town where Vitoria lived as a young student assures us at the very least that he was conscious of the controversy and its consequences in a personal and not merely academic context.[2]

The Provincial Chapter of the Dominican order, which had been held in Burgos in 1506, had assigned Vitoria to studies at the University of Paris. At Paris, Vitoria resided in the convent of St. Jacques, famous for its association with St. Albert the Great and St. Thomas Aquinas. Two Belgian Dominicans, John Fennarius and Peter Crockart, became Vitoria's primary instructors. Crockart is renowned as the first to replace the study of Lombard's *Sententiae* with Aquinas' *Summa*. The introduction of Aquinas into the regular curriculum of theology students began in 1509. Between 1514 and 1519 a number of editions of Aquinas, including commentaries by authorities such as Cajetan, began to circulate at the University of Paris.

Since Crockart greatly appreciated Aquinas' *Summa* and exercised a considerable influence on Vitoria's theological training, it is appropriate to consider the background of Crockart. A description of the evolution of Crockart's thought comes from Ernest Nys, a scholar of the history of jurisprudence, who as a professor of international law at the University of Brussels studied the relationship of Vitoria and the *jus gentium*:

> At first an ardent disciple of the Scot, John Mair, and like him a nominalist, he became a Dominican in 1503 and displayed the greatest zeal for St. Thomas Aquinas; in one of his books, where he treats of questions relating to the logic of Aristotle and touches on one point of the doctrine of the Angel of the School, he styles himself *Divi Thomae doctrinae interpres et propugnator accerimus*. Very close bonds attached Franciscus de Vitoria to the Belgian theologian; for in 1512 he supervised the printing of a work by him, a commentary on the *Secunda Secundae* of the *Summa* of St. Thomas. Crockart, already reader of the *Sententiae*, took the degree of bachelor, and in 1510 he became a licentiate. He died in 1514.[3]

After studying theology at the University of Paris from 1506 to 1509, Vitoria spent the next three years studying the liberal arts under the direction of Crockart. His familiarity with the humanities would distinguish and expand the scope of citations he would come to make in his lectures. Commentators invariably allude to the literary elegance of Vitoria in contrast to the dry and wooden state of scholastic theology that he encountered.[4] His interest and background in the humanities accounts in part for his friendship with Erasmus and the influence of Erasmus upon him as a person and intellectual. A letter of a contemporary Spanish humanist, Juan Luis Vives, indicates that Vitoria frequently defended the intellectual inquiries of Erasmus while he was a student at the University of Paris. Another letter, from Erasmus himself, refers to a *teólogo sorbónico*, apparently a friendly allusion to Vitoria.[5]

In 1512 Vitoria was confirmed by the general chapter of the Dominicans, held at Naples, as a lecturer on the *Libri sententiarum* of Peter Lombard. He would serve in this capacity until 1520 when he was admitted to the Sorbonne. In 1521 he obtained the degree of licentiate in theology and occupied the chair of theology at the Sorbonne until 1523. In addition to Erasmus, Vitoria befriended Josse van Assche and Juan Luis Vives, two prominent humanists of the sixteenth century. His relationship with these literary luminaries serves as evidence that the thomistic revival of which Vitoria would become the eponym was linked with sectors of the Renaissance, such as Erasmus and his following, who were hospitable to Catholic interests.

Just as Burgos, the site of Vitoria's early education, would play a critical role in Spanish self-examination of its treatment of the Indians, so Valladolid, the site of Vitoria's first teaching assignment in Spain, would make history as the center of the great debate over the right or "title" of Spain to colonize the New World between Bartolomé de las Casas and Juan Sepúlveda in 1550-51. Following his appointment as Master of Studies at St. Gregory's in Valladolid in 1523, Vitoria began to discuss in his lectures the issues of Spanish conquest and Indian rights. Once again these issues affected Vitoria in a personal and not merely academic manner, for Valladolid was the seat of the Council of the Indies, the tribunal concerned with the moral aspects of Spanish treatment of Indians in its quest for the gold of the New World.

In 1526 Vitoria assumed the *prima* chair of theology at the University of Salamanca, a position he would hold until his death twenty years later.[6] Vitoria was the unanimous choice of the judges, selected to replace Pablo of Leon, who had held the *prima* chair from 1507 until his death in 1526.

We shall shortly examine in detail the record of extant works attributed to Vitoria but it should be observed in this summary of the historical background that Vitoria did not publish any works of his own. The record we have of his reflections comes in the main from the meticulous notes of his classroom lectures kept by a student, Francisco Triger. The impact of Vitoria as a teacher can be measured in part by the quality of the students he encountered and, as it were, produced in his twenty years at Salamanca. These students included Melchior Cano, Domingo and Pedro de Soto, Bartolomé de Medina and Domingo Bañez.

A laudatory portrait of Vitoria's influence is sketched by the Belgian jurist, Ernest Nys:

> Under his powerful direction the College of Salamanca attained a position unique in Spain. His manner of teaching distinguished him from most of the other professors. Instead of the aridity of scholastic formulas, which he employed only in order to lay the bases of his teaching, he knew how to bring out eloquently their beauty and their grandeur. He did not despise elegance of diction; he loved to support the conclusions of theology by happy citations from the Fathers and by the facts of ecclesiastical history. His courses, made attractive by the grace of his language, rapidly reached universal favor. Solidity of doctrine with elegance of instruction, this is what was afforded by the long professorate of Franciscus de Vitoria.[7]

The fame of Vitoria as a moral theologian is attested to by the fact that he was consulted by the Crown on at least two key questions, one of direct consequence to the Crown, viz., the validity of the arguments of King Henry VIII of England in his attempt to annul his marriage to Catherine of Aragon, the aunt of the Spanish monarch, and the other of direct consequence to our inquiry, viz., the treatment of Indians converted to Christianity. Vitoria's answer to the entreaty of the Crown on the arguments of Henry VIII are contained in his *relectio* entitled *De Matrimonio*, which includes a passage that refers specifically to this historic dispute.

Although the reflections of Vitoria on the marriage of Henry VIII to Catherine of Aragon, solicited by the Spanish Crown, do indicate the degree of confidence he enjoyed as a theologian, they are not otherwise relevant to this study. What does warrant our attention, however, is the response of Vitoria and others on the Salamanca faculty to several inquiries of King Charles V in 1539 and 1541 in regard to the rights enjoyed by the Indian converts following their baptism. The inquiry of 1541 apparently stemmed from a question raised by Bartolomé de las Casas before the *Consejo de Indias*, viz., whether it was lawful to baptize adult Indians according to the manner generally used in the New World, that is, without any preliminary religious instruction. Vitoria, Domingo de Soto and six other professors responded with a statement that underscored the importance of religious instruction before baptism and admonished the *encomenderos* about the spiritual and human rights of the Indians. Vitoria was kept well-informed on the subject of the treatment of the Indians in the New World because a number of his students had become energetic missionaries in the West Indies. Among the students who corresponded with him were the Dominicans Alonso de Veracruz and Domingo de Salazar. Their reports constituted potent eyewitness accounts of the factual setting of the Spanish conquest.

A response of King Charles V remains to this day. It criticizes Vitoria and Domingo de Soto for "irreverent" but unspecified teachings. Written on November 10, 1539, the letter is addressed to the Prior of the Dominican Convent of San Esteban in Salamanca. Charles V complains about "the excessive liberty taken by the theologian Vitoria in problems of such delicacy affecting the greatness of his empire."[8]

Although the complaint of King Charles V was surely serious, it did not prevent the Crown from soliciting Vitoria's advice again on the degree of instruction required by the Catholic faith for baptism. A letter from the Crown, dated March 31, 1541, speaks respectfully of the theologians and seeks guidance on this matter.[9] Nor did the complaint of 1539 prevent his son, Prince Philip, from inviting Vitoria to attend the Council of Trent in February, 1545. Vitoria's frail health prevented him from attending. Vitoria died on August 12, 1546, having suffered from rheumatism for the last two years of his life.

The reflections of Vitoria which bear directly on the issues of slavery and human rights are found in two *relectiones* apparently delivered in 1532. We shall now consider them in the context of the Vitoria bibliography available today.

We can now examine the writings of Vitoria, first in general, and then to examine closely those which pertain to the slavery controversy. Father Luis Getino, OP, makes a useful threefold distinction in his study of the bibliography of Vitoria's published works. Father Getino's system of classification is a response to the fact, already noted, that Vitoria published nothing under his own name. We must rely on the notes of his students, and the inherent danger of inaccuracy in second-hand sources, in order to understand Vitoria's approach to slavery and human rights.

The distinction of Getino consists of (a) works of other authors published by Vitoria; (b) works of Vitoria published by others; (c) works of Vitoria which have until recently remained unpublished.[10]

In the first category of works of other authors published by Vitoria himself, Getino lists the following:

1. The *Secunda Secundae* of St. Thomas Aquinas with commentaries by Peter Crockart, OP (Paris, 1512);
2. The *Sermones Dominicales* of Peter Covarrubias, OP (1520);
3. The *Summa Aurea* of St. Antoninus of Florence, OP (Paris, 1521).

In the second category of works of Vitoria published by others, Getino includes various letters and written opinions on contemporary questions, but the most important works by far are the *Relectiones theologiae*, the first edition of which was compiled by Jacques Boyer in Paris in 1557.

In the third category of works which were unpublished at the time of his writing (1930), Getino listed the *Manuscripts* of his commentaries on the *Summa* of St. Thomas Aquinas. Two years later the commentary on the *Secunda Secundae* was edited and published by Beltran de Heredia, OP.[11]

Since the *Relectiones theologiae* will furnish us with the primary understanding of Vitoria's thoughts on human rights, it is important to ascertain exactly what is meant by the term *relectio* in the context of Vitoria's era. One of the statutes of the University of Salamanca required the *prima* professor of theology to give an extra lecture for two hours on some matter of public concern at the end of each academic year. These public lectures were entitled *relectiones* or "readings." Since Vitoria served for twenty years (1526-1546) as *prima* professor of theology at Salamanca there should technically have been twenty *relectiones*. Getino indicates in chapter fifteen of his text that thirteen are extant. The records extant are not written notes of Vitoria himself but notes written by his students. Inevitably we must rely on the accuracy and adequacy of those notes to ascertain the original intent of Vitoria. It appears that some student notes were lost in the destruction of monastic libraries which occurred during the napoleonic wars of 1835.[12]

In his study of the manuscripts of Vitoria, Father Beltran de Heredia has compiled a chronology of the *relectiones*. The chronology is important because it discloses the manner and direction in which Vitoria's thought matured and progressed.[13] It should be noted in the chronology of Heredia below that the critical *relectiones*, *De Indis* and *De Jure Belli*, are placed near the end of Vitoria's life (1538-39). Other scholars, such as C. H. McKenna, OP, Herbert F. Wright and Ernest Nys, place these critical *relectiones* in 1532. The question of the proper chronology is important if, in comparing the *relectiones* with the commentaries on the *Secunda Secundae*, we are to know which work represents the more mature thought of Vitoria.

Father Getino accepts the Heredia chronology, i.e., a later date of delivery of *De Indis* and *De jure belli* on the following grounds:

> If we take the phrases of Vitoria at the end of a letter we would say that these *relectiones* were delivered in 1532, forty years after the discovery; but these phrases do not refer to the time of discovery but to the years in which the emigration began. The greatest difficulty in adopting this date of 1532 is that it does not explain how Charles V had no knowledge of the *relectiones* until 1539.[14]

Getino's point is compelling: if Charles V was angered by an opinion of Vitoria in a *relectio* of 1532, why would he refrain from expressing his anger until 1539? Knowledge of the theological debates of Salamanca was widespread among Spanish citizens and closely followed by the Court, as illustrated by the inquiry on Vitoria's view on Henry VIII's grounds for an annulment. Despite the erudition of Herbert F. Wright and Ernest Nys, it seems likely that the reference in *De Indis* to "forty years ago" refers to migration, not discovery, the view of Getino, *supra*. Getino's proximity to the archives of Salamanca provides him with a vantage point not enjoyed by other scholars.

In our study of Vitoria's understanding of the *jus gentium* and *dominium*, we will first examine his *Commentaries* on the *Secunda Secundae* and then the *relectiones*. This will be our sequence for two reasons: (1) the scholarship of Heredia and Getino suggests that this is the accurate chronological progression;[15] (2) the nature of the *Commentaries* is more systematic than the *relectiones*, which were by definition limited to a specific topic of current importance. This sequence will thus move from the general to the particular, from systematic understanding to concrete application.

One final note on the different terminology used to describe the *relectiones* needs to be made. *Relectio* number 11 is usually entitled *De Indis*, although it is occasionally referred to as *De Indis Prior* in order to distinguish it from *relectio* number 12, which is then given the title *De Indis Posterior sive De Jure Belli*. We shall use *De Indis*, *De Jure Belli* and *De Potestate Civili* and refer to them by name rather than by number.[16]

1. Vitoria's Understanding of *Jus* and *Jus Gentium*

Vitoria treats the concept of *jus* ex professo in his commentary on the *Secunda Secundae* of St. Thomas Aquinas, in q. 57, a.1.[17] He follows the basic methodology of Thomas' *Summa*, i.e., presenting a proposition in the form of a question, adducing arguments in favor of and then against an acceptance of the proposition, and finally his conclusion in view of the weight, relevance and accuracy of the arguments examined. The sources given greatest consideration in the presentation of arguments are scripture and treatises of canon and civil law.

Vitoria begins by observing that *jus*, or "the just," considered as the object of justice, does not take into account the personal qualities of the agent, e.g., whether he is rich or poor.[18] By providing concrete examples, Vitoria establishes this difference: the condition of the agent is considered in other virtues but not in the case of justice. He accepts as his own the conclusion of St. Thomas that *jus* is the object of the virtue of justice, which is always *ad alterum*.[19]

Vitoria then turns to the meanings which the term *jus* can have. He identifies three: (a) the just deed itself; (b) the skills of juridical art; (c) identity with lex. He accepts the position of Thomas that *jus* stands for what is just or the just deed itself. Justice flows from its object, *jus*, not vice-versa.[20]

After expressing his agreement with the view of Thomas that *jus* stands for "that which is just," Vitoria rebuts the equation of *jus* with *lex* made by John Buridan (d. 1358) in his commentary on Aristotle's *Ethics*. He accomplishes this by citing the view of Ulpian, universally accepted and expressly mentioned in the *Summa*, that justice is the "firm and constant will of rendering to each that which is his due." Since this definition embraces precepts such as the prohibition of murder, it stands for the just thing, the content of justice, not its cause, the *causa justi*, which is *lex*.[21]

Before completing his commentary on q.57, a.1, Vitoria again has occasion to rebut Buridan on a central proposition already alluded to, viz., whether justice is always *ad alterum*. He cites the view of Buridan, expressed in his commentary on Aristotle's *Ethics*, that many moral virtues pertain to the other, e.g., the chastity of a spouse pertains to the other spouse and the intemperance of one spouse, expressed through adultery, refers to the other spouse. Vitoria responds by noting that Thomas does not deny that justice and the other virtues have qualities in common; his concern in his *De Jure* treatise is to identify qualities always present in and proper to the virtue of justice. Accordingly, a relation with another is always proper to the virtue of justice. It denotes an *altérité* or "otherness." Vitoria again cites the example of a debt owed by someone: the debt exists on its own merits, irrespective of the financial condition of the debtor. If someone incurs a just debt, a duty to pay it arises irrespective of the poverty or wealth of the agent. It is clear that Vitoria intends to adhere to an objective view of justice in conformity with the *Summa*. By rebutting explicitly the views of Buridan, a leading exponent of nominalism, Vitoria endeavors to retain the pre-nominalist meaning of *jus* found in Thomas.

It is in his commentary on q.57, a.3 that Vitoria states succinctly his understanding of the *jus gentium*. In considering the question posed by the *Summa*, whether the *jus gentium* can be distinguished from the *jus naturale*, Vitoria responds by presenting the distinction of Thomas that "the *jus naturale* is that which of its very nature is commensurate with something else."[22] He then uses this observation of Thomas to make a further distinction between that which has a sort of equality and justice of itself (*de se*), and that which is made equal in reference to something else (*in ordine ad aliud*). The first kind of justice pertains to natural law; the second, to the *jus gentium*.

Vitoria supplies an illustration. Private property is divided not according to an intrinsic norm of equality or justice, but rather its distribution is ordained to the peace and concord of society, which could not be maintained unless individuals possessed certain goods. It is then according to the *jus gentium* that private property is allocated.

After providing this illustration, Vitoria concludes that those things which are absolutely adequate and just in the first mode described above (*de se*) pertain to the natural law. Those things which are adequate and just in the second mode (*in ordine ad aliud*) pertain to the *jus gentium*. This means that whatever is not inherently just (i.e., morally neutral, not unjust), but whose just character flows from the fact of its enactment by human statutes arrived at by reason, pertains not to the natural law but to the *jus gentium*. That which is just *de se* should be immediately evident to human reason; that which is just *in ordine ad aliud* requires the intervention of human calculation to ascertain whether a practice is reasonably ordered to a worthy end. Vitoria cites another example, war. War does not entail an intrinsic equality but can imply an equality (i.e., in redressing a just grievance) based on the relationship of the belligerent parties (*propter aliquid aliud*).[23]

Having concluded, in agreement with Thomas, that the *jus gentium* is to be distinguished from the *jus naturale*, he moves to the question of whether the *jus gentium* is part of the natural law or the positive law. He cites Thomas (1a2ae, q.95, a.4) to the effect that the *jus gentium* belongs to the positive, not natural law. Vitoria asserts that the jurisconsults appear to have a much broader definition of the *jus gentium*, assigning to it the duties of worship of God, love of country and honoring of one's parents. Vitoria criticizes them for construing the *jus gentium* so broadly. Their reason for extending the realm of the *jus gentium* to include such virtues as religion is because brute animals cannot be said to worship God. In effect, Vitoria is criticizing the jurisconsults for holding the ulpianist view of natural law, i.e., "*quod docuit natura omnia animalia.*" Vitoria holds that worship of God, love of country and honoring parents are just in themselves and thus part of the natural law. He does not attach much importance to the debate about whether various practices, virtues or duties should be classified under the heading of *jus naturale* or *jus gentium*. Indeed he dismisses the question as a debate merely of terminology rather than substance.[24]

When Vitoria denigrates the importance of the debate over whether virtues such as honoring one's parents fall under the category of the *jus naturale* or the *jus gentium* and holds that the question is merely of terminology rather than theological content, it appears that he has taken a fateful if inadvertent step in the direction of separating the *jus gentium* from the *jus naturale*. Although he has provided a standard by which one can determine whether a virtuous practice belongs to the natural law (it is just *de se*) or to the *jus gentium* (it is just *in ordine ad aliud*), he does not explicitly connect the *ad aliud* of a feature of the *jus gentium* with the norm of reason, the pre-eminent standard of the natural law. He omits any guidelines which can or must link a worthy end (*ad aliud*) of the *jus gentium* with some precept of the natural law to which the end should be related. This has the effect of permitting any end, whether reasonable or unreasonable, private or communal, to qualify as the *aliud* toward which a virtue or practice is ordained. The features of the *jus gentium* remain broad and vague, no different from the formulation of the jurisconsults whom he has so forcefully criticized.

While it can be readily conceded that virtues such as religion, patriotism and filial piety are good and desirable whether considered as part of the *jus naturale* or *jus gentium*, and in a sense the question of whether they belong to the former or the latter is secondary since it adds nothing to their content, the matter is not so trivial when a practice which is not a self-evident virtue is involved. Slavery is the principal illustration. It is assuredly not good or just *de se* so it cannot be part of the natural law; indeed we saw that the *Institutes* and St. Thomas deemed it to be repugnant to the natural law. But to be part of the *jus gentium* it must be ordained to some worthy end (*in ordine ad aliud*). Would the private good of the master suffice as a worthy end? Or imperial colonization? Or the instruction of the slave in the faith? Must the goal or end be related to the common good to qualify as a feature sanctioned by the *jus gentium*? What is the relation to *naturalis ratio*? These critical questions are not addressed.

Vitoria has criticized the jurisconsults for extending the range of the *jus gentium* too broadly. They assign to the *jus gentium* any practice or virtue which is specific to human beings because they have accepted the ulpianist view of the *jus naturale* and do not want to classify a specifically human practice or virtue as a feature of the natural law, which extends in the ulpianist understanding to subhuman members of the animal kingdom as well. Animals do not consciously worship God or demonstrate allegiance to a country or display filial piety. The jurisconsults thus recognized that to classify worship, patriotism or piety as virtues of the natural law would be absurd if this classification meant that these virtues would be ascribed to animals.

By saying that anything which is just *de se* or *in se* belongs to the natural law, Vitoria implicitly rejects the ulpianist view of natural law, because some practices (e.g., worship of God) are inherently good but specific only to humans. The jurisconsults are handicapped by their retention of the ulpianist view and are forced to extend the scope of the *jus gentium* too broadly.

At this point one faces a tragic shortcoming in the argument of Vitoria: he did not go far enough in his criticism of the jurisconsults. He simply assumed that slavery was a legitimate feature of the *jus gentium*. Had he applied his general criticism of the jurisconsults to the specific question of how slavery can be justified as a feature of the *jus gentium*, viz., its status vis-à-vis Thomas' repeated standard of *naturalis ratio*, he would surely have concluded that it cannot further any goal or end intrinsically connected to any precept of the natural law. This was the logical conclusion toward which his criticism of the jurisconsults was heading but he accepted without protest the critical assumption that slavery was a legitimate feature of the *jus gentium*.

On the critical question of whether the *jus gentium* belongs to the natural law, Vitoria concludes that it must be considered part of the positive, not natural, law.[25] The background for this distinction is Gaius' understanding of the *jus gentium* as the natural law which is strictly human, in contradistinction to the ulpianist view. Within human law one can distinguish, in the tradition of Gaius and the *Corpus Juris Civilis*, the natural law and the positive law. The natural law is necessary, for it carries with it an intrinsic meaning of *ex natura rei*; it is independent of the judgment and will of any human legislator. That parents must educate their children and children obey their parents is an example of the natural law. In contrast, the positive law is contingent because the norms present do not come from nature itself but "depend on the will and consent of men."[26] Positive law emerges either from a private contract or from public consensus as manifested in enacted legislation.[27] Vitoria will cite the institution of private property, i.e., the uneven distribution of created goods, as an example of the positive law.

Later in his *Commentary* on the *Secunda Secundae* Vitoria will reiterate his view that the *jus gentium* is closer to positive law than natural law. The important point about this inclination of the *jus gentium* more to the positive than the natural law is the fact that positive law can be readily changed, a difference that he explicitly acknowledges, while the natural law is immutable.[28]

The application of this point to the issue of slavery is direct. If slavery is part of the *jus gentium*, which Vitoria repeatedly acknowledges, and if the *jus gentium* is positive rather than natural law, then the institution of slavery can readily be changed, i.e., abolished, through human legislation. The notion that slavery is of human invention or law rather than of divine law is completely consistent with the axiom taken directly from St. Thomas that the divine law which is from grace does not remove human law which is from natural reason.[29]

There are two problems, however, with the proposition that slavery, as part of the *jus gentium*, is merely of the positive law: (1) the positive law cannot contradict the natural law; if slavery is contrary to the natural law, it cannot be a legitimate instance of positive law; (2) the force of the natural law is necessary, deriving its power *ex natura rerum*, whereas the force of positive law derives from the respect due to legislative authority; if legislators enact laws which perpetuate slavery, citizens would be obligated in conscience to respect public authority on contingent matters and thus, prescinding from the judgment of the natural law, accept the judgment of human law that slavery is permissible. We shall examine these problems later.

Vitoria then turns to the question of whether one is obligated to obey the *jus gentium*, i.e., whether a violation of the *jus gentium* is sinful. He answers by distinguishing the two kinds of law which constitute the jus gentium—-private contract and public statute. This distinction flows from the nature of positive law, of which, he has concluded, the *jus gentium* is part. There is one kind of positive law manifested in private contracts, and another sort which is found in public consensus, i.e., enacted by a legislature in the form of a statute. The latter represents a solemn compact among a community of peoples and nations. Both kinds of law give rise to legal as well as moral obligations.

Vitoria cites two examples of provisions or conclusions of the *jus gentium* which are morally binding. First, the *jus gentium* dictates that all nations respect the inviolable status of ambassadors. Treatment of ambassadors illustrates not only a binding provision of the *jus gentium* but ultimately the relationship between the *jus naturale* and the *jus gentium* as well. Vitoria's reasoning is as follows: (a) the role of ambassadors is to achieve and preserve the peace; (b) the attainment of peace is a precept of the natural law; (c) by respecting the inviolability of ambassadors, a precept of the *jus gentium*, nations thereby comply with an important precept of the natural law as well, viz., the pursuit of peace. Thus the *jus gentium* serves the *jus naturale*. Vitoria goes so far as to say that the natural law could not be preserved in the absence of the *jus gentium*. His point appears to be political rather than philosophical: unless individuals and nations are disposed to honor a public consensus on contingent matters there is little hope that the pursuit of good and avoidance of evil can become or remain a reality.[30]

A second precept of the *jus gentium* which is cited by Vitoria as an illustration of a morally binding obligation is the reduction of persons taken captive in a just war to slavery. Although he does not elaborate on the reasons why this precept is binding, the idea implicit in his formulation is that only in wars deemed just through the common consensus of the *jus gentium* could the reduction to slavery be permitted.[31] Vitoria is consistent on this point with the medieval tradition that links slavery with war. Slavery apart from war is forbidden, but a lifetime of slavery is deemed less harsh than death, the ancient and medieval penalty for prisoners of war. Vitoria accepts the traditional notion that slavery under these circumstances is humanitarian and adds the qualification that the war in question must be just, a determination to be made by the application of the princiles and precepts of that part of the *jus gentium* which is public and international. After citing these two examples, Vitoria concludes that it is always illicit to violate the *jus gentium*; to do so would be to violate the common consensus of all peoples.

Vitoria proceeds to make two important qualifications in regard to positions he has taken on the *jus gentium*. First, he asserts that its precepts do not follow necessarily from the natural law. If they did, he argues, they would be part of the natural law and the *jus gentium* would be indistinguishable from the *jus naturale*.[32]

The second qualification pertains to the point he has already made about the role of the *jus gentium* in preserving the natural law. Having observed that the natural law could not be preserved in the absence of the *jus gentium*, he now observes that *jus gentium* is nearly necessary but not wholly necessary for the conservation of the natural law. It would be possible to conserve the natural law in the absence of the *jus gentium* but only with the greatest difficulty, since the likelihood of wars would be much greater were it not for the restraining influence of the *jus gentium*.[33]

The final consideration which Vitoria gives to the meaning of the *jus gentium* in his *Commentary* on the *Secunda Secundae* (in q. 57, a.3) is crucial to our investigation, for it bears directly on the question of slavery. Vitoria now inquires whether the *jus gentium* can be abrogated. He answers that since it represents the virtual consensus of the world, it could only be abrogated in the same way, viz., through a consensus of all the world. Since this is inconceivable, he concludes, the *jus gentium* could not be abrogated.[34]

At this point Vitoria suggests that while the entirety of the *jus gentium* could not be abrogated, it could be nullified in part. The example he cites is slavery! He cites the view of Paludanus[35] that Christians captured in war are captives rather than slaves, the difference being that captives are entitled to defend themselves in a court of law and claim other legal rights denied to a slave. The reason for this was that Christians had been baptized.

The *jus gentium* was understood by Isidore of Seville and subsequent commentators to permit the reduction to slavery of those captured in war. Slavery could result from capture and by inference should occur, as a matter of magnanimity, if the only alternative were death. The position of Paludanus appears to add a third option to the captor in his treatment of the vanquished. The defeated could fall into one of three categories: (a) a captive (some rights), (b) a slave (no rights), (c) death. Thus Frenchmen captured by Spanish soldiers, according to Paludanus, should be treated as captives with legal rights rather than as slaves totally lacking in rights. Vitoria cites the view of Paludanus without any objection.[36]

Vitoria thus makes an implicit distinction between a violation of the *jus gentium*—acting directly against a precept (e.g., the inviolable status of ambassadors)—and the partial abrogation of the *jus gentium*—a public consensus which modifies a traditional precept. Improving the lot of a captured prisoner would certainly be a modification rather than violation of the *jus gentium* and Vitoria appears to signal his approval of Paludanus' humanitarian concern by summarily concluding his commentary on the matter with the remark, "let this suffice on the question."

It thus appears that Vitoria has significantly qualified his earlier position that any violation of the *jus gentium* is illicit. He does so by saying, in effect, that not every modification is *eo ipso* a violation. A modification which has obtained the approval of public consensus becomes a partial abrogation. Such a departure can take place without any unfavorable moral consequences ("*bene potest*[...]").[37]

Vitoria has thus provided two important limitations to the traditional medieval justification of slavery: (a) reduction to slavery can occur only when capture occurs in a just war; (b) if the belligerents partially abrogate the *jus gentium* and treat captives as holders of certain legal rights and not as slaves, their "violation" of the traditional precept of the *jus gentium* is not illicit. The suggestion is implicit in the views of Paludanus and Vitoria that baptism confers certain rights upon Christians, an issue which Vitoria confronts in his *De Indis*.

This implied acceptance of some departures from the *jus gentium* as licit appears to be a more mature opinion than that expressed by Vitoria in an earlier *relectio*, his *De Potestate Civili* (c. 1527, according to Heredia). In *De Potestate* Vitoria had made it clear that the *jus gentium* had the *vim legis* ("power of law") and not merely the authority of positive legislation.[38]

It is not clear whether Vitoria intends by "*vim legis*" the force of natural law or not. We have seen that he distinguishes often between natural law as "necessary" and the *jus gentium* as "positive" or contingent. For this reason it does not appear warranted to infer that he intends to suggest in this early *relectio* that the *jus gentium* has the force of natural law, but only that it has a definite authority.

He also makes clear in the same passage from *De Potestate* that any violation of the *jus gentium* is mortally sinful. If this demonstrates nothing else, it shows that he accords the *jus gentium* a considerable authority.

The partial abrogation that he will countenance later in the *Commentarios* was apparently not acceptable to him in this earlier period, at least in regard to more serious issues ("*in rebus gravioribus*"). The authority of the international community ("*totius orbis auctoritate*") outweighs any right of individual nations to abrogate the *jus gentium*. This does not automatically mean of course that *De Potestate* and the *Commentarios* are inconsistent, for he does not suggest that every departure from the *jus gentium* qualifies as a violation. In particular, there is no suggestion whatever that a more humane rendering of the *jus gentium*, as proposed for instance by Paludanus, counts as a violation.

2. The *Relectio De Indis*

Although there are only several references to the *jus gentium* in *De Indis*, the most celebrated definition given by Vitoria of the *jus gentium* occurs in the passage which opens the third section. Before we examine that, however, we must note again the consistent complaint of Vitoria, which we have seen in several instances in the *Commentarios*, that the jurisconsults and the theologians tend to understand *jus* differently. In the Prologue to *De Indis*, he asserts forcefully that divine law governs the plight of the Indians of the New World, not human law, and that the jurists are not qualified to define the terms of divine law.[39]

We shall see that Vitoria's concern for the rights of the "Indians" will lead to a fundamental axiom: dominion comes from divine law and is not subject to human interference, whereas the rights established by human law cannot simply be abridged on account of a subject's failure to observe the divine law.

Apart from the roles played by divine and human law, one can remark the courage evident in Vitoria's observations. He is neither afraid to criticize the competence of the powerful jurisconsults nor reluctant to defend the property rights of a primitive people against the claims of an imperial power.

The basic issue which served as the catalyst for the delivery of the *De Indis relectio* was baptismal catechesis. As noted above, a persistent and often acrimonious debate engulfed the various religious orders of the time in regard to the degree of readiness needed by a proselyte for baptism. Although this question was of critical importance, the inquiry also led inevitably to related questions of comparable importance which had to do with the fundamental morality of the Spanish conquest: could the Spanish assume dominion of the property of the Indians? Was there any justification for confiscating the land of the Indians apart from a just war? Was there any recognized "title" by which the Spanish could claim a right to the new territory?

It was this last question which provided the context for Section Three of *De Indis*. Having listed and rejected in Section Two a number of illegitimate titles, i.e., claims which could not justifiably support the Spanish conquest on legal or moral grounds, Vitoria now examines titles which might be legitimate. The first title he examines is natural society and fellowship:

> The Spaniards have a right to travel into the lands in question and to sojourn there, provided they do no harm to the natives, and the natives may not prevent them. Proof of this may in the first place be derived from the law of nations (*jus gentium*), which either is natural law or is derived from natural law (*Institutes*, I, 2,1): 'What natural reason has established among all nations is called the *jus gentium*.' For, congruently herewith, it is reckoned among all nations inhumane to treat visitors and foreigners badly without some special cause, while, on the other hand, it is humane and correct to treat visitors well; but the case would be different, if the foreigners were to misbehave when visiting other nations.[40]

One notes that the definition which Vitoria cites is a quotation. The text which he obviously had in mind was the *Institutes* of Justinian which, as examined in Chapter One, enshrined the definition of the *jus gentium* of Gaius: "that which natural reason has established *among all men* is called the *'jus gentium'* (emphasis added).[41] Vitoria changed *inter omnes homines* (the *Institutes* from Gaius) to *inter omnes gentes*.

Ernest Nys has suggested that Vitoria's substitution of *"gentes"* for *"homines"* ("nations" for "humanity") was the inauguration of the Law of Nations or International Law, a century before Hugo Grotius, with whose name the beginnings of International Law are commonly associated. Nys suggests that the substitution was the product of a faulty memory but inspired imagination.[42]

Whether Nys was correct that the substitution was due to a faulty memory—a plausible possibility in view of the fact that Vitoria delivered his *lectiones* from notes—or not, Nys is unstinting in his praise of Vitoria, identifying him as the founder of international law:

> The exact notion of International Law is not found in the writings of the medieval authors; International Law remained during this epoch confused and as it were encrusted upon the natural, both in canonical and roman law. Nor had the Protestant authors of the sixteenth century succeeded in establishing an exact concept. It was a Spaniard who defined it, Francisco de Vitoria, in saying that the Law of Nations is that which nature has established among all nations. On the other hand it is to Suarez that the honor belongs of having expressed precise and definite ideas in respect to the juridical rules which link nations with each other.[43]

A clear consensus exists among jurists and historians of jurisprudence that the shift from the definition of Gaius ("*quod naturalis ratio inter omnes homines constituit*") to the definition of Vitoria ("*quod naturalis ratio inter omnes gentes constituit*") ushered into the arena of jurisprudence an approach which was potentially revolutionary.[44]

There are only two more references to the *jus gentium* in Section Three of *De Indis*, but they are both significant. In speaking of property which may be common both to citizens and strangers, Vitoria asserts that the *jus gentium* confers rights and creates obligations:

> There are many things in this connection which issue from the law of nations, which, because it has a sufficient derivation from natural law, is clearly capable of conferring rights and creating obligations. And even if we grant that it is not always derived from natural law, yet there exists clearly enough a consensus of the greater part of the whole world, especially in behalf of the common good of all.[45]

Vitoria is consistent with his view in the *Commentarios* that the *jus gentium* derives from the natural law but does not follow as a necessary conclusion from the premises of the natural law, for that would render the two *jura* indistinguishable. There is a "sufficient" derivation which, coupled with the legislative force attaching to the global consensus, endows the *jus gentium* with the "force of law," i.e., with the power to confer rights and create obligations binding upon all peoples and nations ("*inter omnes gentes*").

The second reference to the *jus gentium* is important because it involves the question of slavery. In describing the circumstances which would convert the Indians from innocent civilians to combatants, Vitoria alludes to the classic precept of the *jus gentium* that prisoners of war become the property of the victor:

> It is a universal rule of the law of nations that whatever is captured in war becomes the property of the conqueror, as laid down in *Dig.*, 49,15,24 and 28, and in the *Decretum*, pt. I, dist. I, can. 9, and more expressly in the *Inst.*, 2, 1, 17, where it is said that 'by the law of nations whatever we take from the enemy becomes ours at once, to such an extent that even men may be brought into slavery to us.'[46]

Vitoria cites this classic statement of the medieval tradition, both moral and juridical, that prisoners of war become slaves upon capture, not only to make the point that all combatants, whether Christian or pagan, are liable to slavery upon capture, but to demonstrate the point just made above, viz., the *jus gentium* confers rights and penalties. It has the *vim legis* ("force of law") which derives "sufficiently" from the natural law to warrant the consensus of nearly all peoples and the obedience of all citizens.

While the above citation is the second and last reference to the *jus gentium* in *De Indis*, there is one more passage which requires our attention. Vitoria asserts that "bondage" (Bate's translation) is of human, not divine law:

> St. Thomas expressly says (q.2, a.2, q.10, a.10) (that) the Church could free all Christian slaves who are in bondage to unbelievers even if that bondage was in other respects lawful [...] How much more then will he be able to free other Christians who have been reduced to bondage but with less severity than as slaves. Confirmation hereof is also to be found in the fact that a wife is as much bound to her husband as a bondsman to his lord, and even more so, seeing that marriage is a tie of the divine law and bondage is not.[47]

It is not surprising that in a *relectio* which begins with a question of baptismal catechesis there should be some consideration of the possibility that baptism generates a difference between the rights of Christians captured in war and the corresponding rights, or lack thereof, of unbaptized pagans similarly taken as prisoners of war. The suggestion appears that some sort of "bondage," more humane than slavery, is appropriate for Christian prisoners. Vitoria is also consistent with the medieval tradition extending from Augustine and Isidore that "bondage" or slavery are features of the human law, i.e., the *jus gentium*, not of divine or natural law.

In 1537 Pope Paul III issued the bull *Sublimis Deus* which condemned the enslavement of the inhabitants of the New World. Vitoria does not refer to *Sublimis Deus* in either the *Commentarios* or *De Indis* which probably means that he was not yet aware of its existence, even though it touches on some of the same issues that he addresses. It is unfortunate for scholars that the possible effect of *Sublimis Deus* upon *De Indis* will never be known. It was even more unfortunate for those enslaved in the servitude that Vitoria sought to ameliorate, however tentatively and conditionally. We are now ready to turn to his thought on the subject of dominion.

3. Vitoria's Overall Understanding of *Dominium*

Vitoria formally considers the meaning of *dominium* in his examination of the issue of restitution in his *Commentary on the Secunda Secundae*.[48] He begins his commentary in question 62 by noting that one cannot incur an obligation to return an object to another unless it can first be shown that the other has enjoyed dominion over the object. The content of the discussion is property rights and ownership; the context is moral and legal.

The first question examined by Vitoria is the etymology of the term *dominium*. He confesses to past doubts about whether the name is truly Latin, i.e.,, whether it has a classical pedigree, because it is rarely found in the works of the great masters such as Cicero and Livy. His doubts are settled on the matter because the term is found in the *Corpus Juris Civilis* under such titles as "*De adquirendo dominio*" and "*De adquirenda possessione*." He observes that it is also found in the scriptures (Tobias 8.24; 1 Mach. 11.8).[49]

Just as *dominium* must be understood before one can speak intelligently of restitution, so *jus* must be determined before *dominium* can be properly grasped. Vitoria asserts, in the manner of an axiom rather than conclusion, that there is no dominion which is not based on *jus*.

Vitoria cites the constant authority of the jurisconsults that *jus* is that which is permitted by the laws. He refers back to question 57, a.1 *ad 2* in which Thomas holds that *lex* and *jus* are not identical, that *lex* is the *ratio juris*, i.e., the reason by which something is licit. Vitoria accepts the view of Thomas that *jus* and *justum* are the same, an identification, Vitoria notes, which is consistent with Aristotle's *Ethics*.[50] Accordingly, one can speak of both *jus* and *justum* as that which is permitted by the law. Vitoria refers to the sense of common usage to illustrate his conclusion: when we speak of a "right" to use something, we mean "it is permissible" for one to use something.

Vitoria turns to the definition of *jus* given by Conradus Summenhart (d. 1502), a popular German jurisconsult of the era; he is usually cited simply as "Conrad." Conrad's definition is broad: a power or faculty belonging to another according to the law. Conrad had appropriated this definition from the work of John Gerson (d. 1429), a pupil of the nominalist Peter of Ailly, whom he succeeded in 1395 as chancellor of the University of Paris.[51] After citing Conrad and Gerson, Vitoria notes that their understanding of *jus* as a power or a faculty conforms to its meaning in several scriptural passages. He cites 1 Cor. 7.4, which states that a wife does not have power over her body, but that it belongs to her husband ("*Mulier sui corporis potestatem non habet*[...]"), as well as the question directed to Jesus in his expulsion of the money changers in the temple, "by what right do you do this?" ("*Dic nobis, in qua potestate haec facis?*" Mt. 21.24; Luke 20.2).

Moving from the point that *jus* stands for a faculty or power to do something in accord with the law, Vitoria now inquires whether *dominium* and *jus* are the same. He begins by noting that *dominium* can be understood in three ways. First, it can mean a certain eminence or superiority. In this sense some men are cited as *dominii* in regard to subordinates. Vitoria cites Thomas' *De potentia Dei* as an authority for the proposition that dominion always entails a power to compel subordinates.[52] *Jus* is clearly different from *dominium* understood in this sense, he argues, because a child has a *jus* to food and shelter from his parents but is not their *dominus*.

A second understanding of *dominium* occurs in the context of property. This meaning is broader than that of eminence but is still proper ("*latius sed proprius*").   The *Corpus Juris Civilis* employs *dominium* in the context of property rights, distinguishable from use, usufruct and possession. Vitoria quotes the section of the CJC entitled "*de adquirenda possessione*" which distinguishes dominion and possession. Those who enjoy the use, usufruct or possession of property can do so without ownership. But there are limits to their rights: they cannot, for example, alienate the property.   Only those who enjoy ownership of an object can be said to have dominion over it in the sense of being free to use or even dispose of it in any fashion not disapproved by the law. In the context of property law, ownership and dominion are equivalent terms but in the larger scheme of creation dominion is the broader concept, encapsulating the body of rights which rational creatures can exercise. Ownership is one such right.

Because mere possession does not necessarily mean ownership or dominion, the CJC confirms the related distinction between *jus* and *dominium* which is the object of Vitoria's inquiry at this point. One who has possession or use of an object has a *jus* but not *dominium*. One can use an object belonging to another, thus having a *jus*,[53] but one who rightfully uses or possesses the property of another does not have dominion over it.[54]

A third meaning attaches to *dominium* according to Vitoria: a certain faculty to use something according to the laws. Again Vitoria cites Conrad for this proposition.[55] In this manner of understanding *dominium* Vitoria agrees with Conrad that there is a legitimate identity of *jus* and *dominium*. Vitoria adds that most jurists do not subscribe to this position: they are loath to confer dominion on someone who merely uses or possesses the property of another.   But Vitoria quotes approvingly the view of Conrad that in regard to restitution and morality, *dominium* and *jus* can refer to the same reality:

> If we take something from another having dominion, in that manner
> we take the faculty from him of using the thing, and we are therefore
> held to restitution.   In order that I be held to restitution for

something, it is enough that I do injury to someone in a thing over which he has some faculty. That faculty might be anything; if I do an injury against him, I am held to make restitution to him. *Jus* and *dominium* can be defined in this manner.[56]

Vitoria adds that rarely are *dominium* and *jus* viewed chiefly from the standpoint of restitution, which means that they are rarely held to be equivalent terms. Moreover, he acknowledges that this third sense can easily be abused by someone attempting to prove dominion over an object where the relationship is one merely of use or possession.

Vitoria concludes this section by summarizing his view. Although *jus* and *dominium* are in general to be distinguished, on the subject of restitution, the terms can be used indifferently because what is at issue is the injury done to a party and the need to remedy that injury.

Having made the point that *dominium* and *jus* are generally different, Vitoria asks whether someone can indeed be a *dominus* in creation and answers in the affirmative through a series of eleven propositions, followed by several corollaries. The first nine propositions are germane to our inquiry. We shall list them for the sake of completeness and conclude with the eighth proposition which is critical to the issue of slavery, namely, that human dominion in general is granted by divine natural law, not human law, and therefore cannot be withdrawn by human fiat.

The first proposition advanced by Vitoria is that God is our Lord and *dominus* of all creatures and the entire world.[57] God could not have created everything and be called a servant. He owns all things and is properly lord or ruler of creation. Vitoria cites Psalm 23.1 and Judith 9.17 to illustrate the plenitude and dominion of God.

The second proposition holds that all *jus* and *dominium* found in creatures are gifts from God.[58] This means that any power or dominion found in creation must be attributed ultimately to God. Vitoria's third proposition holds that the dominion which in some way belonged only to God, i.e., prior to creation, was not communicated to any irrational creature.[59] In this section Vitoria rejects the contemporary notion that irrational and even inanimate creatures shared in divine dominion. He cites St. Thomas' views that only rational creatures have dominion.[60] He concludes that animals cannot possess a *jus* or any *dominium* since any use of them for human needs would on that account constitute an injury to them and they would be entitled to restitution; only a human owner of an animal could be entitled to restitution.

The fourth proposition holds that the beneficent God has given to human creatures dominion over all other creatures and created goods, with the exception of the angels. He cites Psalm 8 and Genesis 1.26, 28 to illustrate the dominion of humanity entrusted to it by the Creator.[61] God made all things *propter hominem*. "Since man is the end of creation, it follows that he is lord of all," he concludes.

At this point Vitoria makes two important points. First, it is by divine natural (rather than positive) law that man[62] has the right to use created goods for his needs. This is significant because it means that human authority cannot annul the exercise of or right to dominion of every human creature. Moreover God cannot act to change this since it is divine natural law rather than positive law. In the case of divine positive law (Vitoria cites the choice of David to be king of Israel), God can change matters according to His will. But the identity of man as a rational creature endowed with dominion stands as an unchanging reality of creation.

The second significant point which Vitoria makes in regard to the identity of man as end and *dominus* of creation is that his dominion does not empower him to use other creatures without restriction. Man does have dominion over all things but this is not a power to do all things with them. Vitoria specifically cites the relationship of a master and servant as an illustration of the inherent limitation of uses; the master, for instance, lacks the authority to kill his servant.[63]

Vitoria's fifth proposition holds that not only does the universal human community enjoy dominion over created goods, but even in the state of natural justice man was able to "use and abuse" ("*uti et abuti*") other creatures.

The sixth proposition hold that man did not lose dominium through original sin but remains master of all creation. Dominion is entrusted to man through natural law; his loss of paradise through sin in no way ends man's identity as the end and master of creation. Even after sin all things are subordinated to the good and needs of man.[64]

The seventh proposition is that the division of things did not take place on the basis of natural law. It is not the role or task of natural law to determine how property is to be distributed among various peoples. This distribution of property, i.e., the institution of private property, was considered a feature of the *jus gentium*, not the *jus naturale*.[65] The eighth proposition holds that the division of property was not made on the basis of divine positive law. Vitoria writes that scripture, history and reason can verify that this is so. Although in some instances God granted property (e.g., the promised land to the sons of Jacob), He did not undertake the task of dividing material goods among the descendants of Adam or Noah. A corollary follows from this: no one is temporal ruler of all the universe.[66]

The ninth proposition holds that the division and appropriation of property was done according to human law. Neither divine natural nor positive law, nor the angels could be responsible for the varied distribution of material goods. It had to occur through human law.[67]

In summary, we observe that dominion attaches to every human creature. It derives ultimately from divine dominion and cannot be destroyed by either sin or human authority. Dominion belongs to man as the apex of creation; it extends to no irrational or inanimate creature. Although dominion is part of the human identity of all rational creatures, it does contain inherent limitations, e.g., the prohibition against injury or death of a subordinate. Whereas dominion attaches to human beings through divine natural law, the distribution of property (i.e., the institution of private property) occurs through human law.

We shall now turn to the *lectiones* of *De Indis* to see the specific application of these ideas on dominion to the status of the natives of the New World.

4. Vitoria's Understanding of *Dominium* in *De Indis*

The *relectio De Indis* is an extended discussion of the rights of the Indians in the New World. Its immediate focus and point of departure is baptismal catechesis. Vitoria centers his reflections around the Gospel text of Matthew 28.19, "Teach all nations, baptizing them in the name of the Father and of the Son and of the Holy Spirit." The immediate question for Vitoria is "whether the children of unbelievers may be baptized against the wishes of their parents."[68]

Vitoria raises the larger and thornier question of "whether the aborigines in question were true owners in both private and public law before the arrival of the Spaniards." The answer to this question is found, he avers, through reference to the nature of dominion. Vitoria expresses his reluctance to pursue the "numerous utterances of the doctors" on the nature of dominion, noting that he has already dealt with the subject in his commentary on q. 62 in the *Secunda Secundae*.[69]

Despite his expressed reservations about repeating his reflections on dominion found in his *Commentarios*, Vitoria cites several possible reasons why the Indians may be lacking in dominion:

> If the aborigines had not dominion, it would seem that no other cause
> is assignable therefore except that they were sinners or were
> unbelievers or were witless or irrational.[70]

Vitoria proceeds to consider at length the possibility that sin, unbelief, unsound mind or irrational nature might remove the necessary "title" for dominion. We shall examine and summarize his views on these possible explanations for a defective title leading to a non-existence or loss of dominion.

John Wyclif (c. 1330-1384) and the Waldensians had popularized the notion that grace is a necessary title for dominion. This means that anyone in mortal sin necessarily lacks dominion over anything: "no one is a civil owner, while he is in mortal sin."[71]

While Vitoria indicates his familiarity with the distinction of Wyclif between civil and natural dominion, he makes no further reference to Wyclif's understanding of divine dominion, preferring instead merely to link Wyclif with the Hussites, Waldensians and their condemnation by the Council of Constance. In fact, however, L.J. Daly, SJ, has shown that Wyclif's principal concern in linking the dominion of a creature with his moral condition was to preserve the sanctity of divine dominion, i.e., to prevent the attribution of human excess to participation in divine sovereignty. Daly's paraphrase of Wyclif's thoughts on divine dominion shows a fundamental similarity between Vitoria and Wyclif on the limits of human dominion:

> When one speaks of human lordship, then, it is really only a stewardship held from the supreme Lord; for no creature serves another except insofar as he serves his God. Thus no one is placed in servitude unless God as principal lord, first places him there. Finally, the creatures who dispense temporal goods of God need the mutual spiritual help of their brothers for the edification of an integral militant Church.[72]

Vitoria observes merely that Wyclif's opinion on civil dominion was condemned by the Council of Constance (1414-1417). He begins his refutation of the notion that mortal sin deprives the subject of dominion by noting the distinction between civil dominion—power over property granted by human law—and natural dominion—control over activities granted humans by God. Although the civil authority may have the power to remove dominion, there can be no loss of natural, i.e.,

God-given, dominion, for even a sinner has a right to defend his life. Vitoria also cites the example of kings in scripture who were sinners but who did not lose their kingly dominion.[73]

Perhaps most important for our purposes is the explicit rejection by Vitoria of the notion that sinful behavior destroys man's identity as *imago Dei*, thereby imperiling his natural dominion:

> Thirdly, I employ against the opposing party their own argument: dominion is founded on the image of God; but man is God's image by nature, that is, by his reasoning powers; therefore, dominion is not lost by mortal sin.[74]

Vitoria thus concludes that sinful behavior does not suffice to remove dominion.

Vitoria now considers the possibility that unbelief is sufficient to cause loss of dominion. Against this proposition he cites the evidence of scripture that unbelieving kings (e.g., Sennacherib and Pharaoh) were in no way subject to a loss of their royal dominion on account of their clear lack of belief; Joseph, a believer, made all of the land of Egypt subject to the Pharaoh, a pagan (Gen. 47).

Following this scriptural argument Vitoria cites St. Thomas' view in *ST*. 2a2ae. q. 10, a.12 that unbelief does not prevent anyone from being a true owner:

> The proposition is also supported by the reasoning of St. Thomas, namely: unbelief does not destroy either natural law or human law; but ownership and dominion are based either on natural law or human law; therefore they are not destroyed by want of faith[...] Hence it is manifest that it is not justifiable to take anything that they possess from either Saracens or Jews or other unbelievers; but the act would be theft or robbery no less than if it were done to Christians.[75]

Vitoria makes it clear that confiscation of property is warranted neither for unbelief in general nor for heresy in particular: "if ownership be not forfeited on the ground of any other unbelief, it follows that it is not forfeited on the ground of heresy."[76] Although Vitoria cites Conrad, Sylvester and other jurisconsults, it is his invocation of St. Thomas' authority that will dominate the Spanish debate on the morality of colonization after his death:

> From all this the conclusion follows that the barbarians in question cannot be barred from being true owners, alike in public and in private law, by reason of the sin of unbelief or any other mortal sin, nor does such sin entitle Christians to seize their goods and lands, as Cajetan proves at some length and neatly (*Secunda Secundae*, q. 66, a.8).[77]

Two more arguments were advanced to support the view that the Indians could not possess or exercise dominion over property. The first, more general argument was that all non-Caucasians were by definition irrational creatures and therefore incapable of dominion. The second, more specific argument was that the Indians discovered in the New World were as a matter of fact lacking in the mental acumen needed for dominion.

In responding, Vitoria cites the opinions of Sylvester and Conrad that ownership extends to irrational creatures, both sensible and insensible, as well as to rational beings. Conrad's justification for this broad understanding of ownership is that it is "nothing more than the right to put a thing to one's own use." Accordingly, the stars own light and animals own the plants upon which they feed.

Vitoria proceeds to reject categorically the notion that irrational creatures are capable of dominion. Dominion is a right, a *jus*, as Conrad agrees, but irrational creatures cannot possess a right. Therefore they cannot have dominion:

> Wild beasts themselves and all irrational animals are more fully within the ownership of man than slaves are. Therefore, if slaves cannot have anything of their own, much less can irrational animals.[78]

Vitoria then confirms the correctness of his argumentation by citing the authority of St. Thomas to the effect that only rational creatures can have dominion over their acts, and the test of a subject being master of his acts is whether or not he has the power of choice. Since animals are moved rather than move on their own, they cannot say, "it is in my power," in the manner of rational creatures.[79]

Vitoria then examines the question of whether a child or someone suffering from a perpetual unsoundness of mind can be said to have dominion. He answers in the affirmative: a child can suffer a wrong, therefore he has a right over things, therefore he has dominion. The same reasoning applies to a mentally unsound individual.

The critical question now looms: is the status of the "aborigines" of the New World such that they are irrational creatures and therefore lacking in dominion? Because of its importance, Vitoria's answer is quoted in its entirety:

> The Indian aborigines are not barred on this ground [i.e., unsoundness of mind] from the exercise of true dominion. This is proved from the fact that the true state of the case is that they are not of unsound mind, but have, according to their kind, the use of reason. This is clear, because there is a certain method in their affairs, for they have polities which are orderly arranged and they have definite marriage and magistrates, overlords, laws, and workshops, and a system of exchange, all of which call for the use of reason; they also have a kind of religion. Further, they make no error in matters which are self-evident to others; this is witness to their use of reason. Also, God and nature are not wanting in the supply of what is necessary in great measure for the race. Now, the most conspicuous feature of man is reason, and power is useless which is not reducible to action. Also, it is through no fault of theirs that these aborigines have for many centuries been outside the pale of salvation, in that they have been born in sin and void of baptism and the use of reason whereby to seek out the things needful for salvation. Accordingly I for the most part attribute their seeming so unintelligent

and stupid to a bad and barbarous upbringing, for even among ourselves we find many peasants who differ little from brutes.[80]

Having affirmed the essential humanity and claim to dominion of the Indians of the New World, Vitoria establishes a striking historical analogy. In view of the fact that the Spanish had driven the Moors from Granada in 1492, completing the Christian conquest of the Iberian peninsula, and that the Jews were expelled from Spain in the same year, the Spanish were acutely aware of the priority and delicacy of the question of whether sworn enemies of Christianity had rights, such as dominion. Vitoria now makes a classic application of the a fortiori argument:

> The upshot of all the preceding is, then, that the aborigines undoubtedly had true dominion in both public and private matters, just like Christians, and that neither their princes nor private persons could be despoiled of their property on the ground of their not being true owners. It would be harsh to deny to those, who have never done any wrong, what we grant to Saracens and Jews, who are the persistent enemies of Christianity. We do not deny that these latter peoples are true owners of their property, if they have not seized lands elsewhere belonging to Christians.[81]

A final inquiry remains. What of the theory of natural slavery found in book one of Aristotle's *Politics*? Could the Indians be slaves by nature due to an inherent incapacity to achieve self-government? Vitoria's answer is to deny that any are inherently slaves. The method that he uses to assert this principle and make the appropriate application is to provide a benign interpretation of Aristotle's intent:

> Aristotle certainly did not mean to say that such as are not over-strong mentally are by nature subject to another's power and incapable of dominion alike over themselves and other things; for this is civil and legal slavery, wherein none are slaves by nature. Nor

does the Philosopher mean that, if any by nature are of weak mind, it is permissible to seize their patrimony and enslave them and put them up for sale; but what he means is that by defect of their nature they need to be ruled and governed by others and that it is good for them to be subject to others, just as sons need to be subject to their parents until of full age, and a wife to her husband[...]It is clear that he does not mean hereby that such persons can arrogate to themselves a sway over others in virtue of their superior wisdom, but that nature has given them capacity for rule and government. Accordingly, even if we admit that the aborigines in question are as inept and stupid as is alleged, still dominion cannot be denied to them, nor are they to be classed with the slaves of civil law.[82]

This affirmation of the human rights of the Indians concludes section one of *De Indis*. The second section is an inquiry into illegitimate titles for the reduction of the Indians into the power of the Spaniards, while the third section explores legitimate titles by which the Indians could be colonized. These latter two sections focus on the limits of ecclesiastical and civil power. Aside from a strong reiteration of the now established principle of Thomas that "dominion and pre-eminence were introduced by human law[...] not by natural law,"[83] these sections are beyond the scope of our inquiry. They do, however, give further evidence of Vitoria's freedom from any sort of nationalistic bias. He is emphatic in his rejection of blatantly nationalistic arguments that the Spanish are somehow "entitled" to colonize the Indians. He does accept the argument that the Spanish have a right to be in the New World insofar as their presence is based on natural society and fellowship. It is thus clear that Vitoria does not believe the Spanish have any obligation to leave the New World, but merely to treat the Indians with a fundamental human dignity, i.e., at least on par with that accorded Saracens and Jews.

5. Conclusions

It will be the task of Chapter Four to analyze the different understandings of St. Thomas, Vitoria and Soto in regard to the *jus gentium*, dominion and slavery but several observations appear in order at this point. They are drawn from three historians of moral theology and pertain to (1) the impact of nominalism; (2) the radically different meaning of *jus* which accompanied the nominalist influence; (3) a summary analysis of the strengths and limitations of Francisco de Vitoria.

Servais Pinckaers, OP, has described the impact upon moral theology of the surge of nominalism which characterized the fourteenth century:

> If a comparison is permitted that may seem audacious and yet can be very exactly verified, we see with Occam the first atomic explosion of the modern era. The atom which exploded was clearly not physical but psychic: it is the nucleus of the human spirit and its powers which is broken as a result of a new conception of liberty, provoking successive explosions which will shatter the unity of theology and western thought. With Occam liberty, through the claim of radical autonomy which it defines, is completely separated from everything distinct—from reason and sensibility, from natural inclinations and from external events. Multiple separations ensue: on the one hand between liberty and nature, law and grace, and, on the other hand, between morality and mysticism, reason and faith, the individual and society, etc.[84]

When the personal sacrifice of Vitoria entailed by his dogged determination to substitute the *Summa Theologica* of St. Thomas for the *Sententiae* of Peter Lombard as the standard theology text in seminaries is considered, there can be no doubt of his determination to remain faithful to, even to recapture, the thomistic tradition. But it is against this bleak, atomized philosophical background that Vitoria must struggle to retain the metaphysical basis of St. Thomas' understanding of *jus* and *dominium*.

For a summary description of the new meaning of *jus* (as "right" and "title") brought about by the nominalist sea-change which had its roots in the fourteenth century, we are indebted to Eberhard Welty, OP:

> There has been a lamentable confusion, indeed, falsification, of ideas ever since the sixteenth century. Right in its objective sense (meaning the just thing, what is due to others) has fallen into disuse. In its place it has been claimed that what is now called subjective right is right in its proper and original sense. Yet the contrary is the case. Right in the proper sense is what is just; whereas subjective right (legal title) is right in the derived and metaphorical sense. St. Thomas Aquinas, for example, who treats of the question of right thoroughly and in detail, undoubtedly knew what we mean by subjective right, but he did not regard legal title as right. Discussing the question: 'What is right?', he enumerated the various meanings of the term 'right' (Latin: *jus*), without mentioning legal title (see II-II, 57, I). The reason is that right belongs to the category of relations (equality) whereas 'title' signifies moral ability, permissibility, freedom.[85]

Welty's observation that the meaning of "title" is radically different from St. Thomas' understanding of *jus* could in no way be inferred from a reading of *De Indis* no matter how valiantly Vitoria labors to capture the thomistic cast of that critical concept. One wonders what the result would have been if Vitoria had concentrated his enormous analytical powers not on the distinction between legitimate and illegitimate titles but on whether "title" was the appropriate lens with which to view the human rights of the Indians.

In a trajectory of the history of moral theology from St. Thomas to St. Alphonsus, Louis Vereecke and Bernard Häring summarize the contribution of Francisco de Vitoria and the Salamanca school:

The originality of the Salamancan school resides in the fact that it integrated within the framework of St. Thomas' moral theology the acquisitions of nominalism, i.e., a preference for the concrete and adaptations to modern times. This will be its major accomplishment. Vitoria, for instance, knew quite well the major problems of his era. Indeed he can be regarded as the founder of International Law. He placed the economic and political problems of his contemporaries in a thomistic light. Even if he studied numerous cases, they were nevertheless real cases. In a spontaneous affinity with the jurists (and canon law is for them always in full blossom), these theologians share equally the taste of the Renaissance for ancient sources in the manner of Erasmus. Vitoria displays a stunning acquaintance with patristic sources. All of this combines to confer upon the salamancan writings an exceptional depth of wisdom. In a sense it marks an apogee for moral theology.

Nevertheless, we must speak also of their limits. Most of them had as professors deep-seated nominalists. They take from their earliest formation a reserve vis-a-vis metaphysical speculation. They adopt thomism but generally without exploring the depth of its synthesis. In the *Summa* dogma interests them less than moral (theology); they constantly risk reducing moral theology only to the *Secunda Pars*, such as the catalogue of virtues in the *Secunda Secundae*. As an example, in fourteen years of teaching devoted to commentary on the *Summa*, Vitoria reserved ten for the *Secunda Pars* and from this interest the *Secunda Secundae* is the principal beneficiary. This is precisely the danger of a rupture between dogmatic theology and moral theology, which strikes at the very heart of thomism.[86]

With these astute capsulized summaries of the major issues of our study serving for the moment as preliminary reflections, let us now turn to Vitoria's friend and protege, Domingo de Soto.

Notes for Chapter Two

1. Luis Getino, OP, "El maestro Fr. Francisco de Vitoria," *La Ciencia Tomista* 1 (Marzo-Abril, 1910), p. 9.

2. See H. Muñoz, *Vitoria and the Conquest of America*, 2d. ed., (Manila: University of Santo Tomas Press, 1938), p. 41.

3. Ernest Nys, Introduction, p. 66, Vitoria, *De Indis et De Iure Belli Relectiones* in the collection, *The Classics of International Law*, edited by James Brown Scott (Washington: Carnegie Institution, 1917).

4. See Herbert F. Wright, ed. *Francisco de Vitoria: Addresses in commemoration of the fourth centenary of his lectures "De Indis" and "De Iure Belli," 1532-1932*, a compilation of essays delivered at the Catholic University of America, May 1, 1932 (Washington, DC: Catholic University Press, 1932), *passim*.

5. L. Getino, "El Maestro Fr. Francisco de Vitoria," *La Ciencia Tomista* 5 (Nov-Dec., 1910), pp. 12ff. Getino reviews the record of Vitoria's interventions on behalf of Erasmus in his conflicts with the Inquisition. Vitoria was not uncritical of Erasmus' theology but sought to defend him from unfair attacks.

6. The *prima* lecture was delivered at 6:00 a.m., whereas the *vespera* lecture was delivered at 6:00 p.m., an indication of the importance and intensity attached to these *lectiones*. Domingo de Soto, Vitoria's student and protegé, served as *vespera* professor at Salamanca during the last years of Vitoria's life.

7. E. Nys, *op.cit.*, p. 70. The credentials of Nys are relevant so that his praise of Vitoria is understood as professional admiration and not mere puffery. Nys (1851-1920) was Professor of international law at the University of Brussels and a member of the permanent Court of Arbitration at The Hague. He was an editor of *Revue de droit internationale*, and focused on Spanish law in his *Le droit des gens et les anciens jurisconsultes espagñols* (Brussels: Beyaert, 1914).

8. Cited in C.H. McKenna, OP, *Francis de Vitoria: Founder of International Law*, 2d. edition, (Wash. DC: Catholic Association for International Peace, 1930), p. 8.

9. L. Getino, "El maestro Fr. Francisco de Vitoria," *La Ciencia Tomista* 9 (Jul.-Aug., 1911), pp. 364ff.

10. L.Getino, OP, *El maestro fr. Francisco de Vitoria, su vida, su doctrina y su influencia* (Madrid: Covarrubias, 1930), chapter XV.

11. Beltran de Heredia, OP. *Franciscus de Vitoria, OP: Commentarios a la Secunda Secundae de Santo Tomas* (Salamanca, Spain: Universidad de Salamanca Press, vol. I, 1932; vol. II, 1932; vol. III, 1934; vol. IV, 1934; vol. V, 1935).

12. H. Muñoz, *op.cit.*, p. 42.

13. Beltran de Heredia, OP, *Los Manuscritos de Maestro Fray Francisco de Vitoria*, OP (Madrid: Valencia, 1928). The titles and dates of the *relectiones*, as cited in Muñoz, *supra*, pp. 42ff, are as follows:

　　1. *De Silentii Obligatione* (1526-7);
　　2. *De Potestate Civili* (1527-8);
　　3. *De Homicidio* (1528-9);
　　4. *De Matrimonio* (1529-30);
　　5. *De Potestate Ecclesiae* (1530-32);
　　6. *De Potestate Papae et Concilii* (1532-33);
　　7. *De Augmento Caritatis* (1533-34);
　　8. *De eo ad quod tenetur veniens ad usum rationis* (1535-36);
　　9. *De Simonia* (1535-36);
　10. *De Temperantia* (1536-37);
　11. *De Indis* (1537-38);
　12. *De Jure Belli* (1538-39);
　13. *De Magia* [two] (1539-41).

14. L.A.Getino, OP, *El Maestro Fr. Francisco de Vitoria y El Renancimiento Filosofico Teologico Del Siglo XVI* (Madrid, 1933), footnote, p. 100.

15. Luis Getino, OP, dates the commentaries on the *Secunda Secundae* from 1534 to 1540 in *La Ciencia Tomista* 8 (Mayo-Junio, 1911), p. 184. There is no disagreement about these dates that I have been able to discover.

16. In the first, i.e., Boyer edition of the *Relectiones theologicae* (1565), these two lectures are entitled *De Indis recenter inventis relectio prior* and *De Indis, sive de jure belli Hispanorum in barbaros, relectio posterior*. Boyer was a contemporary of Vitoria. He had been the librarian at the University of Salamanca. A second edition of the *relectiones*, prepared in 1565 under the direction of Alonso Muñoz, OP, was printed in Salamanca by Juan de Canova. Its title page states that the edition "has been purged of the prodigious and countless mistakes with which the first edition, that of Jacques Boyer, was filled." Muñoz adds in a prefatory note that he became aware of the errata while aiding Domingo de Soto in the preparation of a commentary on the *Sententiae* of Peter Lombard. To this second or Muñoz edition of the *relectiones* was annexed a four page list of errata in a subsequent edition of 1580 printed at Ingolstadt.

17. Francisco de Vitoria, OP, *Commentarios a la Secunda Secundae de Santo Tomas*. Edicion preparada por el R.P. Vicente Beltran de Heredia, OP. Tomo III: De Justitia < qq. 57-66 > (Salamanca, Spain, Spartado 17, 1934).

18. "In objecto justitiae, scilicet justo, non est considerandum de qualitate agentis, puta si est dives vel pauper qui emit, dummodo det aequale." *ibid.*, q. 57, a.1, num.4, p.2.

19. "Ex his differentiis ponit sanctus Thomas conclusionem principalem: quod jus est objectum justitiae, quia non considerat qualitatem agentis, sed est in ordine ad alterum." *ibid.*, num.4, p.3.

20. "Capiendo ergo jus proprie, ut sanctus Thomas capit in proposito, dicimus quod *jus* non derivatur, id est dicitur a *justitia*, sed potius *justitia* derivatur a *jure*." *ibid.*, num. 7, p. 5. (Emphasis added)

21. "Sed hoc (i.e., Buridan's equation of *lex* and *jus*) facile excluditur ex jurisconsultorum diffinitione, qui dicunt quod justitia est 'firma atque

constans voluntas jus suum unicuique tribuens,' ubi jus non potest capi pro lege ipsa quae est causa justi. Sic etiam dicitur a juristis quod praecepta juris sunt: neminem laedere, jus suum unicuique tribuere. Ecce quo pacto ibi jus non potest capi pro lege quae est causa justi, sed pro justo." *ibid.*, num. 7, p. 5.

22. "Sanctus Thomas ponit distinctionem, scilicet jus naturale est quod ex natura sua est alteri commensuratum." *ibid.*, q.57, a.3, num. 1, p. 12.

23. "Illud quod est adaequatum et justum secundo modo ut ordinatur ad aliud justum, est jus gentium. Itaque illud quod non est aequum ex se, sed ex statuto humano in ratione fixo, illud vocatur jus gentium; ita quod propter se non importat aequitatem, sed propter aliquid aliud, ut de bello et de aliis, etc." *ibid.*

24. "Respondeo ad hoc: et primo dico, quod disputatio est potius de nomine quam de re, nam parum refert hoc vel illud dicere. Secundo dico, quod jurisconsulti nimis extendunt jus gentium et nimis ample capiunt illud, quia ut patet in titulo illo 'De justitia et jure,' extendunt jus gentium ad omnia illa in quibus non communicant bruta animantia, ita quod extendunt illud ad omnia quae sunt communia solis hominibus." *ibid.*, num. 2, p. 13. His criticism of the phrase "de justitia et jure" as too broad is of historical interest, for this became the standard title of manuals of moral theology on questions of justice.

25. "Et sic ad dubium principale respondeo per hanc conclusionem: quod jus gentium potius debet reponi sub jure positivo quam sub jure naturali. Unde theologi non ponunt illa exempla quae ponunt jurisconsulti de cultu Dei et honoratione parentum etc., sed alia vel de proprietate rerum vel de aliis quae de se non habent aequitatem, id est ex natura sua, *utputa manumissiones*, proprietas possessionum, conservatio regni, etc. Disputatio est de nomine, et ideo potestis loqui vel sicut juristae, vel sicut theologi, capiendo terminos largo modo, vel proprie, ut debent capi, et melius." *ibid.*, p. 14 (emphasis added). It is clear from the Latin text cited here that Vitoria believes the meaning of *jus* is "better" comprehended when it is used in a "proper" rather than "broader" ("*largo modo*") sense. It is also clear that he faults the jurists for using the terms too broadly, i.e.,, more broadly than the construction

given *jus* and related terms by the theologians. In view of this clear preference of Vitoria for a strict construction, it is surprising that Francis Crane Macken utterly ignores the words *ut debent capi, et melius* when he translates the last sentence of number 2, p. 14 as follows: "The dispute is one of words, and therefore one may speak as a jurist or as a theologian, interpreting the terms loosely or closely—*however one may consider they ought to be taken*" (emphasis added) in James B. Scott, *The Spanish Origin of International Law: Francisco de Vitoria and His Law of Nations* (Oxford: Clarendon Press, 1934), Appendix V, p. cxii. Macken appears to be exculpating the jurists from taking an overly broad construction and thus departing from the clear import of Vitoria's meaning as disclosed in the Latin translation.

26. Vitoria, *op.cit.*, in q. 59, a.1, nums. 1-2.

27. See R.P.S. Ramirez, OP, *El Derecho de Gentes* (Madrid: Ediciones studium, 1955), p. 138.

28. "Respondetur quod posita necessitate in rebus, mutantur res: et illa quae sunt de jure gentium dicuntur aliquando de jure naturali, et aliquando de jure positivo: et ideo St. Thomas dicit supra esse de jure naturali, et modo de jure positivo. Ex quo patet quod supra diximus, quod jus gentium, licet participet de jure naturali et positivo, tamen *potius spectat ad positivum*: et dixit esse de jure positivo. *Et inde patet, si est positivum, mutari posse ius gentium.*" Vitoria, *op.cit.*, in q. 66, a.2, num. 5 (emphasis added).

29. "Jus divinum quod est ex gratia non tollit jus humanum quod est ex naturali ratione." 2a2ae. q.10, a.10; "Ea enim quae sunt naturalia homini neque subtrahuntur neque dantur homini per peccatum." 1a. q.98, a.2.

30. "Ad hoc respondetur, supposito quod duplex est jus gentium, sicut duplex is jus positivum, ut diximus supra[...] Quoddam est jus positivum ex privato pacto et consensu, et quoddam factum est ex pacto publico. Ita de jure gentium dicimus, quod quoddam factum est ex communi consensu omnium gentium et nationum. Et isto modo legati admissi sunt de jure gentium, et apud omnes nationes sunt inviolabiles; nam *jus gentium ita accedit ad jus naturale ut non possit servari jus naturale sine hoc jure gentium.*" *ibid.*, num. 3, p. 15 (emphasis added).

31. "Idem est de captivis in bello justo, quod efficiuntur servi de jure gentium apud omnes gentes et nationes. Unde ex hoc semper est illicitum violare jus gentium, quia est contra commuem consensum." *ibid*.

32. "Jus gentium, postquam non est necessarium jus et naturale, sed *positivum*." *ibid*., in q. 57, a.3, num. 5 (emphasis added). Vitoria is consistent in identifying the natural law with necessary conclusions and the *jus gentium* with "positive" determinations. These latter pertain to contingent matters (e.g., private property) which are midway between the premises of the natural law and the legislative enactments of the positive law. The firmness of Vitoria's view that the *jus gentium* is more positive than natural law is confirmed by his reiteration later: "Jus gentium est *magis jus positivum quam naturale*, ut supra diximus." *ibid*., in q. 64, a.1, num. 5 (emphasis added).

33. "Nihilominus tamen jus gentium est necessarium ad conservationem juris naturalis. Et non est omnino necessarium, sed pene necessarium, quia male posset conservari jus naturale sine jure gentium. Posset quidem orbis subsistere si possessiones essent in communi, ut est in religionibus; tamen esset cum magna difficultate ne homines in discordias et bella prorrumperent." *ibid*., num. 4, p. 16. The meaning of "nearly" (*pene*) but not "wholly" (*omnino*) appears to correspond roughly with the distinction of *ad melius esse* but not *ad esse*, although Vitoria does not use that terminology; its meaning and force are unclear.

34. "(Q)uando semel ex virtuali consensu totius orbis aliquid statuitur et admittitur, oportet quod ad abrogationem talis juris totus orbus conveniat, quod tamen est impossibile, quia impossibile est quod consensus totius orbis conveniat in abrogatione juris gentium." *ibid*., num. 5, p.16.

35. Peter Paludanus (c. 1275-1342) was a Dominican theologian and bishop. Appointed Patriarch of Jerusalem during the Crusades by the Pope, he may well have had a personal interest in improving conditions for prisoners of war, a pastoral practice consistent with the theory attributed to him.

36. "Secundo dico, quod bene potest ex parte abrogari jus gentium, licet non omnino; sicut jus gentium est quod captivi in bello justo sint servi, sed *Palude dicit quod hoc non tenet inter christianos*. Si enim in bello

Hispani capiant Gallos, Galli sunt captivi, sed non servi, quia possunt comparere in judicio et alia hujusmodi, quae tamen non liceret si essent servi. Item facta, Galli tenerent, et christianus non posset illum omnino vendere. Ecce hic ex parte violatur jus gentium, nam de jure gentium captivi in bello justo sunt servi. Haec dicta sint de isto articulo." *ibid.*, num. 5, pp. 15-16. (emphasis added)

37. Although Vitoria does not address the question of what criteria might clarify the difference between a practice which is merely a modification and thus licit, and a departure which amounts to a violation, one can ascertain an immediate criterion—whether the change is in accord with the *jus naturale* or not. A practice which conforms with the natural law would be an acceptable departure; a practice which violated the *jus naturale* would *eo ipso* violate the *jus gentium*. Ceasing to honor the inviolable status of ambassadors would contravene the *jus naturale* but giving more rights to captive prisoners of war would not.

38. "Jus gentium non solum habet vim ex pacto et condicto inter homines, sed etiam habet vim legis; habet enim totus orbis, qui aliquo modo est una respublica, potestatem ferendi leges aequas et convenientes omnibus, quales sunt in jure gentium. Ex quo patet quod mortaliter peccant violantes jura gentium, sive in pace, sive in bello; in rebus tamen gravioribus, ut est de incolumitate legatorum, neque licet uni regno nolli teneri jure gentium; est enim latum totius orbis auctoritate." *De Potestate Civili*, n. 21.

39. "Secundo dico, quod haec determinatio non spectat ad Jurisconsultos, vel saltem non ad solos illos. Quia cum illi barbari, ut statim dicam, non essent subjecti juri humano, res illorum non sunt examinandae per leges humanas, sed divinas, *quarum Juristae non sunt satis periti, ut per se possint hujusmodi quaestiones diffinire.*" *De Indis*, prologue, n. 3. (emphasis added)

40. Francisco de Vitoria, OP, *De Indis*, trans. John Pawley Bate in James Brown Scott, *The Spanish Origin of International Law: Francisco de Vitoria and His Law of Nations* (Oxford: Clarendon Press, 1934), p. 36.

41. "Quod vero naturalis ratio inter omnes homines constituit, id apud omnes populos peraeque costoditur, vocaturque jus gentium, quasi quo

138

jure omnes gentes utuntur." *Institutes*, I, ii, 1 (*De Jure Naturali*, 1. *Jus autem*) Krueger-Mommsen edition (Berlin, 1905).

42. E. Nys, *Le Droit International*, V, I; Bruxelles-Paris, 1904, p. 52; *Relectiones de Indis et de Jure Belli*, Introduction, pp. 42-43. (Classics of International Law, Washington). On the other hand, it has been suggested that Nys is mistaken in supposing that Vitoria is relying on a faulty memory; it is suggested instead that his substitution of "*gentes*" for "*homines*" was deliberate, that he knew the famous citation from the *Institutes* would be immediately recognized and that his students would perceive the implications of the change he had made: J. Larequi, "Del 'Jus Gentium' al Derecho International," *Razon y Fe* 83 (1928), p. 23.

43. *Idem.*, *Les Origines du Droit International*, Bruxelles, 1894, pp. 9-10.

44. E.g., Ernest Nys, J. Barthélemy, James Brown Scott, J.T. Delos.

45. Vitoria, *De Indis*, p. xxxviii.

46. Vitoria, *De Indis*, p. xl.

47. Vitoria, *De Indis*, pp. xliii-xliv.

48. Francisco de Vitoria, OP, *De Justitia*. Publicaciones de la Asociación Francisco de Vitoria, edición preparada por el R.P. Vicente Beltran de Heredia, OP. Tomo Primero (Madrid: Medinaceli, 1934), q. 62, a.1.

49. *Ibid.*, num. 4, p. 65.

50. Book V. The *Nicomachean Ethics* had been the object of intense study in the fourteenth century. Heredia notes that a preoccupation with ethical and juridical questions was the common denominator that united nominalists, scotists and humanists at the time. Diverse translations and commentaries on the *Ethics* were in circulation. No stronger authority could be cited than Aristotle's *Ethics* to support this critical identification of *jus* and *justum* made by Thomas and accepted by Vitoria. Vitoria, *Comentarios a la Secunda secundae de Santo Tómas*, ed. V.B. de Heredia, tomo III: "Introduction" (Salamanca: Spartado, 1934), p. xxvii.

51. J. Gerson, *De potestate ecclesiastica et de origine juris et legum*, cons. 13 (Antwerp: Dupin, 1706), V, p. 250.

52. Q. 7, a.10, treated in Chapter One.

53. The distinction *"jus in re"* and *"jus ad rem"* will become standard distinctions of the manualist tradition.

54. *Corpus Juris Civilis*, "de adquirenda possessione," 1.41, t. 2, n.12.

55. Conrad, *De Contractibus*, tr. 1.

56. Vitoria, *op.cit.*, num. 8, p. 67.

57. "Non est dubium nisi quod Dominus Deus noster est dominus omnium creaturarum et totius orbis." *ibid.*, num. 9, p. 68.

58. "Omne jus et dominium quod invenitur in creaturis est datum a Deo." *ibid*, num. 10, p. 69.

59. "Hoc dominium quod soli Deo aliquando competebat, scilicet quando solus erat, nulli creaturae irrationali communicavit." *ibid*, num. 11, p. 70.

60. *ST.* 1a2ae. q. 1, a.1, *ad 2*; q. 6, a.2, *ad   2*; q. 17, a.6; 2 *Contra Gentiles* 110.

61. "Deus benedictus ex sua liberalitate, exceptis angelis, dedit omnibus hominibus omnia bona creata et omnes creaturas, id est dedit eis dominium omnium." *ibid.*, num. 12, p. 71.

62. The term "man" is used to signify humankind in general; it thus corresponds with *anthropos*, not *aner*. In general I have attempted to use inclusive language but both fidelity to the language of Vitoria and facility of expression suggest that "man" is the appropriate term in this context.

63. "Ita quod homo non erat dominus omnium rerum ad omnes usus, quia ad habendum verum dominium non oportet quod secundum omnes usus utamur illo, sicut nec dominus est dominus servi ad omnes usus, quia non occidendum." *ibid.*, num. 15, p. 73.

64. "Homo per peccatum non perdidit illud dominium, sed adhuc est dominus omnium." *ibid.*, num. 17, p. 74. The notion that mortal sin destroyed dominion and that material possessions could be freely taken from those not in the state of grace was associated with John Wyclif (c. 1325-1384), an English reformer. Vitoria will examine his idea of dominion in *De Indis*.

65. "Divisio rerum non est facta de jure naturali. Patet, quia jus naturale semper est idem et non variatur." *ibid.*, num. 18, p. 74.

66. "Divisio rerum non facta est de jure divino positivo[...]Ex quo sequitur corollarium: quod de jure divino nec naturali nullus in toto orbe est dominus temporalis omnium, id est proprietarius." *ibid.*, num. 19, p. 75. The corollary tacitly, albeit pointedly, denies that either imperial or papal authority includes total temporal dominion of the world, a view in vogue among some at the time: "Si quis diceret imperatorem non esse dominum et monarcham totius orbis, forte esse haereticus[...]" Bartolus de Sassoferrato (d. 1359), *Tract. de represaliis*, cit. by C. B. Trelles, *Francisco de Vitoria, Fundador del Derecho Internacional Moderno* (Valladolid: Covarrubias, 1928), p. 33.

67. "Divisio et appropriatio rerum facta fuit jure humano[...]et non jure naturali nec divino, ut dictum est, nec angeli fecerunt eam: ergo jure humano facta est." *ibid.*, num. 20, p. 75.

68. Vitoria, *The First Relectio of the Reverend Father, Brother Franciscus de Victoria* (sic), *On the Indians Lately Discovered*, trans. J. Pawley Bate, Appendix A, in Scott, *op.cit.* As noted above, any reference to *De Indis* refers to *relectio* number 11, sometimes referred to as *De Indis Prior*. Any reference to *relectio* number 12, sometimes referred to as *De Indis Posterior*, will designate it as *De Jure Belli*, its more common title.

69. The translator erroneously identifies the commentary as the *Prima Secundae*.

70. *Ibid.*, p. vi.

71. This summary of Wyclif's view on dominion is found in his *De Civili Dominio*. The Council of Constance condemned over 200

propositions identified with Wyclif. John Hus (1372-1415), the Bohemian reformer and disciple of Wyclif, came to Constance under a safe-conduct pass from the Emperor but was condemned as a heretic and burnt at the stake.

72. L.J. Daly, SJ. *The Political Theory of John Wyclif* (Chicago: Loyola University Press, 1962), p. 68. The text from Wyclif's *De dominio divino* (III, vi, 250) is as follows: "Primo quod quilibet creatura rationalis sit improprie dominus, quin potius minister vel dispensator supremi Domini. Patet ex hoc quod quelibet creatura est servus Domini habens quidquid habet ex mera gracia ut dispenset[...] Secundo supponitur quod, sicut nulla creatura servit alteri nisi eo ipso serviat Deo suo, sic nulla creatura in aliquod premiat servum nisi Deus eo ipso principalius premiet in eodem[...] Tercio supponitur quod creature dispensantes bona temporalia Dei sunt egent mutuo spirituali iuvamine confratrum integrancium ecclesiam militantem."

73. E.g., David. *ibid.*, p. viii.

74. *Ibid.*

75. *Ibid.*, p. ix. By his citing of the *Secunda Secundae*, Vitoria lays the groundwork for the later (1550-51) debate at Valladolid between Bartolomé de las Casas and Juan de Sepúlveda. Las Casas will cite the *Secunda Secundae*, q. 10, a.10 and q. 10, a.12 to support the proposition that human law cannot take away natural dominion. Domingo de Soto will have the task of summarizing the arguments of the two partisans. As both student and friend of Vitoria, Soto will naturally present Vitoria's views, adopted and affirmed by Las Casas, in the most favorable light. The selection of Soto as redactor of arguments thus guaranteed that the thought of Vitoria (and indirectly, of St. Thomas) would determine the outcome of the debate.

76. *Ibid.*

77. *Ibid.*, p. xi.

78. *Ibid.*, p. xii.

79. *ST.*, 1a2ae. q. 1, a.1 and a.2; q. 6, a.2; 3 *Contra Gentiles* 110.

80. *Ibid.*, p. xiii.

81. *Ibid.*

82. *Ibid.*, pp. xiii-xiv.

83. *ST.*, 2a2ae. 10.10, cited in *De Indis*, section 2, p. xvii.

84. S. Pinckaers, OP, "La théologie morale au déclin du Moyen-Age: Le nominalisme," *Nova et Vetera* 52:3 (1977), p. 211.

85. Eberhard Welty, OP, *Herders Sozialkatechismus*, Vol. I, *Grundfragen und Grundkrafte des sozialen Lebens*, 2nd ed., 1952, n. 55, p. 185n.

86. B. Häring—L. Vereecke, "La Théologie Morale de S. Thomas d'Aquin a S. Alphonse de Liguori," *Nouvelle Revue Théologique* 77:7 (1955), pp. 682-83.

CHAPTER THREE

Domingo de Soto's Understanding
of the *Jus Gentium* and *Dominium*:
The Conditional Acceptance of Slavery

Domingo de Soto was born in Segovia in 1495. After early studies
in his native city, he matriculated at the University of Alcalá in the field
of liberal arts under the direction of St. Thomas of Villanova. From
1516 to 1519 he studied theology at the University of Paris. Returning
in 1520 to Spain, he became professor of philosophy at the University of
San Ildefonso in Alcalá until 1524 when he became a Dominican at the
Convent of St. Paul in Burgos. Upon entering religious life he changed
his baptismal name of Francisco to Domingo.

In 1525 he was sent to the College of San Estéban in the University
of Salamanca, becoming a professor of dialectics and publishing his
studies in logic under the title of the *Summulae*. During this time he
would substitute for the *prima* professor of theology, Francisco de
Vitoria, during periods of absence or illness. In November, 1532, he
succeeded Bernardo Vasquez de Oropesa as *vespera* professor of
theology at Salamanca, holding that position until March, 1549, when he
became Confessor of Carlos V, Spanish and Holy Roman Emperor.

Soto was active during his teaching career in pastoral problems. He
involved himself in problems of the University, especially the education
of students from poor families, and took an active role in aiding the poor
during the famine of 1540-1544.[1]

In 1545 he went to the Council of Trent at the direction of Emperor
Carlos V and represented the Dominican order for the opening sessions.
(The ill health of Vitoria prevented him from accompanying Soto). He
summarized his approach to the problem of justification dealt with in the
fourth and fifth sessions in his *De Natura et Gratia*.

Apparently weary of conciliar maneuvering, Soto returned to
Salamanca in 1549, having been offered the Bishopric of Segovia by

Carlos V but declining it. He did not spend much time in Salamanca, however, for he was dispatched by the Emperor to Valladolid the following year to present his views on the dispute between Bartolomé de las Casas, OP, and Juan Ginez de Sepúlveda on the morality of colonization of the New World. Soto was charged with the task of summarizing their lengthy argumentation.

In 1552 Soto succeeded Melchior Cano in the *prima* chair of theology at the University of Salamanca. He was unanimously selected to be Cano's successor. Although he remained at Salamanca until his death on November 15, 1560, he was asked by King Philip II, the son and successor of Carlos V, to serve as a mediator between Spain and the Holy See in various ecclesiastical disputes. Among his diplomatic missions, he negotiated a *cessatio a divinis*, governing church revenues, between Cardinal Siliceo of Toledo, King Philip and Pope Paul IV. His reputation was so revered by his countrymen that the phrase "*Qui scit Sotum, scit totum*" was commonplace.[2] Aside from his writings on justification and the sacraments, his principal work remains the voluminous *De Justitia et Jure*, published in 1553-1554 at Salamanca. We will now turn to this treatise for his views on the *jus gentium* and *dominium* in regard to the issue of slavery. After a series of reflections on natural law in Book I and the divine positive law in Book II, Soto begins his analysis of *jus* as the object of the virtue of justice in Book III.[3]

1. Soto's Understanding of *Jus* and *Jus Gentium*

"Quo ergo jure obtinemus imperium quod modo reperitur ultramarinum? Revera ego nescio."[4]

"By what right have we obtained dominion in the New World? In truth, I do not know." An amazing confession of uncertainty on the hotly contested issue! The question posed by Domingo de Soto in a *relectio* entitled *De dominio*, by what right did the Spanish acquire an empire in the New World, and the disarming confession that he did not know the answer in this vital matter, reveals the impact of Vitoria's quest for legitimate titles of conquest in the *De Indis*. It also reveals the intellectual honesty of Soto, searching for a correct understanding of *jus* in his *relectio* on dominion. It is clear once again that these closely related concepts of *jus* and *dominium* had a critical role in providing the justification or lack thereof of Spanish colonization of the New World and treatment of the Indians. Although there are only fragments of Soto's *De dominio* extant at this point, his reflections on both concepts are present in a systematic study entitled *De Justitia et Jure*. Our search thus lead us to Book III of *De Justitia et Jure*.[5]

Soto begins Book III by placing justice within the context of the moral virtues. He accepts and combines the traditional definitions of Aristotle and Ulpian to the effect that justice is the habit which moves the will to seek and do that which is just, namely, to render to each that which is his due.[6]

We shall see that his understanding of *jus* basically adheres to the view of Thomas, and against that of the nominalists. Because Soto's approach to the meaning of *jus* reiterates the traditional distinctions and conclusions of Thomas, it is noteworthy for our purposes only insofar as it underscores his unmistakable intent of aligning his approach with the thomist tradition freshly renewed by Vitoria. There are no unexpected views expressed or positions taken. Soto will follow the lead of Vitoria in placing the *jus gentium* within the category of positive law.[7] We shall see the effect of this classification in his understanding of *dominium* in the second part of the chapter and in the critical analysis of Chapter Four.

After placing justice within the context of the moral virtues, Soto reflects on the proposition that *jus* is the object of justice and endorses that conclusion. He rejects by name the view of John Buridan, a leading contemporary nominalist, that *lex* and *jus* are identical. The concept of *lex* stands for a rule of reason or dictate of prudence of the kind found in authorities governing the community. The concept of *lex* stands for "the just thing" or the course of events which equitably approximates the accommodation of interests of the parties involved. Whereas *lex* is found in the mind, *jus* inheres within objective reality.

In making the point that *jus*, the object of justice, inheres in objective reality, Soto emphasizes that justice entails an equality between two terms, while the other moral virtues entail a balance within the agent between two extremes of excess and defect. Soto selects the virtue of fortitude as an example: it strikes a balance between foolhardiness and cowardice. The standard is subjective, i.e. contingent upon the temperament of the agent. Among the moral virtues, only justice possesses an objective standard, a *medium rei*, not merely a *medium rationis*. He points out that the balance is even more contingent upon the person in the case of temperance: the mean between gluttony and malnutrition depends on the weight and age of the agent. In contrast, justice is an "ad-*just*ment of equality between at least two persons, such as a buyer and a seller. It is thus clear that Soto rejects a purely subjective definition of *jus*.[8]

In order to defend the proposition that *jus* is the object of justice and distinct from *lex*, Soto had to respond to the contrary views of two classical jurists, Ulpian[9] and Isidore.[10] Ulpian had written that *jus* is what results from justice; Isidore had written that *lex* is a species of *jus*. Against Ulpian, Soto employs an argument of etymology: *justum* must come from *jus* because longer forms are derived from shorter; moreover the Greek *dikaion* stands for both *jus* and *justum* without distinction. *Jus*, the just thing, precedes justice as its object both in language and logic. He follows this etymological argument with the theological argument that habits are specified by their object, not vice-versa. Since justice is clearly a habit, it must be specified by an object, namely *dikaion* or *jus*.[11]

In response to Isidore's statement that *lex* is a species of *jus*, Soto responds that while it is true that *lex* can stand for a written form of that which is just, Isidore's view must be taken metaphorically. While *lex* as a rule of practical understanding established by prudence is the reason or *ratio* for that which is just, the relation of *jus* and *lex* can never be that of genus and species. Soto writes that Isidore could not have meant literally that *lex* was a species of the genus *jus*.[12]

In the second article of Question One, Soto concludes that *jus* is divided primarily into the *jus naturale* and *jus positivum*. He rejects both the tripartite division of Isidore of *jus naturale*, *jus gentium* and *jus civile*, a classification common among contemporary jurists, as well as the other common system of four categories--the three above and divine law.

Since he studies the operation of divine natural law and divine positive law in the first two Books of *De Justitia et Jure*, it is not unexpected that in confronting questions of justice that arise from human law in Book Three, he should conclude that *jus* is divided primarily into natural and positive categories. He so concludes in q. 1, a. 2, citing well-known examples of each. The obligation to return a borrowed object arises, for instance, from the natural law whereas the determination of the price of goods in commerce arises from human reckoning and falls within the scope of the *jus positivum*.

In article three of the first question, Soto turns to the pivotal question of under which category--natural or positive--the *jus gentium* falls. He observes first that the *jus gentium* is clearly distinct from the natural law. He cites the view of Ulpian that the natural law is common to all animals, a proposition which precludes the *jus gentium* from being part of the natural law since the *jus gentium* is universally acknowledged as belonging only to humans. Moreover, the natural law gives rise to absolute rights; it is "simply," i.e. radically necessary or independent of any human determination, whereas the *jus gentium* requires the rational calculation of human society. Soto observes that there would never have been any division of property if society had not decided that some should possess this and others that. Thus the *jus gentium* cannot be considered "simply natural" as is the natural law; hence it must be part of the positive law, the only other category in Soto's schema.[13]

Soto expresses the view that St. Thomas considered the *jus gentium* to be part of positive rather than natural law. He cites the responses in 2a2ae. q.57 to the objection that the *jus gentium* is part of the natural law as evidence that Thomas affirmed the rightful place of the *jus gentium* to be within positive law. Nonetheless he recognizes that Thomas did not explicitly include the *jus gentium* within positive law.[14]

Soto also cites St. Thomas' division in 1a2ae. q.95, a.4 of the positive law into the *jus gentium* and the *jus civile*.[15] Even though he concludes that the *jus gentium* belongs to positive law, Soto faithfully paraphrases the thought of Aquinas in 2a2ae. q.57 that there are two ways by which the "ad-*jus*tment" of terms can occur in the natural law:

> This accommodation can occur in two ways, either according to the absolute nature of things (e.g., a man and a woman are suited to produce offspring; a father has the duty to support his son), or else a thing can be accommodated to another not by virtue of its absolute nature but by being ordered to a determined end and established by circumstances.[16]

As an example of the second manner of accommodation, namely, through its relation to a determined end in certain circumstances, Soto cites the example of the cultivation of land. In view of the end of producing fruit and occupying land in peace, natural reason can "immediately deduce," when it takes into account the sinful nature of man, that a division of property to individuals is better suited to the attainment of those goals than an attempt at communal cultivation.

A contradiction is apparent here. It was universally agreed among jurists and theologians of the era that private property was a feature of the *jus gentium*. Soto has concluded that the *jus gentium* belongs to the *jus positivum* as a result of his reading of 1a2ae. q.95, a.4. In syllogistic fashion his views are: (1) the *jus gentium* is positive law; (2) the institution of private property belongs to the *jus gentium*; (3) therefore, private property is a feature of positive law. Why should Soto now advance private property as an example of the second manner of operation of the natural law (in deference to 2a2ae. q.57) since this would align the *jus gentium* with the *jus naturale*? Ulpian's definition provides the explanation for the contradiction: because the *jus gentium* entails rational calculation, it cannot by his definition be part of the natural law since reason does not extend to all animals. It thus appears that the weight of Ulpian's legacy constrains Soto to lapse into a contradiction: Soto defines private property as positive law and describes it as natural law. If we accept Lottin's thesis that the weight of tradition confined Thomas in 1a2ae. q.95, a.4 and forced him to link the *jus gentium* with positive rather than natural law, we can note the irony that the same weight of tradition, including also of course Vitoria at this juncture, will influence Soto to make the same linkage in his commentary on 2a2ae. q.57.

Having posited that the *jus gentium* is part of positive law, Soto now turns to the question of its scope and possible "dispensations" from it. The first question pertaining to its scope is the manner in which the *jus gentium* differs from the *jus civile*. Soto identifies two major distinctions. First, the *jus gentium* is "deduced by way of conclusion from the natural principles of things considered in relation to an end in certain circumstances." Once again Soto uses the example of private property:

> Fields should be cultivated. Men are more industrious when they work for themselves than when they work in common. Therefore it is better that they possess fields privately.[17]

By way of contrast to the rational calculation of suitable means to achieve desired ends, Soto stresses the will of the legislator in the formulation of the *jus civile*:

> The *jus civile* is deduced from a natural principle and another premise which human will supplies. It is not deduced by way of inference but

by the determination of a general principle in a special law, as in ceremonial laws and judicial commands...For example, that things should be sold at a just price is clearly [a precept of the natural law], but ascertaining the correct price in view of circumstances of time and place is of the *jus civile*.[18]

It thus appears that Soto's understanding of the difference between the *jus gentium* and the *jus civile* is that the former occurs through rational inference from the precepts of the natural law, whereas the latter occurs through a voluntary determination from principles not self-evident in the natural law but added by human intelligence and experience through the instrumentality of the law.

Another difference cited by Soto between the *jus gentium* and the *jus civile* is that no legislature is needed to proclaim the *jus gentium* since reason teaches it to all people, but the authority of those governing the community is required for the promulgation of the *jus civile*. It is evident from this that Soto continues to describe the *jus gentium* as an operation of the natural law, under the influence of Ulpian's view of the natural law as "*quod natura docuit animalia omnia*." By identifying the premises of the *jus gentium* with the self-evident precepts of the natural law, Soto is placing the *jus gentium* much closer to natural than positive law, in contradiction to his formal position that it is part of the body of positive law.

A final difference cited by Soto between the *jus gentium* and the *jus civile* is that the former is known by all peoples, whereas civil law is established by the government of each individual community. By noting the universality of the *jus gentium*, in contrast to the particularity of the *jus civile*, Soto continues his de facto alignment of the *jus gentium* with the natural rather than the positive law.

Before completing article 4, Soto levels a sharp criticism at contemporary jurisconsults and considers a final question ("*dubium*") which pertains directly to the issue of slavery. We shall examine first the criticism and then the question of dispensing from the *jus gentium*.

Having explored the relationship between the natural law, the *jus gentium* and the civil law, Soto delivers a pointed criticism of the jurisconsults of his era for construing the *jus gentium* too broadly. This criticism recalls the identical complaint issued by Vitoria in *De Indis*. Without identifying specific theologians or jurists, Soto argues that the "jurisconsults" extend the scope of the *jus gentium* too far because they think that everything "common to all animals" (Ulpian's famous definition) is included within the ambit of the *jus gentium*. Soto holds that such a comprehensive inclusion of natural rights within the *jus gentium* is fallacious. There are many natural rights which belong solely to human nature and not to the animals, e.g., the Decalogue:

> That which is inferred as a necessary consequence of the absolute nature of things pertains to natural right; that which is inferred not from the absolute consideration of things but in relation to a determined end is of the *jus gentium*. Thus the Decalogue is not of the *jus gentium* but the *jus naturale*...When we said that the *jus gentium* is deduced from the principles of nature by way of inference, it was not intended that such an inference be totally necessary, but rather as suitable to the nature of a thing in relation to a certain end.[19]

It becomes unmistakably clear that the basis of Soto's criticism of the jurisconsults for construing the *jus gentium* too broadly is their acceptance of Ulpian's understanding of the natural law as common to men and animals. This definition is fundamental to all of Soto's observations about the *jus gentium* and its relation to natural and positive law. The effect of his agreement with Ulpian is to oppose those who construe the *jus gentium* as coterminous with the natural law (namely, the jurisconsults), and to classify the *jus gentium* as positive rather than natural law. This important decision of classification is made notwithstanding the fact that Soto strongly supports the view, as we have seen, that the *jus gentium* has an inherent universality (common to all peoples, in contrast to civil law), and that it occurs by way of rational deduction from the precepts of the natural law, whereas the civil law, in contrast, adds premises independent of the natural law for its determinations. While he classifies the *jus gentium* overall as positive law, he aligns its key features with natural law.

Soto concludes his consideration of the *jus gentium* in article 3 by raising the question of whether there can be "dispensations" from it.[20] There are some features of the *jus gentium* which are so suitable, he says, to the human community that they could never be dispensed with, such as private property. There are other determinations, however, which can reasonably be dispensed with, such as slavery:

> Slavery is of the *jus gentium* and nevertheless is dispensed with so that Christians, when taken as prisoners of war, are not reduced to slavery...When the philosopher [viz., Aristotle] says that there are men who are slaves by nature, he is not considering the natural law in itself. Since there is no reason for one to serve more than another, if we consider human nature in itself, it can be only when ordered toward some end, such as one being subordinated to the authority of another or to be freed from the penalty of death in a war. This is rather of the *jus gentium*, although the submission of the more ignorant to the wise so that they can be instructed in the manner of living is not of itself contrary to liberty, as we will show in Book IV in the corresponding question.[21]

Soto's benign construction of Aristotle's view of slavery in the *Politics* allows him to reject Aristotle's conclusion that some are by nature suited to slavery and to accept the more limited view that only in some circumstances, i.e. in relation to a determined desirable end, could one be subject to another.

The reference above to "the corresponding question" in Book IV pertains to q.2, a.2, whether one can have dominion over another. Soto will conclude that under some circumstances there can be a master-slave relationship. Because his understanding of *dominium* in this context is intimately connected to the concept of *jus*, and represents his chief contribution to the debate on the issue of slavery, we will now turn to *dominium* in Book IV.

2. Soto's Understanding of *Dominium*

In a prologue to Book IV of *De Justitia et Jure*, Soto observes that Book IV deals with the second species of justice to be studied in his work, commutative justice, which includes dominion over things as well as restitution. Dominion is the basis for the contracts, pacts and agreements which are the principal concerns of commutative justice.

Book IV consists of five questions: (1) dominion in itself; (2) the kinds of dominion possible; (3) the division and transfer of dominion; (4) particular kinds of dominion; (5) changes in dominion. Our study will culminate in question 2, article 2, which explores the question of whether one man can have dominion over another, i.e. the justification for a master-slave relationship. We shall begin with Soto's explanation of dominion in general and then move to its application to slavery through the *jus gentium*.

Question 1, article 1 has for its scope the definition of dominion. The inquiry is described as "whether dominion is the same as the right and faculty of disposing of things."[22] Using the scholastic methodology of examining arguments which will ultimately be modified or rejected, Soto first proposes that "right (*jus*) is the faculty of disposing and using something freely, which is exactly the meaning of dominion."[23]

A second proposition considered by Soto which supports the identity of *dominium* and *jus* is the example of religious mendicants who can be considered "masters" of things such as food and clothes which they have a right to use even in poverty; thus there is no reason to distinguish between right and dominion.

By way of a *sed contra* argument, Soto notes that "master" and "slave" are always correlative terms and in the treatise in the *Institutes* on the rights of persons, men are divided into free and slave. It can be deduced from this distinction that whoever has a free person (i.e., not a slave) under his authority has a right (*jus*) to order him but does not have dominion over him. One could not, according to the logic of the *Institutes*, have dominion over a free person.

The stage is now set for Soto's examination of the relationship of *jus* and *dominium*. Adhering to the custom popularized by Isidore's *Etymologies*, Soto begins with the etymology of *dominium*. He observes that "*dominium*" is rarely used among classical orators and the ancient Latin writers. Instead, the words "*dominatus*" and "*dominatio*" are used, and generally in a pejorative sense. They "usually mean a form of tyranny exercised when one abuses those subject to him for personal advantage."[24]

Apart from the classical Latinists who rarely use the term, *dominium* is employed by the jurisconsults to mean ownership of things, as distinguished from mere possession, use or usufruct. It is used in the field of commerce to describe goods or property bought, sold or transferred. It is also used in Sacred Scripture: Soto cites Tobias 8 and 1 Maccabees 11 as typical texts. Finally Soto cites the *Digest* which treats of different titles on the manner of acquiring dominion over things.

After examining these classical *loci*, Soto acknowledges that "the moderns" justifiably insist that more consideration be given to the meaning of *dominium*. He cites Gerson and Conrad's treatise on contracts as examples of modern writers desirous of greater clarity. These "moderns" understand dominion to be exactly the same as *jus* when taken as authority over a person or thing. Soto summarizes this "modern" view of dominion as the power or proximate faculty of appropriating things, putting them at one's disposal for a licit use according to those established laws which conform with reason.[25]

Soto proposes now to consider whether this modern identity of *dominium* and *jus* is correct or not. He furnishes an example which, he believes, refutes the position of Conrad that *jus* and *dominium* can be understood as synonymous terms:

> A father has a *jus* over his sons, but does not have dominion, if it is properly understood. It is just and equitable, therefore a *jus* exists, that a father, for the good of his children, exercise dominion over the sons whom he loves as his own, and that he instruct and educate them. But dominion does not mean any *jus* or any power except that which is held over a thing which we are able to use freely for our own benefit; this is what the word *dominium* clearly means to me. The correlative of "master" is "slave," i.e. that which belongs entirely to the master, as though a beast.[26]

In support of his contention that a father has a *jus* but not *dominium* over his son, Soto cites Aristotle's distinction in Book I of the *Politics* between a civil (or real) *dikaion*, on the one hand, and a despotic *dikaion*, on the other hand. While the soul exercises a "despotic" *dikaion* over the body, as would a master over a slave, he who controls an appetite exercises a "civil (or real) *dikaion*," which is not a *dominium*. While the father has authority over his son until the son reaches majority, the father is not a *dominus*, analogous to a master-servant relationship, because the son is "part of himself." Soto accepts Aristotle's "living instrument" theory, i.e., that the slave is comparable to an instrument in the hands of the master, a relationship which the son, a part of the father, could not have. Here Soto does not follow the reasoning of Thomas that the *ad alterum* relationship required for a just relationship is lacking in the father-son relation: he speaks of the father having a *jus* over his son. Nor is he consistent with Thomas' explicit analogy in 2a2ae. q.57, a.4 of the master-slave relation with the father-son relation. Soto implies that the slave could not enjoy the same status as a son with a father.

Two reasons explain Soto's departure from Thomas on this key analogy: (1) the status of a slave in the New World is so different from the feudal serf-like slavery envisioned by Thomas that to maintain the father:son :: master:slave analogy would be factually untenable; (2) Soto has adopted the modern terminology of a moral agent "having" a *jus* instead of a *jus* existing as an objective condition.

Having provided an example which challenges the identification of *jus* and *dominium* favored by the "moderns" such as Gerson and Conrad, Soto now furnishes his definition of dominion, giving careful attention to each of its constitutive elements:

> Dominion, if defined technically, is the faculty and proper right which each one has over something in virtue of which he can use it for his own benefit in any use permitted by the law.[27]

The first point which Soto makes in his explanation of his definition is that the genus of "faculty" is selected instead of "power." The concept of "power," taken as a genus, is too broad for "dominion" because it includes or comprehends instances which are clearly not examples of *dominium*. Soto cites two such examples: (a) a thief who has power over stolen property but does not exercise true dominion over it since he is not the owner; (b) a tyrant through whose power the goods and rights of citizens are abused. Both the thief and the tyrant have the power to use the goods or rights in question but lack the faculty, i.e. a proper right, over them. The mere exercise of power does not confer dominion in the absence either of valid ownership or the permission of the owner.

The next point which Soto considers is the question of whose benefit is intended by the *jus* or dominion exercised by the agent. Dominion entails far more, he says, than merely the use or enjoyment of something; it includes "returning, donating, selling, abandoning, etc."

The use of the faculty (*jus*) must be "permitted by the law." Soto cites the example of a minor who has dominion over goods before reaching majority but who nevertheless lacks the faculty, i.e. the proper right of disposing freely of those goods until he reaches an age of maturity specified by the civil law. This limitation of the civil law is also linked to the question of whose benefit or utility is intended by the use of the right: the law makes a presumption that the minor is incapable of exercising the faculty for his own benefit until he has reached the age of reason and legal majority. It is thus clear that the existence and exercise of dominion is not independent of the civil law. To prevent the possibility of a child squandering something of value, the civil law witholds permission for the child to act; his power to dispose of goods is unaffected by civil law but not his dominion. Soto's distinction is clear and consistent. Mere power does not confer dominion, neither in the case of a thief and stolen property, for the thief lacks the proper right to use the goods, nor in the case of a minor who lacks the capacity to exercise the right even though it is his.

Soto has justified his definition by an analysis of the constitutive elements: it is a faculty, not a power; the benefit of the *dominus* is the end; the civil law sanctions its use.

He now moves beyond elements of definition to some broader philosophical issues of great importance to our study. He warns the philosophers that dominion is a real relation which must be based on a genuine title. His admonitions are noteworthy not only because of their content but because of their tone. Soto displays frustration with the efforts of the *terministas*, the heirs of Occam's nominalism whose penchant for hair-splitting caused them to multiply terms endlessly. He implicitly warns those concerned with the philosophical basis for juridical terminology that they must exercise vigilance in the debate over fundamental terms and the concepts which they express. We shall now examine his first major admonition to the philosophers on the character of dominion as a real relation.

Before finishing his study of dominion in general in question 1, article 1, Soto says:

> Far be it from me to engage in the trivia of whether dominion is the same thing as possession, or in the master rather than in the relation.

But I cannot fail to admonish the philosophers to act to avoid the extraneous expressions of the terminalists, because who can endure the debate about whether the dominion of a horse is in the horse or the rider? Dominion is a real relation between the possessor and the thing which is possessed. Dominion is defined by its act, which is the particular mode of defining potencies. Just as vision is the potency which distinguishes colors, and hearing the potency which perceives sounds, so dominion is the faculty to use and enjoy, etc. a thing.[28]

Although Soto rejects the absolute identity of *jus* and *dominium*, the prevailing view of the jurisconsults, he places *dominium* in the category of relation, in continuity with the view of Saint Thomas, thereby making clear that the relation of *dominus-servus* must be governed by the dictates of justice, whose object, *jus*, requires that each agent in a relation render to the other (*ad alterum*) that which is the other's due. Although they are not logically identical, both *jus* and *dominium* entail a relation. Thus neither can be considered merely as a subjective right without reference to another party.

By directing his observations explicitly at philosophers, Soto surely intended it to be understood that the definition of dominion could not occur without the contribution of philosophy. Jurisprudence, the philosophy of law, could not be reduced to the level of grammar or even legal argumentation. He thus calls for a dialogue between philosophy and law, the proper arena for the jurisconsults. If dominion were defined merely as a kind of possession, the larger philosophical framework of relation would have been lost and the implications entailed by the meaning of relation.

Next Soto turns to the matter of title. As we saw in the study of Vitoria's *De Indis*, the question of title loomed large in sixteenth century moral theology. Title was understood to supply the moral justification or lack thereof for actions. Upon Vitoria's search for a just title for the Spanish conquest of the New World depended his conclusion regarding its moral foundation. Soto exhibits the same regard for title as Vitoria and uses it as a limit upon the kinds of dominion which could justifiably be said to exist.

Soto's reference to title occurs near the end of question 1, article 1:

> Title is effectively the basis for dominion, or the root from which it springs. The titles of dominion can come from nature, law, contract, election, etc. For example, the title of dominion which man naturally has over the fruits of the earth is natural life, since without food man cannot survive. By giving these to man along with the desire for survival, God naturally conferred on man the right to make use of necessary food, in the same way as the title of right (I will not say dominion) which fathers have over their children is natural generation. The title of the right of property is the *jus gentium* through which the division of goods was made. Thus the title of a bishop is election. The title of ownership of a house is either natural inheritance, purchase, prescription, etc.

By requiring dominion to rest upon a legitimate title such as nature, reason, or law, Soto lays the groundwork for limitations on the scope of any authentic dominion, but at a great price. As the text above reveals, he departs from St. Thomas' view in 2a2ae. q.57, a.4 that the deficiency of an *ad alterum* character in the father-son relation prevents it from being a just relationship in a strict sense. He concludes that a legitimate title exists for a *jus*, namely natural generation or simply nature, but since the child is an extension of the parent there is not an *ad alterum* relationship, hence no dominion. For Thomas the absence of an *ad alterum* character meant the absence of a *jus*, not just the absence of *dominium*. The scope of *jus* is vastly greater than before and the son-slave analogy is further eroded.

He now alludes to the difference between *dominium plenum*, the total right to use or dispose of an object in an unrestricted fashion, and *dominium utile*, the right merely to use something but not to alienate it. He cites the distinction and adds that it is not important to his study. While Soto is no doubt correct about the relative unimportance of the *dominium plenum/dominium utile* distinction to his inquiry, it will be this distinction which will govern the manualist tradition on the issue of slavery through the twentieth century. Almost without exception the manuals will countenance slavery as a *dominium utile*, i.e. the right to the product of a slave's labors, but not as a *dominium plenum*, i.e. ownership of the individual in violation of certain rights such as worship and marriage.

Soto replies to the second proposition submitted at the beginning of the question—that mendicants have dominion over the food and clothes they use—by responding that mendicants cannot be said to have dominion over the food and clothes they use because they do not have the faculty or right to dispose of them; they can merely use them as necessities. The mendicants are not owners, because they cannot alienate the necessities they use. Soto uses this example, taken from religious life, to clarify and summarize his view at the end of the article:

> Dominion and *jus* are not the same thing. The word '*jus*' is more
> general than dominion.[29]

Following this summary conclusion that *jus* is broader than *dominium*, Soto begins the second article of question 1, whether dominion is proper only to God and rational creatures. Although the content is not directly related to our inquiry, two aspects of this article are important in elucidating Soto's line of reasoning, namely, his continuing criticism of the "moderns, guided by Gerson," and his rejection of a distinction between real and natural dominion. His criticism of Gerson is scathing:

> The moderns, guided by Gerson, invent many things which barely
> conform to reason. This author, otherwise respectable, has multiplied
> greatly the species of dominion...Many of these he attributes to the
> brutes and many others even to insensible things.[30]

Soto's attribution of dominion to God as sovereign provides an outline for his thought:

> To dominate is proper only for those who enjoy reason and free will and therefore only they have dominion over things. In the first place it belongs to God, then to those with naturally intellectual, angelic nature and finally to man. God, from whom is the earth and its fullness, by right of creation has dominion and sovereignty over all things created by Him, as the passage from Wisdom affirms, 'You are Lord of all things...' Dominion over exterior things belongs to no one except by reason of being lord of his own acts, since dominion over one's own acts is the cause and root of dominion, which can be held over many things. According to St. Thomas in I-II, q.1, only man is master of his acts through will and intelligence. For the same reason he alone possesses dominion over other things.[31]

It will be noted at this point that while Soto's conclusions about the scope and extent of dominion are identical to St. Thomas, whom he cites, he does not speak of human participation in divine dominion, the metaphysical basis in St. Thomas' thought for human dominion. Soto predicates human dominion on the basis of the possession of reason and free will, a psychological rather than metaphysical foundation. It could be argued that this theme of human participation in divine dominion is present implicitly; that may well be so. But it is not an explicit feature of Soto's understanding of human dominion.

The second point to be considered in this article is Soto's rejection of the validity of the distinction between real and natural dominion:

> Although some distinguish between real dominion and natural dominion, stating that the first requires liberty but the second does not, there is no basis for such a distinction, since nature itself does not make anyone master of something apart from his action or the thing itself.[32]

By rejecting this distinction as specious, Soto denies the possibility of one possessing natural dominion through birth but lacking in real dominion, which requires liberty. The implication is clear that one could neither claim a "natural" dominion on the basis of race or deny "natural" dominion to another on the basis of race.

Whether Soto had the condition of the New World Indians in mind or not we can only speculate. But the subject could not have been far from the mind of Soto as question 2, article 2 will shortly show.

Soto now moves to question 2 of Book IV, "on the things which are the object of man's dominion." The first two articles are central to our inquiry. Article 1 concerns "whether man in some manner is master of all things in the world," while article 2 asks directly "whether one man can have dominion over another man." Question 2, article 1 is important as much for what it denies as for what it affirms. It denies that man is a sovereign of the universe with unrestricted authority; man's dominion cannot be separated from the plenary sovereignty of God:

> After having established that among the corporeal creatures only man has dominion over things, it follows that we examine the manner of this dominion and over what things it extends...The first question...affirms that man is not absolute *dominus* over all things which have been created in the world. Such dominion would come either from natural right (*jus naturale*), or divine right (*jus divinum*) or human right (*jus humanum*). But man does not have it through natural right since universal dominion was not granted to him by God in creation. Neither does he have it through divine right because in this case man would be master of whatever he might need through grace and if grace were lost, dominion would disappear with it.[33]

What remains to be defined is the human *jus* which serves as the basis for human dominion. Soto will demonstrate in this article that human dominion is not absolute but contingent upon the *jus gentium* and the *jus civile*. Before examining this dichotomy of human right, *jus gentium* and *jus civile*, Soto continues his attack upon "the moderns" for their proliferation of classes and kinds of dominion:

> In this question the modern masters, whom we have already mentioned, accumulate many classes of dominion. Thus Gerson has enumerated six; others have mentioned up to nine. Conrad had the pleasure of enumerating twenty-three. They say that there is a beatific dominion in which the daring are masters of glory. Another is gratifying dominion, which is what the just have over created things, through which they can make use of them in accord with the words of Paul to the Romans, 'to those who love God, all things work together unto good.' And there is natural dominion and evangelical dominion. But they multiply without reason these classes of dominion for two pernicious reasons. First because they continue to believe that *dominium* is the same thing as *jus*, and second because they separate dominion from its objects. Since this division is lacking in any rules, it can continue infinitely. Dominion can be divided only according to the titles from which it originates.[34]

Once again dominion is linked with the concept of "title" and distinguished from the concept of *jus*.

Soto now proceeds to enumerate four conclusions on the relationship of the *jus gentium* and dominion:

> Let this be the first conclusion on this matter: dominion is only of four classes, namely, natural, divine and human. The latter is divided into two, namely, that which arises from the *jus gentium*, and that which arises from the *jus civile*. This conclusion is so clear that there are not many reasons needed to demonstrate it. Essentially any dominion owes its origin to some class of right (*jus*), and as we have seen in the earlier articles there cannot be any *jus* other than natural, or human, that is, of the *jus gentium* or the *jus civile*, or one which has been added by divine positive law, that is, one which does not belong to man through the exigency of his nature but has been added to it by God...As a result there cannot be any more than these classes

of dominion since there are no other *jura* than these through which one can acquire dominion. Therefore no reason exists which authorizes us to distinguish dominion into original, beatific, etc.[35]

It is thus unmistakably clear that any claim to dominion must be based either on natural law, human law (civil or the *jus gentium*), or divine positive law, in Soto's understanding of dominion. No exercise of rights or authority over others is permissible if it contravenes any of these laws.

Soto's second conclusion is that man has natural dominion not only over the fruits of the earth but in a certain manner also over the terrain which is his domicile. This conclusion is derived from a reading of Genesis 1.26ff—"Let us make man in our image...Be fruitful, multiply and subdue the earth." Soto considers man's dominion over the earth to be of natural rather than of divine positive law because food and terrain are needs related to man's nature and not given over and above human nature.

The third conclusion identifies the *jus gentium* as a source of different kinds of dominion:

> By human right (*jus humanum*), which we have already divided into *jus gentium* and *jus civile*, man also enjoys many dominions. By the *jus gentium*...he was introduced to the division of property...By virtue of the civil law, i.e. the law proper to a specific city or kingdom, men are masters of many things, e.g., by way of the right of prescription, or inheritance, or primogeniture, etc. All these things are clear and manifest.[36]

The institution of private property remains the principal example cited by St. Thomas, Vitoria and Soto of the operation of the *jus gentium*.

Against those who hold that grace is either a prerequisite for or a basis of dominion, Soto delivers a fourth conclusion. Although aimed at the Wyclifites, it is directly relevant to those in Spain who had adopted the discredited view of Wyclif that dominion presupposes grace and applied it to the New World. By citing instances of idolatry or sexual excess or cannibalism on the part of some of the Indians, these proponents of the Wyclif view argued that the Indians lost any claim to dominion on account of their immoral conduct.

Soto could not have been unaware of the application of the Wyclif view to the New World situation:

> Gerson and Ricardo say in effect that those in friendship with God have a dominion on account of his grace over things which they do not possess by any other title, e.g., over all the things of any other owner since in virtue of grace they can take possession of them. But against them I state a fourth conclusion: whoever is in the grace of God does not have more dominion or right to use the things of others than he who is in mortal sin. Both in the case of extreme necessity can make use of things which they need which belong to some other owner. But aside from this one case neither of them can do so. To affirm the contrary is false and dangerous. Certainly grace is not the title in virtue of which man has received dominion over things, as the Wyclifites and Armachanus falsely thought...Dominion has been received according to the *jus naturale* or the *jus humanum*. God makes the sun to shine on the good and the evil alike...For the same reason, that grace is the title for dominion over things, the Wyclifites...take the view that no one except those in the state of grace can possess dominion over spiritual or temporal goods. But this represents a stupid heresy, many times condemned. Although the evil are unworthy, lacking the dignity of merit in the bread they eat and the life they live...they nevertheless continue to have the natural right to enjoy the sun that God lets shine on the evil also.[37]

Although Soto does not explicitly cite St. Thomas (*ST.* 2a2ae. q.10, a.10, 10.12), it was the view expressed by St. Thomas that dominion is neither conferred by grace nor removed by sin that became the most powerful weapon in the arsenal of arguments used by Las Casas in is debate with Sepúlveda at Valladolid in 1550-51 on the subject of the rights of the Indians in the New World. It was of course Soto who was designated by the Council to summarize the lengthy arguments of Las Casas and Sepúlveda. His *De Justitia et Jure* was published after the debate at Valladolid. We have seen that Vitoria used *ST*. 2a2ae. q.10, a.10, q.10, a.12 in direct reference to the rights of the Indians in *De Indis*. Whether Soto omits any reference to this salient text from St. Thomas out of a sense of diplomacy or a desire not to confuse the Wyclifite dispute with the dispute over Spanish colonization or for some other reason is a matter for speculation.

3. Soto's Application of *Dominium* to Slavery

We now come to the *locus classicus* of Soto's consideration of the issue of slavery. The form of the question—"whether a man can have dominion over another man"—will become the standard inquiry of the manualist tradition in the centuries after Soto's *De Justitia et Jure*. The question will almost without exception be answered in the affirmative, even after two Popes raise the identical question and answer it in the negative: Pope Gregory XVI in his bull entitled *In Supremo* of 3 December 1839, and Leo XIII in the encyclical *In Plurimis* of 1888.[38] Because this question lies at the heart of Soto's view on slavery, it will be quoted extensively.

Soto begins Question 2, article 2 in the customary fashion of scholastic dispute, considering arguments which will ultimately be modified or rejected:

> In this second article we speak of one of the particular species of dominion, viz., whether a man can dominate over another man. Against this proposition it is alleged primarily that natural rights cannot be abrogated by any other right. This is so. For by natural right all men are born free, as the legislators have plainly stated in the *Institutes* (*de ju. person. et ff. de stat. homi. l. libertas*): slavery, wherein one is subject to the dominion of another, is contrary to nature. Saint Gregory affirms the same when he said that it is against

nature that some dominate others. The argument also stands since man surpasses the other animals precisely in the fact that he enjoys reason and liberty. Therefore there can be no right (*jus*) for slavery to be introduced among us. As is clear from Ecclesiastes 15, God made man and placed him in the hands of providence. For this reason...he was placed by the same God at the head of all creatures but not in charge of other men.

Secondly, (the proposition) is confirmed principally among Christians because it is not suitable that those to whom Christ gave liberty, making them sons of God, should be permitted to become as slaves. As Christ Himself suggested in Matthew 17, sons are free.

On the other hand, a *jus* (of slavery) is established in certain titles (*De Statu homin.*; *Institutes*), and Aristotle in the *Politics*, book II, distinguishes and approves many species of slavery.[39]

By citing contradictory texts in the *Institutes* in the affirming and *sed contra* arguments, Soto regrettably lapses into an inconsistency that characterized classical Roman jurisprudence and its medieval progeny, viz., the assertion that slavery contradicts the *jus naturale* but is sanctioned by the *jus gentium*. The larger issue of whether the *jus gentium* contradicts the *jus naturale* is tragically avoided. It is present, at least by implication, in the argumentation cited by Soto above, and will be addressed in a legal rather than philosophical context in his last conclusion of Question 2, article 2.

Soto presents four conclusions. The first three pertain to the three classes of slavery which Soto considers: (1) "natural" slavery as described in Aristotle's *Politics*, i.e. a natural pre-eminence among some who *ex natura* must direct the slower for the good of all; (2) contractual self-enslavement whereby one sells himself on account of indebtedness in order to survive, termed the first of two classes of "legal" slavery in the Aristotelian schema; (3) slavery as a penalty for capture in war, termed the second of two classes of "legal" slavery in the Aristotelian schema and sanctioned by the patristic tradition. The fourth conclusion pertains to the relationship of "natural" slavery and the *jus gentium*.

The citations given will be lengthy both because of the detail and examples provided by Soto himself but also because of the importance of Question 2, article 2 in providing a serious explanation of the moral reasoning of a premier moral theologian in addressing the burning issue of his era.

The first conclusion is that a man can have dominion over another man both by natural right and the *jus gentium*. Aristotle rightly recognized in Book I of his *Politics* two classes of slavery, natural and legal. The natural is that which men of keener talent exercise over those who are more sluggish and primitive. This occurs in the same way as the soul surpasses the body, as Comico said. Within the human genus there are men who excel in many ways over others; natural wisdom was given to some men of talent to rule, while, on the other hand, strong bodies were given to some to serve. Thus it is proved that this natural slavery is just and suitable. It is natural to man to live according to reason and to be subject to it. Just as the perfection of the sensitive appetite in man consists in obeying reason, so also among men the perfection of the knowledgeable over the primitive consists in being subject to the direction of the wise.

The other class of slavery is legal and can occur in two ways according to the *Institutes* (*de jur. pers.*). Some are slaves because, having reached maturity, they contract voluntarily (to be slaves) and to receive a salary. This slavery was practiced in the old law since we read in Exodus 21, 'if you buy a Hebrew, he will be your slave during six years but on the seventh he will become free...' There was thus a difference between slaves taken from the Gentiles, who were slaves for a lifetime, and the Hebrew slaves, whose servitude could only be temporary.

Concerning this slavery we offer a second conclusion: this class of slavery is licit. Although men have been created free by God, the desire and right to survive is so innate in all living creatures that necessity can compel slavery. Although liberty is worth more than all the gold, nevertheless it is worth less than life, which is more precious than all gold. Even fathers obligated by necessity were authorized under the old law to sell their sons, as recorded...in Leviticus 25...The *Institutes* speak of the power of the country (*patria potestas*) in the *glossae*, although among Christians these laws are not in use. It is said that this custom still survives among the Ethiopians, where the Portuguese with their ships capture them in order to sell them. If they sell themselves freely there is no reason why this commerce should be considered criminal. But if it is true, that these practices go too far, that is, if it is coercion, we must conclude otherwise. There are those who state that the primitive people are seduced with lies and bribes and attracted and taken to the port unknowingly through gifts and games, sometimes forced to board the ship and sold without knowing what is happening to them. If this is true neither those who overpower them nor those who buy them, nor those who possess them can ever have a tranquil conscience while these slaves are deprived of liberty, nor can [the owners] recover their cost. If anyone retains something of another, even though he acquired it in the market, or by means of some other just title, as soon as he knows it cannot be his, he is obligated to return it to its owner, no matter the cost. How much more is one obligated to return liberty to a man born free who has unjustly been made a slave! If anyone alleges as a pretext that enslavement is a great benefit to the pagans because the slaves are converted to Christianity, I believe that he does injury to the faith which must teach and persuade with the utmost of liberty. Let him be so far away that only God can accept his excuse.[40]

We may certainly inquire as to why Soto would cite the Portuguese capturing slaves on the west coast of Africa but omit the practice of the *encomenderos* of compelling Indians in the New World to operate the gold mines of the Spanish. While the motive of nationalism is an obvious possibility, it must be remembered that Soto and Vitoria were already on record as having serious misgivings about Spanish colonization, as the irate letters of Carlos V to the Salamanca faculty described in Chapter Two illustrate. Moreover, the raging debate at Valladolid on the rights of the Indians preceded the publication of Soto's *De Justitia et Jure* by little more than two years. The controversy was far from stale when these words were written. One might speculate that Soto chose not to make the obvious application because of the freshness of the controversy and the role that he had personally played in summarizing the opposing arguments of Las Casas and Sepúlveda for the Council.[41]

The third class of slavery considered by Soto—the penalty of capture in war—will occasion his third conclusion in the article:

> The third class of slavery is also legal, and as we are taught in the law cited and in the *Institutes* (*de stat. hom.I, libertas*), this is how the word *servitus* is described. It arises from those who conquer, not given either to sell or to kill prisoners of war, but to save them. These slaves are called prisoners of war because the conquerors, entitled to impale them with the sword, take them to save them. Concerning this species of slavery, we add a third conclusion: not only is it licit, it is the fruit of mercy. If one can survive though deprived of liberty, it can be reasoned that it is more advantageous to become a prisoner than to be subject to death.[42]

Having concluded that the three kinds of slavery examined are licit, Soto now distinguishes among them according to two key issues, viz., the extent to which the slave is obligated to serve and the question of whether the relationship is for the mutual advantage of master and slave (the rationale of Aristotelian natural slavery) or for the sole benefit of the master. He also touches on whether there is a right to flee in the three classes of slavery:

> There is a great difference between these kinds of slavery. Dominion and natural slavery do not encompass the entire reality which the word signifies...In the second and third species of slavery (voluntary indebtedness and capture of a prisoner of war) the slave is not free

and everything belongs to the master. The master does not use the slave for the benefit of the slave himself but rather for his own personal advantage, as he would use a beast of burden. As the *Institutes* say (*Per quas pers. nobis. acqui, n. item nobis, et de acquir, rerum dominio. I etiam invitis.*), all that the slave acquires is deemed to be his master's...Those who are obligated by necessity to become slaves, since they are sold freely for a price, cannot in justice flee...But I do not believe that prisoners of war are obligated not to flee.[43]

Soto also states that the identity of a slave as Christian or infidel is irrelevant to the question of whether he is free to flee. The reason why the religious faith of the slave is irrelevant is that "the *jus gentium* is the same for all persons."[44] But if the religious faith of the slave is unrelated to any right to flee, it does have a bearing on the duties of servitude:

It seems to me that there is a legitimate difference between these species of slaves in regard to the things that they are obligated to do for their masters. Christians made prisoners of war by other Christians are not obligated to serve as slaves, nor do their goods belong to their masters...Neither do I think that slaves taken in war from the infidels by the Christians are entirely their masters' in such a way that all that they own through gifts or inheritance or licit earnings belong to their masters. Since they did not fall into slavery voluntarily, their misfortune does not merit that they be punished at such a great penalty. According to the rules (of interpretation) of a *jus*, favors should be expanded and punishments restricted. In the case of those who have sold themselves it remains to be seen whether there is any reason for all that they have to belong to their master according to the prescription of the laws which we have briefly cited. The judgment on all these things must be left to the jurisconsults.[45]

By placing restrictions on the duties of the slave, Soto illustrates in practice what he has already stated in principle: *dominium* is not an absolute right but a real relationship. He also makes it clear that he does not believe it possible to speak of slavery as a generic institution; one must identify the species or class of slavery involved, for different duties and rights correspond to each class.

Soto now returns to the issue upon which he attaches great weight: whether natural slavery is for the mutual advantage of master and slave or for the sole benefit of the master:

> The first kind of slavery must be judged in a very distinct manner. He who is master by nature cannot make use of those who are naturally slaves for his own profit, as if they were things belonging to him. They must be used by him as free and independent men for their own benefit and advantage. For example he must instruct them and train them in the customs of society. They are not obligated to serve their masters as slaves but with a certain moderation and natural dignity, unless of course they have contracted themselves into slavery.[46]

Although Soto stops short of prescribing any duties on the part of the master in regard to the slave, such as an obligation to foster the slave's right to marry and worship, he places limits on the duties incumbent upon those who might be classed as "natural" slaves. The logical question raised by this analysis is of course, who constitutes a "natural" slave or "natural" master? Presumably the answer is provided in some way by the operation of the *jus gentium*. But against those who seek to classify non-Christians as presumptive "natural" slaves, Soto now addresses the central issue of *De Indis*, the rights of those who are the object or victim of imperial conquest:

> We can now answer satisfactorily those who ask if Christians, by virtue of the *jus* of natural dominion, can make an armed invasion of those infidel countries which on account of the primitive nature of their customs appear to be natural slaves. There is no reason why we acquire any right over them to dominate them by force, since their inferior condition does not deprive them of liberty as does the

condition of those who sell themselves into slavery, or those who were prisoners of war. Since liberty is the basis of dominion, (these infidels) preserve a *jus* over their goods. Aristotle not only posited this slavery between one nation and another but also between persons of the same city and family. There are among Christians of the same city slaves by nature who nevertheless cannot be deprived of their goods, even though they refuse to obey those who are naturally their superiors.[47]

In short, Aristotle's theory of natural slavery cannot automatically be pressed into service to justify the colonization of non-Christians. No matter how primitive the customs of the pagans of foreign lands, they cannot automatically be deemed "natural slaves" since they possess the liberty which constitutes the prerequisite of true dominion.

Soto now moves to the question of whether slavery is contrary to the natural law. Tragically, he will not address the overarching issue of whether or how the *jus gentium* can be in conflict with the *jus naturale*; such an analysis may well have led him to conclude that slavery, a feature of the *jus gentium*, must be abolished for all and not merely for Christians since the *jus gentium* applies to everyone and the condition of servitude which it has sanctioned in the past could be seen to contravene the precepts of the *jus naturale* from which the determinations of the *jus gentium* are derived.

Nevertheless Soto asks if slavery is inconsistent with the natural law. He uses one of the early texts of St. Thomas to conclude that it does not violate the "secondary intention" of the natural law. This was the *propter peccatum* theory of slavery (slavery is permissible as a punishment for original sin) given credence by the patristic tradition:

Slavery neither abridges nor repeals the natural law. The natural *jus* does not prohibit slavery as a sin for if it did so it would never be licit. But as St. Thomas said in 4 *Sent.* d. 36 something can be intended by nature in two manners: one in the primary intention...and in another way by a secondary intention...Slavery is

contrary to nature in regard to the primary intention of nature, which
consists in the precept that all men be virtuous according to reason.
But when such an intent fails, punishment follows upon sin, which is
part of fallen nature. One of the kinds of punishment is legal slavery.
From original sin the need (for punishment) arose whence came the
countless wars which reduce men to slavery.[48]

It may well be asked why Soto chose an earlier text of St. Thomas and
chose not to cite some of the texts from the *Secunda Secundae*, examined
in Chapter One, which reveal the clear distaste of Thomas in his mature
thought for the institution of slavery.

Soto will now refer to the household codes of the New Testament
to demonstrate that legal slavery (voluntary self-enslavement for
indebtedness and capture in war) was sanctioned by the early church:

Slavery of this (legal) species is not repugnant among Christians
themselves. Christ only freed us from the law of sin and death, as
St. Paul affirmed in Romans 8; He did not exempt us from the *jus
gentium*. On the contrary, in the Letter to Titus, 3, Paul admonishes
us to obey our masters, and St. Peter adds, whether they be rigorous
or even infidels who do not belong to the church. In I Corinthians
he admonishes that whoever has been called to the faith as a slave
should continue as a slave. It is true however that for the decorum
of Christian liberty the custom has long been followed that Christians
made prisoners of war not serve as slaves, as shown by Bartolus (*l.
hostes de capt. et post. l. rever.*). But natural slavery did not exist
in the state of innocence, as it exists now, since no one was
ignorant...Neither was everyone born with the same facility of mind.
Slavery thus made its entry into the world by sin itself, just as St.
Paul said that death entered the world. St. Ambrose affirmed this (*d.
35, can. sexto die.*) when he called the slave a drunk who being
deprived of the use of reason became a beast.[49]

These are the only references to the New Testament in this pivotal article
of Soto's *De Justitia et Jure*! Presumably he cites the household codes

rather than some of the key passages on baptism which underscore the freedom and equality of those baptized into the Risen Lord, such as Galatians 3.28, because he felt that a fundamental spiritual freedom and personal dignity could be held inviolable notwithstanding one's material condition of servitude.

Nevertheless, it is ironic that in view of his close association with Vitoria, and possessing the knowledge that questions of baptismal catechesis had served as the catalyst for *De Indis*, he did not choose to cite any of the passages from the Gospel or St. Paul which concern the new identity of the baptized Christian.

Soto concludes question 2, article 2 with a final explanation that slavery does not contradict natural reason. Ironically, his explanation links the *jus gentium* with the *jus naturale* by underscoring the universality of the *jus gentium* and its derivation from natural reason:

> It seems to some that the texts on *jus* cited above are contradictory since, on the one hand, they assure that slavery was established by the *jus gentium*, but, on the other hand, say that it (the *jus gentium*) is merely an imposition of rulers. Nevertheless there is no contradiction. Slavery exists in effect through the *jus gentium*, as constantly expressed by St. Gregory (*can. cum Redemptor, 12, q.2*), who said that the men whom nature made free the *jus gentium* subjected to slavery. We call it the *jus gentium* because all people can know it through natural reason, and it is called the constitution of the Emperor because rulers have considered it valid and confirmed it through custom and practice.[50]

In view of Soto's robust attacks on the jurisconsults, in which he identifies his antagonists by name and struggles to define *dominium* correctly by rejecting their equation of *jus* and *dominium*, it is surprising that he shows such deference to them in accepting their construction of the *jus gentium*, even stating at one point, cited above, that the exact conditions of servitude should be determined by the jurisconsults. We may speculate that his initial premise of placing the *jus gentium* within the positive law led him to defer to the judgments of those who specialized in the study of the positive law. Although he wanted a dialogue of philosophy and law, it appears that considerations of legal construction overwhelmed precepts of philosophy.

Notes for Chapter Three

1. V. Beltran de Heredia, "Dominique de Soto," *DTC* (Paris: Librairie Letouzey et Ané, 1941) 14:2, coll. 2423.

2. *Ibid.*, coll. 2428.

3. In the prologue Soto summarizes the contents of the ten books: "We have divided the work into ten books: the first two of which pertain to law, i.e. *de legibus*, which are the supreme norm of justice. The third is of *jus* insofar as it is the object of justice, its substance and its connection with distributive justice. The fourth book deals with the preambles of commutative justice, those, namely, from injurious actions, such as homicide and the like. The sixth is of usury, contracts and rates of exchange. The seventh covers vows. The eighth pertains to oaths; the ninth of simony and the tenth of the domicile of prelates."

4. Soto, *De dominio*, a *lectio* which remains unedited, cited by V.D.Carro, OP, *Domingo de Soto y su doctrina juridica*, 2d. ed. (Salamanca, 1944), p. 60.

5. Domingo de Soto, O.P., *De La Justicia y Del Derecho* en diez libros. Tomo Segundo. Introduccion historica y teológico-juridica por el V.D. Carro, O.P., version española del M.G. Ordónez, O.P.(Madrid: Valencia, 1968). This Spanish edition of *De Justitia et Jure* will be the text cited hereafter. The only Latin editions that I have been able to locate are folios in the Library of Congress in calligraphic form. The Ordónez translation parenthetically inserts Latin terms or phrases wherever germane. Thus there is virtually no likelihood of any loss or change of meaning in using the Spanish in place of the Latin text.

6. Book III consists of two questions, the first of which corresponds to the *ST*. 2a2ae. q.57, while the second question focuses on 2a2ae. q.58. There are four articles which accompany the first question and eight articles which accompany the second question. Our inquiry will concentrate on the first question. The second question is important in demonstrating the vehemence with which Soto criticizes the nominalists in general and Occam and Buridan in particular. His defense of the conclusions of St. Thomas in 2a2ae. q.58 against their attacks indicates clearly the priority attached by the Salamanca school to fidelity to the thomistic tradition.

7. Book III, q.3, a.1.

8. Book III, q.1, a.1.

9. Ulpian, *Institutes*, I, 1, "*si quis.*"

10. Isidore, *Etymologies*, lib. V, cap.2, dist. 1.

11. Soto, *loc.cit.*

12. *Ibid.* Again we see the mischief created by Isidore's fanciful metaphors. Soto charitably dismisses his argument by asserting that its intent could not have been literal. He can thus dismiss the argument without dismissing the author.

13. Book III, q.1, a.3: "Efectivamente, tener aprehension de una cosa en absoluto no solo conviene á los hombres, sino tambien por natural instinto á los animales. Y por esto el derecho simplemente natural, como la sociedad entre el hombre y la mujer y la alimentacion de los hijos es comun á todos los animales. Pero juzgar de las cosas en orden á algun fin y en ciertas circunstancias no compete a todos los animales, sino peculiarmente al hombre, quien en virtud de su razon puede comprender la relacion que una cosa tiene con otra. Pues el derecho que brota asi de calculo uniforme de muchos, se llama derecho de Gentes, es decir, el derecho que todos los hombres, por lo que tienen de racionales, establecieron para si."

14. *Ibid.* "Aunque Santo Tomas no formule expresamente esta conclusion, sin embargo, en las respuestas á las dificultades con que al principio de la cuestion arguye que el derecho de Gentes es natural, se ve claramente que su pensamiento es negar esto, y en consecuencia afirmar que es de derecho positivo."

15. The view of Dom O. Lottin will be recalled that Thomas was constrained in 1a2ae. q.95, a.4 to preserve the reputation of Isidore while rejecting his classification, whereas in 2a2ae. q.57 he no longer had to struggle with this problem, producing a freer and more mature formulation of the problem of classification.

16. Soto, *loc.cit.*

17. *Ibid.*

18. *Ibid.*

19. Book III, q.1, a.3.

20. It will be recalled that Vitoria raised the same question in *De Indis* but used the term "abrogation" rather than "dispensation." The example cited by Vitoria was the same as that now given by Soto—slavery.

21. Soto, *loc.cit.*

22. "Dominion" is translated from the Spanish *dominio* whereas "right" is translated from the Spanish *derecho*, which stands for the Latin *jus*.

23. Book IV, q.1, a.1.

24. *Ibid.*

25. *Ibid.*

26. *Ibid.*

27. *Ibid.*: "Dominio, pues, si se define segun las reglas del arte, es la facultad y derecho proprio que cada uno tiene sobre una cosa cualquiera para servirse de ella en beneficio suyo mediante cualquiera uso permitido

por la ley.

28. *Ibid*.

29. *Ibid*.

30. Book IV, question 1, article 2.

31. *Ibid*.

32. *Ibid*.

33. Book IV, question 2, a.1.

34. *Ibid*.

35. *Ibid*.

36. *Ibid*.

37. *Ibid*.

38. J. Dutilleul, "Esclavage," *DTC* t. 5, col. 501-504.

39. Book IV, question 2, article 2.

40. Book IV, question 2, article 2.

41. The Spanish chaplains who accompanied the *conquistadores* to the New World were for the most part Dominicans and Franciscans, while the chaplains who accompanied the Portuguese in their colonization of Africa were mostly Jesuits. The writings of Luis Molina, SJ, on slavery in his *De Justitia et Jure* shortly after Soto will include copious correspondence from Jesuit missionaries on the conditions of Portuguese colonization. The differing paths of Spanish and Portuguese colonization thus account for the difference in focus between Vitoria and Soto, looking to the New World, on the one hand, and Molina, looking to the west coast of Africa, on the other hand.

42. *Ibid*.

43. *Ibid.*

44. *Ibid.*

45. *Ibid.*

46. *Ibid.*

47. *Ibid.*

48. *Ibid.*

49. *Ibid.*

50. *Ibid.*

CHAPTER FOUR

Analysis of the Concepts of
Jus and *Dominium* in Aquinas, Vitoria and Soto
In Regard to Slavery

As we now turn to the analysis of the concepts of *jus*, the *jus gentium* and *dominium* in Aquinas, Vitoria and Soto, we shall attempt to locate each of these vital terms within the historical and theological context of their usage by the respective theologian. By taking account of the changing context of the terms, we can appreciate their application to the issue of slavery, which was similarly subject to the forces of history. The system of medieval serfdom known by Thomas as part of the domestic or "household" economy of Europe was radically different from the forced labor imposed upon Amerindians and Africans in the New World, the setting for the writings of Vitoria and Soto. Indeed his own brother, Aimo, was a slave.[1] It is our hope that the illumination of the content of these terms through the historical context will disclose the points of similarity and dissimilarity, convergence and divergence between Aquinas, on the one hand, and Vitoria and Soto, on the other hand.

Thomas was the mentor both of Francisco de Vitoria and Domingo de Soto. When Vitoria was forced to teach both the *Sententiae* and the *Summa*, his health began to suffer. But his desire to replace the *Sententiae* with the *Summa* was so great that he endured this double burden until his exhaustion became such that the administration of Salamanca relented and allowed the *Summa* to become the premier text for seminary training. Vitoria spent a decade of his life writing a commentary on the *Secunda Secundae*. Vitoria and Soto demonstrated their adherence to the Angelic Doctor by opposing vigorously and frequently the attacks upon the thomistic approach by a nominalist such as Buridan. Both of these stalwarts of Salamanca used key passages from the *Summa* to challenge the claims levelled by imperialistic countrymen in the Spanish *siglo de oro*. The paean to human rights which Vitoria composed in *De Indis* drew from the inspiration of the *Summa*; the role of Soto in aiding Bartolomé de las Casas against Sepúlveda at the Council of Vallodolid was made possible by an appropriation of the thomistic principle that human law cannot abrogate a natural right.

In view of their concern for human rights and their self-conscious fidelity to Thomas it is difficult to assert, as I shall, that they did not fully utilize the metaphysical foundation of Thomas to conclude on thomistic principles that slavery in any form was repugnant to the Christian conscience. Nevertheless, their delineation and advocacy of human rights deserves the gratitude of all for the courageous contribution that it represented at a critical time when far too few gave any thought to the needs and rights of the natives of North America and the slaves captured from the west coast of Africa.

I shall attempt to show that the meanings attached by Thomas to the terms *jus* and *dominium* have a direct bearing upon the issue of slavery as a moral problem and that his understanding can be grasped under four related headings: (1) analogous relation; (2) finality; (3) relation to the common good; (4) inviolability of the *lex aeterna*. Although Francisco de Vitoria and Domingo de Soto were admirers and self-conscious adherents of Thomas' theology, their approach to the issue of slavery diverged substantially from his because of the different context of their theology. The role of metaphysics in the thirteenth century was largely supplanted by the role of law in the sixteenth century. While Vitoria and Soto struggled to maintain a metaphysical foundation for their enterprise against the nominalists and *"terministas,"* their theological method attests to the force of the contemporary focus on "titles" and "rights" at the expense of the metaphysical foundation which flourished during the golden age of scholasticism.

The approach of Vitoria and Soto to slavery can be grasped also under four headings which serve to contrast the orientation of thirteenth and sixteenth century scholasticism: (1) univocal right; (2) legal title; (3) subjective power; (4) *jus positivum*.

We can schematize the different approaches as follows:

EMPHASIS OF AQUINAS	EMPHASIS OF VITORIA, SOTO
Analogous Relation	Univocal Right
Finality of Acts of Agents	Legal Title
Relation to Common Good	Subjective Power
Inviolability of *lex aeterna*	*Jus positivum*

We shall now critique and compare the views of Thomas Aquinas, on the one hand, and those of Vitoria and Soto, on the other hand, in regard to the moral issue of slavery. The respective emphases of each, as schematized above, will provide the eight headings which will be employed.

1. Aquinas and the Issue of Slavery

For Aquinas the concepts of *jus*, the object of the virtue of justice, and *dominium*, a human perfection, are analogical. The analogical nature of these terms sheds much light on the kind of activity which might qualify as a just relationship or an authentic exercise of dominion.

To appreciate the analogical meaning of *jus* (and *dominium*) we can profit at the outset from a summary of Aquinas' profound understanding and skillful use of analogy.

Analogy is an habitual relation (*habitudo*) between objects which have something in common. It is helpful to recall the fundamental meaning of the terms "univocal" and "equivocal" in contradistinction to the analogical vis-à-vis *jus*.   Henri Renard provides a thorough explanation of these critical terms:

> A univocal term is one predicable of many things according to precisely the same concept.   Not only the spoken and written word, but the concept remains identical and signifies the same essence in its diverse predications...   An 'equivocation' is the use of an ambiguous word; it is a play on words...The scholastics define an analogous concept as one which is simply (*simpliciter*) different, and somewhat (*secundum quid*) the same thing.   The subjects of analogous predication, or those things to which the analogous term is referred, are called "analogates"...We distinguish between a primary analogate and secondary analogates.   The primary analogate is that to which the analogous term is principally referred.[2]

There are two classes of analogy: the analogy of attribution and of proportionality:

> The analogy of attribution is had, when a term is attributed to diverse beings only because of the relation they have to the primary analogate, so that the nature signified by this term is found actually (intrinsically) only in the primary analogate...
>
> The change...which must be found in every analogous predication of attribution does not take place in the predicated perfection, the concept of whose nature remains always the same; rather, it is found in the whole predicate (including the verb), and is had by a modification of the meaning of the verb--a modification which effects a new determination in the mode of attribution. The significant words of Thomas, *secundum intentionem et non secundum esse*...are clear.   The mind predicates a certain perfection of the secondary analogates merely because of the relation which it sees (*secundum intentionem*) to the first analogate, and not because such perfection actually exists in them (*non secundum esse*). Never, therefore, in this analogy of attribution could the predicated perfection exist (intrinsically) in the subject, since the only reason for such predication is *secundum intentionem*.[3]

A classic example of an analogy of attribution cited by Thomas at the beginning of the *Summa* (1a. q. 13, a. 5) is the use of the term "healthy" to describe a person, food which is salutary, and a physical appearance which betokens good health.

In addition to the analogy of attribution, there exists the analogy of proportionality. This latter kind is very important to our study since it was the analogy of proper proportionality that Thomas employed to describe human perfections which humanity enjoys by virtue of participation in the infinite perfection of God:

> The analogy of proportionality is had when a term is intrinsically predicated of diverse subjects, because the perfection signified is found intrinsically in these subjects according to a certain proportional similitude.[4]

It should be noted that the analogy of proportionality is based not on a simple proportion but on a comparison of proportions themselves. In an analogy based on a simple proportion between two things the analogates are on a single plane of reference, like a line between the two points which define and originate it. The two kinds of relationships can be illustrated as follows:

> A simple proportion is constructed like a single wheel. The hub of the wheel is like the primary term of the relationship and the spokes radiate from the center as from their point of origin...A proportionality, on the other hand...is like two wheels. Any two wheels are related to each other because within each wheel there is a proportion of one part to another. The wheel of a toy automobile is like the wheel of a locomotive. The two wheels have a relationship to each other because their parts are proportionately distributed...Because it involves a duality of proportions, a proportional relationship can be a more effective basis of analogical terms that are to be applied to transcendental perfections that are found in both the finite and infinite orders. There is no continuity between the one order and the other; the unity between them is one of similarity.[5]

Having examined the difference between a simple proportion and an analogy of proportionality, we must recognize as well the distinction made by Thomas between an analogy of metaphorical (or improper) proportionality, and one of proper proportionality:

> Sometimes the name implies something belonging to the thing primarily designated which cannot be common to God and creatures...This would be true, for example, of anything predicated of God metaphorically, as when God is called lion, which cannot be attributed to God. At other times, however, a term predicated of God and creatures implies nothing in its principal meaning which would prevent our finding between a creature and God an agreement of the type described above. To this kind belong all attributes which include no defect nor depend on matter for their existence, for example, being, the good, and similar things.[6]

Analogy based on metaphorical proportionality is useful in expressing images which cannot be expressed as vividly in literal language. But metaphorical proportionality is lacking in a simple common concept; the analogates are compared only on the basis of an extrinsic relation to a form that exists properly in only one term. To say that a landlord has a "heart of stone" conveys a vivid image even though the landlord and the stone have no concept in common.

By way of contrast, in an analogy based on proper proportionality, both the common term that is predicated and the reality which is signified are truly present in the analogates. Because the analogy of proper proportionality is both by intent and being (*secundum intentionem et secundum esse*), it is the most useful and productive kind of analogy possible.

One reason is that the perfection spoken of exists formally and intrinsically in both members of the analogy, while this is not found in analogy according to signification only. Since the metaphysician treats of existence as well as of meaning, analogy based on proportionality both according to signification and existence is most properly used to convey a true judgment about the transcendental properties of being.

It is appropriate that Aquinas should refer to the preference of Aristotle for the analogy of proper proportionality in the context of goodness and the end of the agent in his *Commentary on the Nicomachean Ethics* (I, lesson 7, no. 96). Both *jus* and *dominium* entail the good desired and possessed by the agent:

> Thus [Aristotle] says that goodness is predicated of many things, not according to a meaning that is entirely different, as happens in those things that are equivocal by chance, but rather according to analogy, that is, they are proportionately the same insofar as all good things depend on one principle of goodness, or insofar as they are all ordered to one end. Or also all good things are analogously good, that is, according to a similar proportion, as vision in the eye is a good of the body and vision of the intellect is a good of the soul. Therefore [Aristotle] prefers this kind of analogy, because it is taken to refer to the goodness that is really inhering in things.

We can now make a specific application of Thomas' analogical understanding of perfections to the meaning of *jus*. It has been shown in Chapter One that *jus*, the object of the virtue of justice, necessarily entails a relation of moral equality which arises from a *res debita* (e.g., *ST*. 2a2ae. q. 57, a. 1; q. 79, a.1 *ad* 1; q. 80, a.1; q. 81, a. 6 *ad* 1). This relation of moral rather than mathematical equality is found in the objective reality of just relationships. Equality is both the mean of justice (*medium justitiae*) and the mean of reason (*medium rationis*), as shown, for instance, by *ST*. 2a2ae. q. 58, a.10 and q. 81, a. 6 *ad* 1. This objective equality of the agents is what causes the due (*res debita*) to come into existence. The agents are not equal because something is due; something is due another because the parties are equal.

Thomas recognizes that in some cases it is impossible to attain equality in rendering what is due. For example, it is impossible to worship God fully or in an equal measure, yet worship is due Him. Thus the virtue of religion constitutes a potential part of justice. Similarly one is unable to return fully or render equally that which is due to one's parents: the virtue of piety constitutes a potential part of justice. Nor can one return adequately the reward due virtue; the virtue of observance constitutes a potential part of justice. Because religion, piety and observance cannot attain the equality constitutive of the just relationship, they are potential parts of the virtue of justice. Equality remains the formal cause of justice in all human relationships (*ST.* 2a2ae. q. 80, a.1; q. 81, a.7).

It should be noted parenthetically that religion, piety and observance do not constitute justice in the strict sense because the equality required is beyond what the agent can render. There is no comparable annexed virtue or potential part of justice which falls below the standard of equality because an agent is excused from rendering it. Our examination of Thomas' texts on justice shows that the equality of justice is due to all, irrespective of social status. In short, some virtues require "more" equality than the agent can render but in no case is the duty (*debitum*) of equality absent. The slave is in some sense an equal.

In 2a2ae. q. 79, a.1, Thomas cites the objective of justice to be *"facere aequalitatem."* While all the virtues have as their end *"facere bonum,"* the modality of *facere bonum* in the case of justice is *facere aequalitatem*. In Chapter One we saw the schematic representation of P.D. Dognin of this equality to be: *persona/persona = res/res*.[7] The subject of a *jus* and the person who owes the *res debita* are morally equal in the same measure as the claim of the subject of the *jus* is proportional to the debt of the party obligated to render that debt. Since the concept of equality is present in both the parties and the *res debita* in intent as well as in being (*secundum intentionem et secundum esse*), the relation between the parties in a just relationship is an analogy of proper proportionality.

We can now bring together earlier considerations of *dominium* and apply them directly to Thomas' views on slavery. The status of a person as *dominus* in relation to another who is a *servus* is analogical, not univocal. It is analogous to the providential dominion of God over creation and to the control of the moral agent over his acts, as we have seen in several texts (e.g., *ST*. 2a2ae. q. 103, a.3c; 1a2ae. q.6, a.2 ad 2).

The analogy of proper proportionality which is found in the relation of perfections in the creature with divine perfection discloses also the exemplary causality of divine perfection, as Thomas shows in *De Veritate*, q. 21, a.4:

> Every agent is found to effect something like itself. If, therefore, the first goodness is the effective cause of all goods, it must imprint its likeness upon the thing produced; and so each thing will be called good by reason of an inherent form because of the likeness of the highest good implanted in it, and also because of the first goodness taken as the exemplar and effective cause of all created goodness.

If perfections in the creature are images of divine perfection, caused in fact by divine perfection, it remains to be seen whether these human perfections such as goodness are univocal, equivocal or analogical. To answer this question we must turn again to Thomas' *De Potentia Dei*, q. 7, a.7:

> It is impossible for anything to be predicated univocally of God and a creature. This is made plain as follows: every effect of an univocal agent is adequate to the agent's power. No creature, being finite, can be adequate to the power of the First Agent Who is infinite. Wherefore it is impossible for a creature to receive a likeness to God univocally. Again, it is clear that although the form in the agent and the form in the effect have a common meaning (*ratio*), the fact that they have different modes of existence precludes their univocal predication: thus though the material house is of the same type as the house in the mind of the builder, since the one is the type of the other; nevertheless "house" cannot be univocally predicated of both, because the form of the material house has its being in matter, whereas in the builder's mind it has immaterial existence...
>
> Wherefore it is evident that a different relation to being precludes an univocal predication of being. Now God's relation to being is different

from that of any creature's: for he is his own being, which cannot be said of any creature. Hence in no way can it be predicated univocally of God and a creature, and consequently neither can any of the other predicables among which is included even the first, being, for if there be diversity in the first, there must be diversity in the others. Wherefore nothing is predicated univocally of substance and accident.

Having thus established that a human perfection cannot be univocally predicated both of God and the creature, Thomas moves to the question of whether the perfection found in the creature is equivocal or analogical. Later in the same text, he concludes that human perfections constitute an analogy of proper proportionality:

> Others...held that nothing is predicated of God and a creature by analogy but by pure equivocation...This opinion, however, is false, because in all purely equivocal terms...a term is predicated of a thing without any respect to something else: whereas all things predicated of God and creatures are predicated of God with a certain respect to creatures or vice versa...
>
> We must...hold that nothing is predicated univocally of God and the creature, but that those things which are attributed to them in common are predicated not equivocally but analogically. Now this kind of predication is twofold. The first is when one thing is predicated of two by reason of a relationship between these two: thus being is predicated of substance and quantity. In the first kind of predication the two things must be preceded by something to which each of them bears some relation. Thus substance has a respect to quantity and quality, whereas in the second kind of predication this is not necessary, but one of the two must precede the other. Wherefore since nothing precedes God, but he precedes the creature, the second kind of analogical predication is applicable to him but not the first.

It is patently clear that human dominion, like all other human perfections, constitutes an identity which is analogous to the dominion of God. Any form of dominion which contravenes or violates divine dominion cannot be considered a proper exercise of human dominion, for the proper proportionality between divine and human dominion would have been broken.

One more element of human dominion must be clarified: whence originates its nature? The answer of Thomas is that human perfections come about through the participation of created beings in the life of Uncreated Being. Thus human dominion is a participation in divine dominion according to the mode of existence of the particular (created) being, as Thomas specifies in the *ad* 2 of q. 7, a. 7 of *De Potentia Dei*:

> The likeness of creatures to God falls short of univocal likeness in two respects. First it does not arise from the participation of one form, as two hot things are like by participation of one form, because what is affirmed of God and creatures is predicated of him essentially, but of creatures, by participation: so that a creature's likeness to God is that of a hot thing to heat, not of a hot thing to one that is hotter. Secondly, because this very form of which the creature participates falls short of the nature of the thing which is God, just as the heat of fire falls short of the nature of the sun's power whereby it produces heat. (Emphasis added)

It is instructive to note that Thomas' analysis of human perfections in the *Prima Pars* is utterly consistent with his views expressed earlier in *De Potentia Dei*. There can be no possible misunderstanding of Thomas' intent on the grounds of inconsistent texts. Although it is, like the earlier texts cited, somewhat lengthy, our record would not be complete without an explicit consideration of *ST*. 1a, q. 13, a. 5, the *locus* for Thomas' examination of analogy and human perfections:

> Univocal predication is impossible between God and creatures. The reason for this is that every effect which is not a proportioned result of the power of the efficient cause receives the similitude of the agent not in its full degree, but in a measure that falls short; so that what is divided and multiplied in the effects resides in the agent simply, and in

an unvaried manner. For example, the sun by the exercise of its own power produces manifold and various forms in these sublunary things. In the same way, as was said above, all perfections existing in creatures divided and multiplied pre-exist in God unitedly. Hence, when any name expressing perfection is applied to a creature, it signifies that perfection is distinct from the others according to the nature of its definition; as, for instance, by this term "wise" applied to a man, we signify some perfection distinct from a man's essence, and distinct from his power and his being, and from all similar things. But when we apply "wise" to God, we do not mean to signify anything distinct from His essence or power or being. And thus when this term "wise" is applied to man, in some degree it circumscribes and comprehends the thing signified; whereas this is not the case when it is applied to God, but it leaves the thing signified as uncomprehended and as exceeding the signification of the name. Hence it is evident that this term "wise" is not applied in the same way to God and to man. The same applies to other terms. Hence, no name is predicated univocally of God and of other creatures. (Emphasis added)

Thomas demonstrates not only that a human perfection such as dominion is analogical but that it is distinct from the "essence," "power" and "being" of an individual. Although Thomas accepts the notion of Aristotle that some men are naturally more gifted than others and that it is appropriate for these individuals to exercise authority over those who are slower, Thomas in article 5, cited above, rejects the idea that a human perfection is part of a person's essence. One is not *ex rerum natura* a master or lord, but only in comparison with others and their respective talents in specific things.

Dominion is not a univocal essence or state but rather a participation in the divine essence according to the creature's mode of being. Unlike Aristotle, Thomas does not attribute the leadership of dominion to any group on the basis of race or ethnicity. By contrast, Aristotle makes his opinion clear in Book I of his *Politics* that non-Greeks are naturally barbarians. In Thomas, dominion is always *secundum quid* rather than *simpliciter*, proportioned to an end and limited by that end, as we shall shortly see.

It may be supposed that the analogical meaning of *dominium* is without practical effect in the matter of slavery. Nothing could be further from the truth. To say that a human being has the perfection of dominion in a way analogous to God's dominion over the universe means that human dominion must imitate (e.g., Genesis 1.26ff) divine dominion. Divine dominion is the exemplary cause of human dominion; human dominion participates in divine being, as is shown in the *ST*. 2a2ae. q. 103, a. 3:

> Man participates in a certain likeness to divine dominion according to which he has a particular power over another man or over another creature.

Because human dominion is a participation in divine plenary dominion it is limited to the sphere of activity proper to the human agent. In the citation above from the *Secunda Secundae* we see that dominion involves a particular power. This is consistent with the metaphysical basis for dominion provided by Thomas in *De Potentia Dei* where the master is said to have a specific (*tale*) power.[8] The inherently limited scope of dominion evident from these texts is underscored also by the fact that the actions of the master necessarily are oriented toward the common good, as we shall see.

This means that any form of human dominion which aspires to be authentic (viz., morally good and praiseworthy) must be analogous to the dominion which God exercises over creation.

Dominion in short must be providential to be authentic: this is the clear inference of Thomas' thought. The *dominus* must act in a manner that foresees and advances the human good of those who are subject to him. A failure to "provide" for the needs of those in his charge would be violative of the inherently analogous relation to divine dominion. This understanding of dominion is radically different from the emphasis upon power and subjective "right" which dominated theological discussion in Europe after the discovery of the New World.

It is now possible to direct our attention to the issue of slavery by combining the content of *jus* and *dominium*, which can be rendered as a *jus dominativum* or a "right to dominion." *Jus* is, of course, the object of the virtue of justice and *dominium* is human participation in divine dominion. There are two salient texts where these two terms are combined in the writings of Thomas to refer to the right of one individual to rule another.

In his *Commentary on the Nicomachean Ethics*, Thomas compares the right of a lord over his servant to the authority of a father over his son.[9] He contrasts these two species of *jus* with "political" rights, that is, the ensemble of objects and ends which necessarily pertain to and promote the common good, which is justice in the absolute sense: *justum simpliciter*, or for Aristotle, the *dikaion politikon*. Since political rights are ordained to the common good they are absolute; every aspect of life pertains in some respect to the common good or community of life, its spiritual goods and human interests.

In both cases there is a relation which cannot be considered just in a strict sense because there is a lack of the otherness (*altérité*) required for a just relationship. Just as the son is "part of" the father, so the servant is "part of" the master. The relationship does not fail to be just on account of a defect of equality, but rather a defect of otherness.

Because the relationship of a master to his servant entails a unity or at least compatibility if interests, it is not essentially *ad alterum*, so there is not a *jus* present. Thomas' usage of *jus* here illustrates the fundamental meaning which the term has for him: it stands for *justum*, the just thing itself, objectively considered. It stands apart from the subjective power or moral faculty of any agent. It is a relation which inheres in the actions of individuals; it is not a possession which belongs to one of them.

Does the fact that the servant is "part of" the master mean that the master is therefore permitted to treat the servant in a dictatorial way?

Thomas' answer is clear: the dominion of the master over his servant is analogous to his dominion over himself and his own actions. No one can reasonably choose to injure himself; no one can reasonably choose to injure an extension of himself, whether son or slave.

It is clear from this that the *jus dominativum* which one may have over another is inherently limited by two things: (1) its ordination to the totality of "political" rights which constitute the spiritual and material well-being of all individuals in community; (2) the unity of interests which exists between the master and servant (or father and son).

The second salient text which links *jus* and *dominus* occurs in the 2a2ae. q. 57, a.4, where servitude is discussed. Once again the relationship between a master and his servant is compared with that of a father and son. There is not a just relationship present, strictly speaking, because neither relationship (father-son; master-servant) is truly *ad alterum*. It is only "sort of" ("*quoddam*") a just relationship.

Thomas refers to the "living instrument" theory of Aristotle's *Politics* (I,2. 1253b32, 1254a14), viz., that the slave is a "living instrument" of the master. It is clear though that the metaphor of an organism does not have the effect of reifying the slave, i.e. reducing him to the status of a tool in the hands of his master, for Thomas categorically states (*ad 2*) that the servant possesses all of the rights due him as a human being. As a human being he is entirely distinct from the master and the bearer of rights. This analysis is given definitive form in *ST.* 2a2ae. q. 57, a.4, *ad 2*, where both the son and slave are recognized as distinctive beings with a legitimate degree of autonomy vis-à-vis father and master. They are "persons," not merely "individuals," to use the neothomistic terminology of Jacques Maritain in his *The Person and the Common Good*.[10]

We can quickly infer from these two texts, simultaneously consistent and complementary, that no master has an unrestricted right to the use of a servant's labors. The right of the master is analogous to the right of a father to the filial piety due him from his son. There is a convergence of rights, a unity of goods, a virtual identity of interests, to the point where perfect justice exists only in the metaphorical sense that one can treat himself justly. A father cannot reasonably injure himself; nor can there be an *agere contra* relationship of a just master toward his servant.

Thomas thus provides us with three vivid analogies for the relationship of a master and servant: (1) the providential relation of God over creation; (2) the reasonable dominion of an agent over his own acts; (3) the dominion of a parent over a child. As an imitation of and participation in divine dominion, each of these human relations is meant to be the reasonable exercise of power or authority within a limited context and oriented toward the good of both agents in the relationship.

In his treatise on human actions in the *Prima Secundae* of the *Summa*, Thomas observes that in voluntary actions the will has a double activity, viz.,, the interior action of the will and the external action. Each of these actions has its object as he shows in q. 18, a. 6:

> The end is properly the object of the interior act of the will, while the object of the external action is that on which the action is brought to bear. Therefore just as the external action takes its species from the object on which it bears, so the interior act of the will takes its species from the end intended, this being its proper objective...

The part played by the will shapes the performance of the external deed, for the will applies members like instruments to the execution of an action; indeed our outward acts possess no moral significance save insofar as they are voluntary. Consequently the species of a human act is considered formally with regard to the end, but materially with regard to the object of the external action.

The end of the agent denotes the final causality of human actions and it is from this end that the action formally receives its specific character. The intrinsic meaning and value of actions proceeds from the end to which the agent is oriented and from the rational character of the act itself. The end or final causality of the action is always critical:

The form of morality consists in a relationship to the perfect and intelligible good which is the ultimate end of human activity, and to its subordinate goods, *ea quae sunt ad finem*. It is a relationship, *ad aliquid*...an opening out of subject to object, of the self to an 'other' which above all is God. A relationship of conformity means that the activity is morally good, a relationship of nonconformity, or rather of disconformity, means that the activity is morally bad.   This is a real relationship founded on the nature of the activity performed as entering or not the final causality bearing us to our ends, not merely a logical relationship...[11]

In a comprehensive study of the role of the end in the moral theology of Thomas, one of the great contemporary scholars of Thomistic theology, Servais Pinckaers, has written:

Because of the intervention of finality, the thomistic moral theologian considers human activity not as an alignment of isolated actions, but as the integrating parts of a true spiritual organism, directed by a hierarchy of ends, empowered by the intention of a supreme end. In this view the human act appears as something profoundly dynamic and creative of spiritual progress through all of its elements.[12]

The role of final causality is especially important when the subject is justice and its object, *jus*, since justice necessarily entails a relation *ad alterum*. As Thomas Gilby writes above, every human action is done *ad aliquid*, viz., with an end in mind. Thus a just act or relationship is not only *ad alterum* but *ad aliquid*. If there is a separation of the person to whom something is due and the end for which the agent acts, a nonconformity or disconformity occurs, destroying the just character of an action or relationship.   What remains, in the telling phrase of Pinckaers, is the mere "alignment of isolated actions."

In his *Commentary* on Aristotle's *Politics* (book III, lect. 10), Thomas observes that when one considers political rights, namely, Aristotle's *dikaion politikon*, "it is important in a setting of this nature to have a norm over which it is directed. Such a norm is the end of the political good." The context of "political good" is clearly "common good," the *bonum commune* toward which the actions of all citizens must tend.

Elsewhere in his commentary on Aristotle's *Politics* (book II, lect. 7), Thomas makes the point that the worth of a just action depends on its ordination to an end. It derives its worth from being ordered to the worthy character of the end.

The end of the agent likewise has a bearing on the means used by the agent to achieve his end. That which is done is ordained to an end, and must have an intrinsic proportion to the attainment of that end. Actions actually derive their *raison d'être* from the end contemplated.[13] This means not only that the master must bear in mind the end of the common good, the end or goals of the servant, and the relationship between the good of all and his private good, but he is constrained to use means that are proportionate to the attainment of worthy ends. It is ludicrous to suppose that a *dominus* would be free in Thomas' eyes to consider the servant solely as an instrument for the attainment of his personal end and private good.

On the basis of Thomas' concern about the final causality of agents' actions, and the connection between the *ad alterum* status of justice with the *ad aliquid* status of all human activity, we cannot but conclude that in Thomas' schema the master in a *dominus-servus* relationship was limited in the demands that could be placed upon the servant. Since Thomas emphasizes, as we saw above in the *ST*. 2a2ae. q. 57, a.4, that the servant is a person in his own "right," a bearer of rights, we need to recall that the person is "the creature most especially ordained to the good of the universe," an application to the realm of justice of a systematic insight found at the beginning of the *Summa* (1a q. 23, a.7).

Since the creature, whether master or servant, is ordained to the good of the universe and ultimately to God, the *Summum Bonum* of every creature, it is evident that his orientation extends beyond himself to relate to a good which includes but transcends his personal good. Justice does not create a good or confer an end on him; it orders his relation to these pre-existing perfections of Divine Being in which the creature participates as created effect of an Uncreated Cause.

In the beginning of his *Politics* (1253a, 35-38), Aristotle remarks that in Greece, the crossroads of many traditions, the same term is used to designate the order of the civil community and the rights (*dikaion politikon*) enumerated by the legislative tribunals. He says that "justice is an ordering of political association."

At the beginning of his *Commentary on the Nicomachean Ethics* (book I, lect. 1), Thomas builds on the same line of thought in writing that the "good of the multitude is greater than any individual good." Every human good is oriented toward the happiness of the group. Just deeds are intrinsically related to the community. The determination of the law looks to the well-being of the multitude, namely the common good.[14]

It is especially significant that in this commentary Thomas refers to "external goods and things of this sort," for external goods are the material cause of a *jus* coming into being.

Whereas Aristotle speaks of the common good as the ultimate *telos* of human society, Thomas will recognize God as the *Summum Bonum* of human life. While Aristotle proposes nature as the ultimate term of reference, nature becomes an intermediary term for Thomas, since nature in turn is oriented toward grace, and the relation which constitutes the goal of life is a living contact of the person with the Creator, i.e., beatitude.

Despite the shift in perspective, Thomas is in complete agreement with Aristotle that the common good is the end of human society. The orientation of human goods and actions to the common good is part of the reality of general or legal justice, as he notes in article 5 of question 5:

All who are contained in a community are related to it as parts to a whole. A part as such belongs to the whole, so that any good of the part can be subordinate to the good of the whole. Accordingly the value in each and every virtue, whether it composes a man in himself or whether it disposes him in relation to others, may be referred to the common good, to which justice orders us. In this way the acts of all the virtues can belong to justice in that it orders a man to the common good. It is in this sense that justice is called a general virtue. And since it is for law (*quia ad legem pertinet ordinare in bonum commune*) to regulate for the common good, as we have seen (1a2ae.q.90, a.2), such general justice is called legal justice, for thereby a person accords with law which directs acts of all the virtues to the common good.

Thomas then observes (q. 58, a. 7) that legal justice ordains the individual in matters of justice immediately to the common good and mediately to the good of another (*ad alterum*) individual. These reflections echo the point of 1a2ae. q.90, a.2 that *lex* is always ordained to the common good.

Lest it be thought, however, that individual actions lose their own value or force because they bear an inherent ordination to the common good, Thomas observes that individual actions are certainly undertaken in a particular setting but are implicitly related to the common good as a matter of final causality.

Human activities indeed always take place in particular situations; these, however, are relevant to the common good—common here involves acting for a universal final cause, not coming under a general classification according to genus or species. Common good spells common end, as he eloquently notes in *ST*. 1a2ae. q. 90, a. 3 *ad* 2.

In commenting on this text, Thomas Gilby, OP, observes:

The common good is not a generic class-heading...it is an analogical concept, variously modulated according to the degrees of participation in being as good, and good as cause, that is, as final cause...It follows that law as a theological concept is also analogical.[15]

We saw that Thomas understands just actions to be *ea quae sunt ad finem*. We now see that one end toward which all actions involving a *jus* are oriented is the common good. Since it is not a genus but a final cause, the actions in question are not to be classified generically but analogically. They are related to the common good either immediately or mediately, i.e., through their relation to the good of another individual.

In short, any action which entails a *jus* or exercise of dominion is inherently ordained to the common good. One cannot speak of a *dominium utile* in isolation of the common good. Whatever private good of a master is served, it must relate to and promote immediately the common good of all. It must promote mediately the good of the servant. Any action or status which fails to do so falls short of the standard of *lex* which is the efficient cause of *jus* and which is itself ordained to the common good.

Like law and dominion, the common good is an analogical concept. If it were univocal, it could become the basis for a totalitarian state, where each part would promote only the totality and not the good which is the legitimate *telos* of the individual part. The person in community is not a means for the attainment of the end of the common good. In some respects the person is an end, relating to the community not as *pars ad totum* but as *totum ad totum*, in the distinction of Maritain.

Slavery constitutes a prime example. The inherent and inviolable dignity of a person cannot be violated for the supposed good of a society. The Aristotelian notion of natural slavery was accepted by Thomas with the understanding that the common good would be furthered by the promotion of the good of the weaker or duller servant by the skill of the stronger or keener master. The final causality of the common good did not eliminate the final causality of the good of the servant. On the contrary, promotion of the good of the servant was the *mediate* objective of legal justice and promotion of the common good the *immediate* objective.

In the previous section we examined the connection between *lex*, the efficient cause of all *jura*, and the common good. The common good is the final cause of human legislation. Through the enactment of human laws the common good and its effect, virtue, are to be promoted in such a way that individual rights advance or are conducive to the common good and virtue (e.g., *ST*. 1a2ae. 100.9 ad 2; 90.2; 92.1).

We shall now examine the position of Thomas that "all laws insofar as they share in right reason derive from the *lex aeterna*" (*ST*. q. 93, a.3). In quoting Augustine to the effect that nothing is just which is not derived from the Eternal Law, Thomas makes it plain that any human rule or relationship which contravenes the Eternal Law is to that extent unfair or unjust.

Augustine had shown how the extent of this principle in Book XIX (chapter 21) of his *Civitas Dei*, the same book in which he describes slavery as a consequence of man's sin:

> What is rightly done is justly done; what is done unjustly cannot be done by right. We are not to reckon as right such human laws as are iniquitous, since even unjust lawgivers themselves call a right [*jus*] only what derives from the fountainhead of justice, and brand as false the wrong-headed opinion of those who keep saying that a right [*jus*] is whatever is advantageous [*utile*] to the one in power. It follows that, wherever true justice is lacking, there cannot be a multitude of men bound together by a mutual recognition of rights.

In view of the fact that every just human law is derived from Eternal Law, it follows that no provision of the *jus gentium* can be in violation of the Eternal Law. Was not slavery violative of the Eternal Law? In his early writings Thomas held that slavery runs counter to the "primary intention" of nature but not its "secondary intention."[16] Although God created every person free in the state of original justice, the onset of sin meant that some must cede their freedom as a penalty. Like suffering and death, slavery was introduced into human existence *propter peccatum.* This patristic view had a long lineage back at the very least to Book XIX of Augustine's *City of God.*

In his treatise on natural law in the *Summa* (1a2ae. q. 94, a. 5 *ad* 3), Thomas regards slavery in a slightly different sense, viz., as an addition to natural law intended to promote the usefulness of human life through reason:

> You speak of something being according to natural right in two ways. The first is because nature is set that way; thus the command that no harm should be done to another. The second is because nature does not command the contrary; thus we might say that it is of natural law for man to be naked, for nature does not give him clothes; these he has to make by art. In this way common ownership and universal liberty are said to be of natural law, because private property and slavery exist by human contrivance for the convenience of social life, and not by natural law. This does not change the law of nature except by addition.

It is interesting that there is no reference to the *jus gentium* in this article since slavery and private property were considered features of the *jus gentium* from the time of Isidore of Seville. When we recall Lottin's theory that Thomas was constrained by the terminology of Isidore from expressing his unfettered view of the *jus gentium* in his treatise *De Legibus* (1a2ae. qq. 90-97), we can appreciate the possibility that he did not want to dwell on the *jus gentium* at this point.

It may be argued that the question is left unaddressed in this article of what happens when a provision of the *jus gentium* is in conflict with the *jus naturale.* But Thomas has in effect answered the question implicitly. Whatever is added to natural law (such as private property and slavery) is done *"per hominum rationem ad utilitatem humanae vitae."* In other words, whatever is contrary to human reason or the usefulness of human life cannot be considered as a just addition to the natural law.

Thomas thus holds that the fundamental equality of all men is preserved notwithstanding the consequences of sin. This equality does not preclude the political ascendancy of some over others, however, for he holds in 2a2ae. q.10, a.10 that *dominatio* per se is not a consequence of sin. This is of course the text made famous by Vitoria in *De Indis* and by Soto at the Council of Valladolid in support of Las Casas' struggle for the rights of the Amerindians on the grounds that human law cannot remove rights conferred by divine grace.

Since *lex* is not identical to *jus* but is the *ratio* of human legislative enactments, it is clear that all *lex humana* must be not only consistent with the *lex aeterna* but analogous to Eternal Law, the exemplary cause of all law. In his consideration of the *jus gentium* in the *Secunda Secundae*, Thomas essentially speaks of *lex* as the *ratio sub qua* human law is enacted, the paradigm of excellence for human choices and deeds, comparable in its way to an artistic conception in the mind of the artist (*ST*. 2a2ae. q.57, a.1 *ad* 2):

> An idea in the mind of the maker, which is called the rule and pattern of art, exists before the production of external works of art, and likewise an idea in the mind, a rule or pattern for prudence or practical wisdom, prescribes what is a just deed according to reason. If this be set down in writing, it is called a law; a law, says Isidore, is a written regulation. And so, properly speaking, it is not a right itself, but a design for a right.

Human law (*lex humana*) is the "*lumen sub qua*" hur ian legislation is enacted. Thomas has already made it clear in the *Prima Pars* (q. 21, a. 2) that *lex*, a rule of reason, relates to *jus* as a conception of excellence in the artist's mind relates to an actual work of art.

In the same article Thomas uses the phrase "*ordo justitiae*" to speak of the relationship of *jus* to *lex*. Toward the end of the *Secunda Secundae* he will speak of peace as the "flourishing of order," which human law is able to realize.[17] *Lex* is an ideal whereas *jus* is the determination of a concrete act. *Lex* has priority over *jus* in the order of nature as a cause has over an effect.

Thomas refers in *ST*. 1a2ae. q.93, a.4 to two issues which are directly relevant to the question of slavery: (1) the moral limits of human lawmaking; (2) the immoral nature of a *lex* which violates reason. On the first issue, the extent of human lawmaking, Thomas observes that man cannot legislate in regard to his own constitution, which lies beyond his liberty:

> Human government encompasses that which can be done by man but the elements which constitute human nature do not belong to that government, e.g., it is not part of our initiative that man have a soul, hands, feet, etc.

Since dignity is an inherent element of human life, it follows that no civil legislation can legitimately impinge on it, for to do so would contravene the *lex aeterna*. The *lex aeterna* stands not only as the exemplary cause of human legislation but as an unchanging standard which precludes any sort of law which strikes at the nature of man.

The second issue, the existence of laws which violate the *lex aeterna*, flows from the first. Thomas sharply modifies the adage that "the prince's will has the force of law" by noting in *ST*. 1a2ae. q. 90, a. 1, *ad* 3 that to have the quality of law an enactment must be in conformity with reason; otherwise it is "iniquity." Six questions later he describes (1a2ae. q.96, a.4) how laws can be unjust and therefore do not bind in conscience:

> Laws are unjust in two ways, as being against what is fair in human terms and against God's rights. They are contrary to human good on...three counts...from their end, when the ruler taxes his subjects rather for his own greed or vanity than the common benefit; from their author, when he enacts a law beyond the power committed to him; and from their form, when, although meant for the common good, laws are inequitably dispensed. These are outrages (*magis sunt violentiae quam leges*) rather than laws.

Again, explicit mention of the *jus gentium* is missing, but the severity of this text surely amounts to a forceful invitation to legislators to examine the justice of laws from the standpoint of end, authority and application. Since all provisions of the *jus gentium* entail a rational determination to achieve a desirable end, it is surely implied here that any provision lacking in rational content or orientation toward a desirable end must be re-examined.

While it is true that there is no explicit condemnation of slavery as an institution, it must be recalled from 2a2ae. q.57, a.4 that the master-slave relationship was considered analogous to a father-son relationship, viz., so closely approximating a unity of interests that no *ad alterum* aspect existed. This understanding of *servitus* is quite different from the factual setting of North America in the time of Vitoria and Soto. The factual brutality toward the Amerindian and African slaves described by correspondents of Vitoria and Soto surely constituted the kind of "law" Thomas here decries as "violence" and "iniquity." Thomas provided the standard which needed to be applied by those conversant with the facts: conformity with the *lex aeterna*.

When we synthesize the four aspects of Thomas' approach to social questions examined (analogous relationality, finality of agents' actions, relation to the common good, and the inviolability of the *lex aeterna*), we see that it is impossible to justify the kind of coercion which existed toward Native Americans and African slaves on the basis of Thomas' overall methodology. Nevertheless, such a justification occurred for centuries. We shall now turn to two faithful disciples of Thomas who struggled with the issue of human rights and analyze their respective approach.

2. Vitoria and Soto on Slavery

There is no doubt that each of the three theologians we have studied attempted in his own way to clarify and fortify the concern of moral theology for human rights. Although their approaches to the moral problem of slavery occurred in two different continents and two different centuries, these three men were guided by principles of scripture, history, patristic tradition, philosophy, law and pastoral needs.

Domingo de Soto was a self-conscious disciple of Francisco de Vitoria in the same way that Vitoria continued and, in a sense, recovered the theological tradition of Thomas. Because there are virtually no differences of content or context in the writings of Vitoria and Soto, their thought will be analyzed together. We will now study the effect of their understanding of the critical concepts of *jus* and *dominium* on slavery.

We have attempted above to analyze four emphases or orientations within Thomas' approach (analogous relationality, finality of action, relation to the common good and the inviolability of the *lex aeterna*) which need to be understood in order to grasp his view of the moral implications of slavery. It is necessary to abstract those four orientations or themes so that a comparison can be made across two continents and three centuries.

I shall attempt to show that the theological currents of the sixteenth century situated Vitoria and Soto in a much different setting than that of Thomas. The four themes abstracted from his thought will be seen in contrast to four dominant themes of sixteenth century Catholic moral theology: (1) univocal right (in place of analogical relation); (2) legal title (in place of finality of action); (3) subjective power (in place of relation to the common good); (4) focus on *jus positivum* (rather than the *lex aeterna*).

In contradistinction to the analogical meaning of *jus* in Thomas, the concept of *jus* in both Vitoria and Soto will denote instead a univocal right. The two approaches are not only centuries apart but poles apart in starting point and application. We have seen how the concept of *jus* stands for a "reality to be done"[18] in Thomas. Wherever a *jus* exists, a relation also exists, and rights are in analogous relation to each other. The notion of *jus* becomes univocal rather than analogical in Vitoria's approach:

> As traditional authorities maintain, *jus* is nothing other than that which is licit, or what is permitted by law. This is clear from Thomas...q. 57, a.1 ad 2, where he says that *lex* is not properly *jus*, but rather a *"ratio juris,"* i.e., that by reason of which something is licit. This is clear in the same place in the body of the article, where he says that *jus* and *justum* are the same, as witness Aristotle in Book V of the *Ethics*. *Justum* is that same thing, viz., what is permitted by the laws. Therefore *jus* is also the same, that which the law permits. He says therefore that *jus* is that which is licit through the laws. Thus we use that word when we speak. We say, 'I do not have the right to do this, that is not permitted to me'; again, 'I use my right, it is permitted.'[19]

Vitoria goes on to cite without contradiction, dispute or qualification the view of Conrad that *jus* can be broadly defined "under two definitions which coincide in one: *jus* is a power or faculty belonging to someone according to law."[20] Vitoria notes that Conrad received this definition from John Gerson (+ 1429), a leading nominalist influence.

This definition of *jus* which Vitoria accepts without qualification from Gerson, through Conrad, carries with it a number of salient implications: (1) as a faculty or power, *jus* becomes a univocal term; (2) the basis for a *jus* resides in determinations of human law separated from the originating justice of divine law; (3) there is no objective point of reference (whether denominated as a *telos*, or *ad aliquid* or *lumen sub quo*) to identify a *jus* as proper or improper, broad or narrow, communal or personal, etc. aside from precepts enacted by civil or positive law; (4) the focus is on the subject or agent, with the emphasis attaching to his individual power; the relationship to the community or the common good is attenuated.

In his treatise on dominion in Book IV of *De Justitia et Jure*, Soto stresses that *jus* and *dominium* are not identical. He proceeds to narrow the scope of *dominium* to the genus of "faculty" rather than "power." Like Vitoria, he accepts the meaning of *jus* to be a right or a power permitted by the law.[21]

His intent is to show that dominion is not any power over someone or something but only a proper power, which he terms a "faculty." The critical difference between an improper power (e.g., the control of property by a thief) and a proper power or faculty is that a faculty must be in accord with the civil law while a power may or may not be. In addition to the case of a thief in control of stolen property, he cites the example of a child who has dominion in the broad sense over property (i.e., the power to dispose of it) but lacks dominion in the strict sense (i.e., the faculty granted by civil law) to dispose of property. Until the child reaches majority, he lacks the faculty of dominion over property otherwise in his control.

By speaking of dominion as belonging to the genus of faculty rather than power, Soto reveals his understanding of dominion to be generic rather than analogical. The meaning of a *jus* or *dominium* is univocal, viz., whatever the definition of it provided by the civil law happens to be.

Soto does acknowledge at the end of q.1, a.1 of Book IV that dominion always entails a relation, i.e., *dominus-servus*, which must be governed by the dictates of justice, but there is no express reference to the common good or the good of the servant. The content of the "good" and final causality of the relationship must be supplied by the civil or positive law. The metaphysical foundation of an analogy of proper proportionality is lost, which causes a contradiction to arise from the use of a univocal term (either *jus* or *dominus*) as part of a relation (*dominus-servus*) which calls for an analogical term (namely, *dominus servi = Dominus creationis = dominus actus sui*).

Such a contradiction becomes apparent in Soto when he says that a son cannot be an "instrument" in the hands of his father in the way that a slave can be an instrument in the hands of his master. We saw that Thomas' comparison in *ST*. 2a2ae. q.57, a.4, of a son and a slave was analogical: the son was "part of" the father and the slave "part of" the master, which meant that the *ad alterum* relation was absent since the relation of these terms or agents approximated a unity of interest. In Book IV, q.1, a.1 Soto seems to brush aside the comparison of Thomas and simply says that the son could not be an instrument in the hands of his father. He implicitly suggests that the slave can justifiably be an instrument in the hands of his master but offers no clarification. When the analogical reality of *dominus* is eroded, there is a consequent erosion as well of the link with those analogous relations (e.g., father: son; Creator: creatures) whose humane and providential character require at least in logic that the human dignity of the slave be analogously present.

The implicit point is that a master-slave relationship is literally sui generis. In the schema of Thomas it could be argued, logically and theologically, that some rights of a slave are analogous to the rights of a son. This analogical framework is missing in the thought of Vitoria and Soto. The one who exercises dominion is not explicitly bound, in their schema, to exercise the same kind of providential concern as that shown by God (*Dominus* of creation) or by a person in control of his activities (*dominus actus sui*).

In contradistinction to the approach of Thomas, the justification or moral orientation of individual actions is specified not by their final causality but by their sanction through the conferral of a "title" by civil law.

Let us recall the observation of Bernard Häring (with L. Vereecke) on the compartmentalized approach to Thomas' *Summa* taken in the sixteenth century:

> Most of [the Salamancan writers] had as professors deep-seated nominalists. They take from their earliest formation a reserve vis-a-vis metaphysical speculation. They adopt thomism but generally without exploring the depth of its synthesis. In the *Summa*, dogma interests them less than moral theology; they constantly risk reducing moral theology only to the *Secunda Pars*, such as the catalogue of virtues in the *Secunda Secundae*. As an example, in fourteen years of teaching devoted to commentary on the *Summa*, Vitoria reserved ten for the *Secunda Pars* and from this interest the *Secunda Secundae* is the principal beneficiary. This is precisely the danger of a rupture between dogmatic theology and moral theology, which strikes at the very heart of thomism.[22]

The view of Häring is borne out by the absence of references to the *Prima Secundae* in the works of Vitoria and Soto. This prevents them from having the precise focus of Thomas on final causality as he is about to consider the psychology of human actions and their morality (1a2ae. qq. 6-21).

What happened since the thirteenth century to shift the focus away from final causality to legal title? One explanation lies in the influence of William of Occam (1295-1349) who denied that an agent acts for an end.[23] While the Salamancan School certainly did not deny the principle of finality as did Occam, the orientation toward final causality is conspicuous by its absence in the commentaries on moral questions. The lengthy commentary on the *Prima Secundae* written by Bartolomé Medina, OP (+1581) would not appear until the seventeenth century. Even then a complete synthesis of the elements of the *Summa* remained more of an aspiration than accomplishment.[24]

It was the position of Vitoria that human law, derived from social consensus, could confer rights and create responsibilities. This is a position closer to John Locke's theory of social contract than Aquinas' understanding of *jus gentium*:

> There are many things in this connection which issue from a law of nations, which, because it has a sufficient derivation from the natural law, is clearly capable of conferring rights and creating obligations. And even if we grant that it is not always derived from natural law, yet there exists clearly enough a consensus of the greater part of the whole world, especially in behalf of the common good of all.[25]

While it is universally recognized that *some* laws enacted by human legislatures are so empowered to confer rights and create responsibilities, it was the view of Thomas that a *jus* or right was a reality to be done, not merely an enactment of a legislature.

Some rights inhere naturally in the objective order, such as the right to worship God or the right to an honorable reputation, quite independent of the will of any legislature. Other rights arise solely through the authority of a legislature, such as the right to drive a car on a green light, and the duty to stop a car for a red light. The distinction *malum in se* and *malum prohibitum* of criminal law in Anglo-American jurisprudence summarizes the difference between actions which have an inherent value and others which receive their value entirely from legislation.

By simply holding that rights come into existence through human enactments, Vitoria leaves the impression that the authority of a legislature is sufficient to pronounce on the morality of issues such as slavery.

In leaving unqualified the authority of human law to generate rights and responsibilities, Vitoria's approach has the unintended and unhappy effect of attenuating the teleological orientation of rights so carefully constructed by Thomas in the *Prima Secundae*. Legal title rather than teleological ordination becomes the basis for rights and responsibilities. This new orientation increases the power of human legislatures since it looks to the will of the lawgiver rather than to the ultimate, remote and proximate ends and fundamental nature of human agents. An authoritarian basis for slavery cannot be maintained for long if the orientation of human actions is steadfastly teleological *secundum rationem*. When this teleological framework is lost, the power and potential for abuse of human lawgivers sadly increases.

Domingo de Soto elucidates the importance of the concept of title and ascribes the existence of dominion to it:

> Title is effectively the basis for dominion, or the root from which it springs. The titles of dominion can come from nature, law, contract, election, etc. For example, the title of dominion which man naturally has over the fruits of the earth is natural life, since without food man cannot survive. By giving these to man along with the desire for survival, God naturally conferred on man the right to make use of necessary food, in the same way as the title of right (I will not say dominion) which fathers have over their children is natural generation. The title of the right of property is the *jus gentium* through which the division of goods was made. Thus the title of a bishop is election. The

title of ownership of a house is either natural inheritance, purchase, prescription, etc.[26]

Domingo de Soto was faithful to the thomistic tradition in seeking to restrict the scope of *dominium* and by distinguishing *lex* from *jus*, as we have seen. But since "title" is a concept of jurisprudence, one must look to the jurisconsults to define and distinguish it. Consideration of the moral quality of actions is ceded almost exclusively to lawyers and positive law.

There is no effort made to locate the concept of "title" in scripture, patristic sources, tradition or philosophy. It was purely a legal term, taken from the jurisprudential terminology of that era. The multiplication of titles had the predictable effect of "atomizing" rights (in the powerful metaphor of Pinckaers cited earlier), i.e., multiplying them into countless entities, subject only to the will of human lawgivers.

We will now examine the role of one end in particular, that of the common good. In recasting the Law of Nations to encompass "all nations" and not just "all men," Vitoria signalled a revolutionary change in the scope of the common good. He is justly hailed as the Founder of International Law for the role he played in expanding the horizon of consciousness from national to global welfare. The example which Vitoria frequently cites of the safety of ambassadors being a prescription of the *jus gentium* attests to the importance he attaches to communication among nations.

There is nevertheless an irony present in the fact that a focus on the global good of many nations occurs at the same time that the correlation between private goods and the overarching common good of society appears to suffer in the understanding of dominion which Vitoria and Soto manifest.

The standard justification of slavery which had begun to emerge in the sixteenth century was based on a limited form of servitude classified as a *dominium utile*, a control over the "uses" or works of the slave, in contradistinction to a total control over his person, a *dominium plenum*, which was rejected as immoral. By holding that the purpose of natural slavery entailed the good of the community, the good of the slave and the individual good of the master, Thomas implicitly proposed the common good as a standard by which any form of servitude was to be judged. If it served the common good, encompassing the good of master and slave, the arrangement could be justified. If it did not promote the common good, it could not be justified.

In his *Commentary on the Secunda Secundae*, Vitoria recognizes that the meaning of *dominium* is limited. There are some uses to which the master cannot put the slave. He cites the murder of the slave as an obvious usurpation of the authority of the master.[27] While it restricts the power of the dominus to say that he cannot justly put the slave to any use whatever, there is no standard provided to illustrate what uses are permissible and which ones lie beyond the pale of moral conduct. The standard for Thomas was of course the common good. The *bonum utile* of the master had to be subordinated to the *bonum commune* insofar as it included the *bonum honestum* of the slave.

In a similar way Domingo de Soto argues that natural slavery, while permissible, must be for the good of both the master and the slave. He reminds his readers that the master must instruct the slaves, treating them with moderation and the natural dignity "of free and independent men." They are to be instructed in the way of society "for their own benefit and advantage (*utile*)."[28] Again, however, there is no explicit reference to the common good. This has the effect of leaving the interpretation of the good of the slave to the master. The objective standard of the *bonum commune* is ceded to the scope of subjective power and perception of the master in providing the framework of permissible and impermissible "uses" to which the slaves could be put.

In a sense the diminished role of the common good is merely a corollary to point two above, the absence of final causality as an overarching orientation of actions. It deserves special attention, however, because of its inherent importance.

One final example from Soto demonstrates this importance. In arguing that a father has a *jus* but not dominion over his sons, Soto compares dominion to the "despotic" *dikaion* which Aristotle describes in his *Politics*, and a *jus* to the "real" or "civil" *dikaion* of Aristotle's schema. Soto's point is of course that a father is to act with reasonable authority (*jus*) but not in a despotic fashion (*dominium*) toward his son. But left unspoken are the bounds of conduct which restrict a master toward his servant. Had Soto pursued the terminology of Aristotle in the Politics, he could have provided some limits on the "despotic" *dikaion* of the master over the slave, because Aristotle subordinates every form of *dikaion*, whether despotic, real or civil, to the overarching *dikaion politikon*, the common good of society. This omission shifted the focus from the attainment of the common good as a *mensura mensurans* to the subjective power of the master as the *mensura mensurans* in regard to the rights of the slave.

How do these considerations impinge upon the verdict of the *jus gentium* on slavery, as understood by Vitoria and Soto? We have examined the view of Dom Odon Lottin, OSB, that the vagueness in Thomas' approach to the *jus gentium*, including the apparent contradiction between *ST.* 1a2ae. q.95 and *ST.* 2a2ae. q.57, on whether the *jus gentium* is part of the *jus naturale* or *jus positivum*, is due to his concern for preserving the reputation of Isidore of Seville. Had he rejected the terminology of Isidore in 1a2ae. q.95, he would have impugned the theological reputation of a classic writer.

We have also seen from the writings of both Vitoria and Soto that the proper placement of the *jus gentium* was still an issue in the sixteenth century. Vitoria dismisses the question as nothing more than an argument over a name.[29] At the same time though he criticizes the jurisconsults for construing the *jus gentium* too broadly; he places it in the category of positive rather than natural law. He reveals a concern in some texts for the question of the derivation of the *jus gentium*, concluding that it is sufficiently derived from the natural law to have the force of law.[30] He speaks of the *jus gentium* as an authority which compels adherence under the force of mortal sin yet one which is capable of partial abrogation through the expressed consensus of the community at large. Indeed he cites the treatment afforded Christians captured by other Christians as one instance where a refinement can in effect be legislated through practical behavior by Christian combatants. Insofar as the *jus gentium* stands for the consensus of the civilized world on matters which do not derive "necessarily" from the natural law (e.g., private property), it is "necessary" for the conservation of the natural law in society.

Vitoria contributed a powerful limitation on the use of slavery when he held that prisoners of war could be reduced to slavery only when they were combatants in a just war. By describing servitude as a precept of the *jus gentium*, i.e., positive law, he laid the groundwork for the abolition of slavery, since what is enacted by human legislators can be repealed by them as well.

Soto follows the lead of Vitoria in placing the *jus gentium* within the category of positive law. He uses Vitoria's distinction between things which are true *de se* and things which are only desirable insofar as they promote an end (*in ordine ad aliud*) to list slavery as an enactment of positive law and to focus on the *jus gentium* as the arena for contingent realities which do not necessarily follow from the natural law.

In reducing the *jus gentium* to the level of positive law, Vitoria and Soto never really confronted the implications for slavery that flowed from their view that the *jus gentium* derived from social convention or human legislation.

Why were they reluctant to state that the precepts of the *jus gentium* derived from the natural law? An answer is not hard to see: iff its precepts necessarily followed from the natural law, then the *jus gentium* would be indistinguishable from the *jus naturale* and thus deal only with contingent matters. The tragic irony emerges that Vitoria and Soto conferred upon the *jus gentium* the stature of the *jus naturale* but proceeded to separate it from the *jus naturale* in regard to the derivation of precepts and conclusions of paramount importance for social questions such as slavery.

By stating that all human laws were effects of the *lex aeterna*, i.e., that the *lex aeterna* is the efficient and exemplary cause of all just human laws, Thomas did not have to consider either the derivation of the *jus gentium* nor the possibility that it could contravene the *lex aeterna* as a problem. We have seen that his treatment of the *jus gentium* in *ST*. 2a2ae. q.57, a.4 consists in an understanding of rational determinations which are human calculations designed to promote the ends of the natural law. In adopting the view of Gaius that the *jus gentium* is the human component of the natural law, Thomas was able to align the *jus gentium* much more closely to the natural law than to positive law.

The otherwise splendid work of both Vitoria and Soto must be charged with internal inconsistency as a consequence of their decision to classify the *jus gentium* as a branch or aspect of positive law. In the case of Vitoria it is the ambiguity of his position that the *jus gentium* is "nearly" but not "wholly" necessary for the conservation of the natural law.[31] Presumably this means that the community will ònly honor the natural law if it exhibits the kind of consensus which Vitoria attributes to the *jus gentium*. But we are left to conjecture about how one law "sufficiently" derived from another is necessary for its conservation.

The inconsistency which confronts Soto is the universality of the *jus gentium*. He alludes in several texts to the universal practice of private property, a precept of the *jus gentium*. But it is only the *jus naturale*, not positive law, which is universal. Although Soto adopts the view of Vitoria that the *jus gentium* applies solely to contingent, non-necessary truths and precepts, in fact he attributes to the *jus gentium* a universality which it ought not to have if it is merely positive law.

The dilemma of Soto is attributable to the weight of Ulpian's understanding of the natural law as applicable to the entire animal kingdom, human and subhuman. If the *jus gentium* is part of the natural law, it would apply to all of the animal kingdom. Soto attacks the jurisconsults for holding this view and attributing dominion to every species of creature.

The greatest difficulty of the view held by Vitoria and Soto that the *jus gentium* is merely positive law is the question of whether the *jus gentium* can contravene the *jus naturale*. For Thomas this would have been an impossibility since the *jus naturale* and the *jus gentium* are derived from the *lex aeterna*. But since the derivation of the *jus gentium* is not clearly presented in Vitoria and Soto, the question looms large. Neither addresses the question of whether the *jus gentium* can be in conflict with the jus naturale. The failure to address such a critical issue constitutes a serious judgment of inadequacy of philosophical and theological method against the prime expononents of Salamancan scholasticism.

This movement away from the *lex aeterna* as the ultimate *norma normans* of all human legislation delayed the inquiry of whether slavery could be reconciled with the dictate of the natural law that all human beings are born free and deserve during the course of their lifetime a freedom consonant with human dignity. Human laws were allowed to proliferate without reference to an ultimate standard. This tragic "atomization" provided slavery with a veneer of justification as a "precept" of the *jus gentium*. The confrontation of such "precepts" with the primary precepts of the *jus naturale*, human participation in the *lex aeterna*, was postponed.

3. Conclusion

Those who suffered the indignity of slavery in the New World greatly benefitted from the attention to human rights which Francisco de Vitoria and Domingo de Soto forced upon the consciousness of the Catholic community in sixteenth century Spain, including the Crown. Nevertheless the shift from a metaphysical foundation in the thought of

Thomas, of whom they sought to be faithful disciples, to a system of legal "titles" in the context of moral theology following Occam, had the tragic consequence of leaving the morality of slavery as an institution unexamined.

Far from being a distraction or irrelevance with respect to social issues, the metaphysical principles upon which Thomas relied were fundamentally sound. The basic framework for understanding equality, justice and dominion was suffficiently textured to allow for application and development in different settings. The loss of a horizon of overarching goods and implementing principles proved disastrous. Those desirous of following Thomas' theological framework had to negotiate uncharted terrain without any compass.

For Thomas, metaphysics provided a mediation between theological principles and legislative enactments. The metaphysical underpinnings of *dominium* and *jus* constituted a hermeneutic of moral discourse. This metaphysical foundation aimed at the perfection of human goods, not their perversion. The rupture of metaphysics and law exacted an incalculable price in human suffering.

Notes on Chapter Four

1. J. A. Weisheipl, OP, *Friar Thomas D'Aquino: His Life, Thought and Works* (Garden City, NY: Doubleday & Co., 1974), p. 7.

2. Henri Renard, *The Philosophy of Being*, Second Edition revised (Milwaukee: Brucke Publishing Co., 1947), pp. 93-94.

3. Renard, *op.cit.* He cites *In I Sent.*, XIX, d. 5, a.2, *ad* 1 as a good example of the difference.

4. Renard, *op.cit.*, p. 97.

5. Herman Reith, CSC, *The Metaphysics of St. Thomas Aquinas* (Milwaukee: Bruce Publishing Co., 1958), pp. 53-54.

6. *De Veritate*, q.2, art. 11, c.

7. P.D. Dognin, OP, "La justice particuliere comporte-t-elle deux espèces?" *Revue Thomiste*, 65:3 (1965), p. 401ff.

8. *De Potentia Dei*, q. 7, a.10, ad 4: "qui consequitur talem potestam..."

9. *In Ethic. ad Nicomachum*. L. V, lectio xi: Dicit ergo primo, quod justum politicum consistit in quadam communitate vitae, quae ordinatur ad hoc, quod sit per se sufficientia eorum, quae ad vitam humanam pertinent...Deinde cum dicit "dominativum autem." Manifestat quod supradictum est de eo quod non est justum simpliciter, sed secundum similitudinem.   Et primo quantum ad justum dominativum, et paternum...Circa primum tria facit. Primo proponit quod intendit. Et dicit quod dominativum justum, quod scilicet est domini ad servum, et paternum quod scilicet est patris ad filium, non est idem his justis, quae sunt politica; sed habet aliquam similitudinem eis, secundum quod aliqualiter est ad alterum...Ostendit quod dictum est quantum ad hoc quod dominativum vel paternum justum non est simpliciter justum: manifestum est enim quod non potest esse simpliciter injustitia hominis ad ea quae sunt ipsius, sicut neque justitia quia utrumque est ad alterum. Sed servus est domini sicut possessio, et filius quousque est pelicon, idest magnus, et separetur a patre per emancipationem, est quasi quaedam pars patris. Et quod non sit injustitia ad seipsum, patet per hoc quod nullus eligit nocere sibi ipsi. Unde patet quod simpliciter loquendo non est justitia vel injustitia ad filium vel servum...Ostendit quod dominativum et paternum justum, etiam si esset simpliciter justum non esset politicum justum quia justum politicum est secundum legem, et in quibus nata est esse lex. Et hujusmodi sunt illi quibus competit aequalitas quantum ad hoc quod est principari et subjici; ita scilicet quod unus eorum subjicitur alteri, sicut servus subjicitur domino, et filius patri. Unde in his non est politicum justum.

10. Jacques Maritain, *The Person and the Common Good*. Translated by John J. Fitzgerald (Notre Dame, IN: University of Notre Dame Press, 1966), pp. 15-30.

11. Thomas Gilby, OP, ed., *Summa Theologiae*. Vol. 18 (NY: McGraw-Hill, 1966), pp. 166-67.

12. S. Pinckaers, "Le Role de la fin dans l'action morale selon Saint Thomas," *Revue des sciences philosophiques et théologiques*, 45 (1961), p. 421.

13. *ST.* 1a2ae. q.102, a.1: "Oportet quod id quod est ad finem sit proportionatum fini. Et ex hoc sequitur quod ratio eorum quae sunt ad finem, sumitur ex fine..."

14. *In X Libros Ethic.* L. V, lectio ii: "Et quia omnis utilitas humana finaliter ordinatur ad felicitatem, manifestum est quod...justa legalia dicuntur ea quae sunt factiva felicitatis et particularum ejus, id est eorum quae ad felicitatem ordinantur, vel principaliter sicut virtutes, vel instrumentaliter sicut divitiae et alia hujusmodi exteriora bona, et hoc per comparationem ad communitatem politiciam, ad quam respicit legis positio."

15. Thomas Gilby, OP, ed., *Summa Theologiae.* Vol. 28 (NY: McGraw-Hill, 1966), p. 12.

16. *In II Sent.* d. 44, q.1, a.3; *In IV Sent.* d. 36, q.1, a.1 ad 2.

17. Question 180, a. 2 *ad* 2. This is an apparent echo of Isaiah 32:17, viz., peace is the work of justice.

18. This phrase comes from Louis Lachance, OP, et al. in A.M. Henry, OP, ed. *The Virtues and States of Life*, trans. Robert J. Olsen et al. (Chicago, IL.: Fides Publishers Assoc., 1957), p. 252ff. I am deeply indebted to Lachance's *Le Concept de Droit selon Aristotle et St. Thomas* (1933) for the development of themes and distinctions in Chapter Four.

19. Francisco de Vitoria, OP, *Commentarios a la Secunda Secundae de Santo Tomas.* Edicion preparada por el R.P. Vicente Beltran de Heredia, OP. Tomo III: *De Justitia* [qq. 57-66] (Salamanca: Spartado 17, 1934), q. 62, p. 64.

20. Conradus Summenhart (+1502), *De Contractibus*, Venetiis, 1580, tr. 1, q.1 *in principio*.

21. Domingo de Soto, OP, *De La Justicia y Del Derecho en diez libros.* Tomo Segundo. ed. M.G. Ordónez, OP (Madrid: Valencia, 1968), Book

IV, q. 1ff.

22. B. Häring-L. Vereecke, "La Théologie Morale de S. Thomas d'Aquin a S. Alphonse de Liguori," *Nouvelle Revue Théologique* 77:7 (1955), pp. 682-683.

23. William of Occam, *Quodl.* IV: "Non potest probari quod tale agens agat propter finem." Occam's influence was also powerful in removing human laws from the ambit of divine exemplary causality: "It cannot be proved by natural reason that God is the efficient cause of any effect." *Quodl.* II, q.1.

24. Bartolomé Medina, OP, *Scholastica Commentaria in D. Thomae Primam Secundae.* (Cologne, 1618).

25. Vitoria, *De Indis*, p. xxxviii.

26. Soto, *De Justitia et Jure*, Book IV, q.1, a.1.

27. Vitoria, *op.cit.*, num. 15, p. 73: Ita quod homo non erat dominus omnium rerum ad omnes usus, quia ad habendum verum dominium non oportet quod secundum omnes usus utamur illo, sicut nec dominus est dominus servi ad omnes usus, quia non occidendum.

28. Soto, *De Justitia et Jure*, q.2, a.2.

29. Vitoria, *De Justitia*, num. 2, p. 13.

30. Vitoria, *De Indis*, p. xxxviii.

31. Vitoria, *De Justitia*, num. 4, p. 16.

SELECT BIBLIOGRAPHY

I. Primary Sources

Albertus Magnus. *In octo libros Politicorum*. Paris: Vives Edition

_____. *Super Libros Sententiarum*. Paris: Vives Edition

Aquinas, Thomas. *Commentary on the Metaphysics of Aristotle*. Translated by John P. Rowan, 2 vols. Chicago: H. Regnery Co., 1961.

_____. *Expositio in X libros Ethicorum*. Ed. Spiazzi. Turin: Marietti, 1949.

_____. *In octos libros Politicorum Aristotelis*. Rome: Marietti, 1959.

_____. *On Kingship*. Translated by G.B. Phelan and I.T. Eschmann. Toronto: PIMS, 1949.

_____. *On the Power of God*. Literally translated by the English Dominican Fathers. Westminster, MD: The Newman Press, 1952.

_____. *Quaestiones disputatae de veritate*. Rome: Marietti, 1949.

_____. *Scriptum in IV libros Sententiarum*, ed. by P. Mandonnet and M.F. Moos. Paris: Lethielleux, 1929- 1947.

224

_____. *Summa Contra Gentiles*. Translated, with an introduction and notes, by Anton C. Pegis. Garden City, NY: Image Books, 1955.

_____. *Summa Theologiae*. Blackfriars, NY: McGraw-Hill Book, Co., 1964-1967.

Aristotle. *Nicomachean Ethics*. Translated by W.D. Ross. Oxford: Clarendon Press, 1925.

_____. *Politics*, ed. and translated by H. Rackham. (Loeb Library.) NY: G.P. Putnam's Sons, 1932.

Augustine, Saint. *The City of God*. Books XVII-XXII. Translated by G.G. Walsh, SJ and D.J. Honan. Vol. 24. NY: Fathers of the Church, Inc., 1954.

Soto, Domingo de, OP. *De justitia et jure libri decem*. Salamanca, 1553-1554.

Vitoria, Francisco de, OP. *Commentarios a la Secunda Secundae de Santo Tomas*. ed. R.P. Vicente Beltran de Heredia, OP, Salamanca: Spartado, 1932-1935.

_____. *De Indis Noviter Inventis*. Salamanca, 1541.

_____. *De Jure Belli*. Salamanca, 1538-39.

_____. *De Potestate Civili*. Salamanca, 1527-8.

II. Secondary Sources

A. Books

Allard, P. *Les Esclaves Chrétiens* (2nd ed.). Paris: Didier, 1876.

Ashley, W. *The Theory of Natural Slavery According to Aristotle and St. Thomas.* Dissertation. South Bend: University of Notre Dame Press, 1941.

Brokhage, J.D. *Francis Patrick Kenrick's Opinion on Slavery.* C.U.A.Studies in Sacred Theology. Ser. 2, n. 85, Washington, DC, 1955.

Buckland, W.W. *The Roman Law of Slavery.* NY: AMS Press, Inc., 1908.

Carro, V. *Domingo de Soto y su doctrina jurídica.* Madrid: Valencia, 1944.

Coffey, P. *Ontology or the Theory of Being: An Introduction to General Metaphysics.* NY: Peter Smith, 1938.

Croix, Geoffret de. "Early Christian attitudes to property and slavery," in *Church, Society and Politics* edited by D. Baker.Oxford: Blackwell, 1975.

Daly, L.J., S.J. *The Political Theory of John Wyclif.* Chicago, Il: Loyola University Press, 1962.

Davis, D.B. *The Problem of Slavery in Western Culture.* Ithaca: Cornell University Press, 1966.

_____. *Slavery and Human Progress*. NY: Oxford Univ. Press, 1984.

Del Vecchio, J. *Philosophie du Droit*. Trans. from the Italian. Paris: Dalloz, 1953.

Eschmann. I., OP. *A Catalogue of St. Thomas' Works*. NY: Random House, 1956.

Figart, T. *A Biblical Perspective on the Race Problem*. Grand Rapids, MI: Baker, 1973.

Finley, M. *Ancient Slavery and Modern Ideology* NY: Viking Press, 1979.

_____. *Slavery in Classical Antiquity*. NY: Barnes and Noble, 1960.

Gerson, J. *De potestate ecclesiastica et de origine juris et legum*. Antwerp: Dupin, 1706.

Getino, L.A., OP. *El Maestro Fr. Francisco de Vitoria y El Renancimiento Filosófico Teologico Del Siglo XVI*. Madrid: Valencia, 1933.

Gosselin, B. Roland. *La Doctrine politique de S. Thomas d'Aquin*. Paris: Riviere, 1928.

Hamilton, B. *Political Thought in Sixteenth Century Spain: A Study of the Political Ideas of Vitoria, DeSoto, Suarez and Molina*. NY: Oxford University Press, 1963.

Hanke, L. *Colonisation et conscience chrétienne au XVI siecle*. Paris: Plon, 1957.

Henle, R., SJ. *St. Thomas and Platonism*. The Hague: Nijhoff, 1956.

Heredia, B. de, OP., ed. *Franciscus de Vitoria, OP: Commentarios a la Secunda Secundae de Santo Tomas*. Salamanca: Spartado, Vol. I, 1932; Vol. II, 1932; Vol. III, 1934; Vol. IV, 1935; Vol. V, 1935.

_____. *Los Manuscritos de Maestro Fray Francisco de Vitoria, OP*. Madrid: Valencia, Spain, 1928.

Hoffner, J. *La etica colonial española del siglo de oro: Christianismo y dignidad umana*. Madrid: Cultura hispanica, 1957.

Jarrett, B., OP. *Social Theories of the Middle Ages (1200-1500)*. London: E. Benn, 1926.

Jolowicz, H. *Roman Foundations of Modern Law*. Oxford: Clarendon University Press, 1957.

Klubertanz, G., SJ. *St. Thomas Aquinas on Analogy*. Jesuit Studies, Chicago, Il: Loyola University Press, 1960.

Lachance, L., OP. *Le concept de Droit selon Aristote et St. Thomas*. Paris: Librairie du Recueil Sirey, 1933.

Langdon-Davies, J., ed. *The Slave Trade and its Abolition: A Collection of Contemporary Documents*. (Jackdaw series, n. 12). NY: Grossman, 1969.

Leclercq, J. *Leçons de Droit Naturel IV: Les Droits et Devoirs Individuels*. Louvain: Societe d'Etudes Morales, Sociales et Juridiques, 1946.

Lengelle, M. *L'esclavage.* (Coll. 'Que sais-je?') Paris: Presses Universitaires de France, 1955.

Lottin, Dom O. *Le Droit Naturel chez Saint Thomas d'Aquin et ses prédécesseurs.* 2nd. ed. Paris: Charles Beyaert, 1931.

Kenna, Charles, OP. *Francis de Vitoria: Founder of International Law.* Second edition. Washington, DC: Catholic Association for International Peace, 1930.

Maritain, J. *The Person and the Common Good.* Translated by John J. Fitzgerald. Notre Dame, In: University of Notre Dame Press, 1966.

Mason, P. *Christianity and Race.* London: Lutterworth Press, 1956.

Mauquoy, J. *Le christianisme et l'esclavage antique.* (Collection "Etudes Religieuses," n. 171-172). Liege, La Pensee Catholique, 1927.

Maxwell, J. *Slavery and the Catholic Church: The History of Catholic Teaching Concerning the Moral Legitimacy of the Institution of Slavery.* London: Barry Rose Publishers, 1975.

Muñoz, H. *Vitoria and the Conquest of America.* 2d. ed. Manila, Phillipine Islands: University of Santo Tomas Press, 1938.

Murphy, F.and Vereecke, L. *Estudios sobre historia de la moral.* (Antropologia y moral cristiana, n. 3) Madrid: Catedra moral 'San Alfonso.' El Perpetuo Socorro, 1969.

Nys, E. *Les Origines du Droit International.* Brussels: Beyaert, 1984.

Reith, H. CSC, *The Metaphysics of St. Thomas Aquinas*. Milwaukee: Bruce Publishing Co., 1958.

Renard, H. *The Philosophy of Being*. Second edition. Milwaukee: Bruce Publishing Co., 1946.

Rice, M.H. *American Catholic Opinion in the Slavery Controversy*. Dissertation. NY: Columbia University Press, 1944.

Russell, K. *Slavery as Reality and Metaphor in the Pauline Letters*. (Pont. Univ. S. Thomae in Urbe, Diss. theol. Extr.), Rome: Officium Libri Catholici, 1968.

Scott, J.B. *The Catholic Conception of International Law*. Washington: Georgetown Univ. Press, 1934.

_____, ed. *The Classics of International Law*. Washington, DC: Carnegie Institution, 1917: *De Indis et De Iure Belli Relectiones by Francisco de Vitoria*.

_____. *The Spanish Origin of International Law: Francisco de Vitoria and His Law of Nations*. Oxford: Clarendon Press, 1934.

Ullman, W. *The Individual and Society in the Middle Ages*. Baltimore, MD: Johns Hopkins Press, 1966.

Wallon, H. *Histoire de l'esclavage dans l'antiquite*. 3 vols. Paris, 1847.

Weisheipl, J., OP. *Friar Thomas D'Aquino: His life, thought and works*. Garden City, NY: Doubleday & Co., 1974.

Welty, E., OP. *Grundragen und Grundkrafte des sozialen Lebens*. Second edition. Bonn: Herder, 1952.

Wright, H.F., ed. *Francisco de Vitoria: Addresses in commemoration of the fourth centenary of his lectures "De Indis" and "De Iure Belli," 1532-1932.* Washington, D.C: Carnegie Foundation, 1932.

B. Articles

Amann, E. "Occam," *Dictionnaire de Théologie Catholique*. Paris: Librairie, Letouzey et Ane, 1924, XI, col. 864-904.

Arbus, M.R. "Le droit roman dans l'oeuvre de Saint Thomas," *Revue Thomiste* 57 (1957), 325-349.

Bedouelle, G. "L'or et l'evangile: l'eglise et la conquete du nouveau monde au XVI siecle," *Sources*. Fribourg (nov.-dec., 1975), 42-48.

Besiade, T. "L'ordre social selon saint Thomas d'Aquin," *Revue Des Sciences Philosophiques et Théologiques* 13 (1924), 5-19.

Bourke, V. "Foundations of Justice," *Proceedings of the American Catholic Philosophical Association* 36 (1962), 19-28.

Brennan, E. "Ideology of Imperialism: Spanish Debates regarding the Conquest of America, 1511-51," *Studies* 47 (Spring, 1958), 66-82.

Briancesco, E. "Tomas de Aquino, maestro de vida social," *Teologia* 11 (1974), 7-23.

Bricout, J. "Esclavage," *Dictionnaire Pratique des Connaissances Religieuses*. Paris: Librairie Letouzey et Ane, 1926, III, col. 3-8.

Brucker, J., SJ. "Negres (La traite des) et Les Missionaires," *Dictionnaire Apologetique de la Foi Catholique*. Ed. A.D'Ales, III, Paris: Gabriel Beauchesne, 1916, col. 1069-1073.

Brufau Prats, J. "La nocion analogica del dominium en Santo Tomas, Francisco de Vitoria y Domingo de Soto," *Salmanticensis* 4 (1957), 96-136.

Burt, D. "St. Augustine's Evaluation of Civil Society," *Augustinianum* 3 (1963), 87-94.

Carro, V. "Las controversias de Indias y las ideas teologo-juridicos medievales que las preparan y explican," *Annuario de la Asociation Francisco de Vitoria*. 8 (1948), 13-53.

Coniglio, G. "Le concept d'esclavage dans St. Thomas d'Aquin," Translated by R. Herval. *Bulletin Cercle Thomiste* (Caen), 15 (1953), 40-44.

Coulton, G. "Slavery and the Roman Church," *Review of the Churches* 47 (1927), 366-372.

Degler, C. "Slavery in Brazil and the United States. A Comparison," *American Historical Review* 75 (1970), 1004-28.

DeLuca, L. "Nocion de la ley en el Decreto de Graciano: legalidad o absolutismo," *Jus Canonicum* 7 (1967), 65-94.

Diaz-Nava, A.F. "El dominio segun la doctrina del Cardinal Lugo (1583-1660)," *Estudios Eclesiasticos* 36 (1961), 35-55.

Dognin, P. "La notion thomiste de justice face aux exigencies modernes," *Revue des Sciences Philosophiques et Théologiques* 45 (1961), 601-640.

Dunbabin, J. "The Two Commentaries of Albertus Magnus on the Nicomachean Ethics," *Recherches Théologique Ancienne et Medievale* 30 (1963), 232-250.

Dutilleul, J. "Esclavage," *Dictionnaire de Théologie Catholique*. Paris: Librairie, Letouzey et Ane, 1924, V. col. 457-520.

"Esclavitud," *Enciclopedia de la Religion Catolica*. Barcelona: Dalmau y Jover, 1952, III, col. 599-604.

Folgado, A. "Los tratados [De Legibus] y [De justitia et jure] en los autores españoles del siglo XVI y primera mitad del XVII," *Ciudad de Dios* 172 (1959), 275-302.

Gaudemet, J. "Contribucion al estudio de la ley en la doctrina del siglo XII," *Jus Canonicum* 7 (1967), 25-40.

Getino, L., OP. "El maestro Fr. Francisco de Vitoria," *La Ciencia Tomista*, nos. 1-16, 1910-1912.

Ginsburg, N., "Metaphysical Relations and St. Thomas Aquinas," *New Scholasticism* 15 (1941) 238-254.

Guillou, M. "La morale de saint Thomas," *Vie Spirituelle, Supplement* (15 mai 1951), 171-184.

Hanke, L. "Pope Paul III and the American Indians," *Harvard Theological Review* 30 (1937), 65-102.

Häring, B. and Vereecke, L. "La théologie morale de St. Thomas à St. Alphonse," *Nouvelle Revue Théologique* 77 (1955), 673-692.

Heredia, B. de, OP. "Dominique de Soto," *Dictionnaire de Théologie Catholique*. Paris: Librairie Letouzey et Ané, 1941. 14:2, coll. 2423.

Hernandez, R. "Las Casas y Sepúlveda frente a frente," *La Ciencia Tomista* 102 (1975), 209-247.

Imbert, J. "Reflexions sur le Christianisme et l'Esclavage en Droit Romain," *Revue Internationale des Droits de l'antiquite.* (Bruxelles) 2 (1949), 445-476.

Jarlot, G. "Dominique Soto devant les problemes moraux de la conquete americaine," *Gregorianum* 44 (1963), 80-87.

Kaczynski, E. "Il 'naturale dominium' della II-II, 66, 1, e le sue interpretazioni moderne," *Angelicum* 53 (1976), 453-475.

Keating, J. "The Survival of Slavery," *Month* 160 (Oct., 1932), 354-356.

van der Kroef, J. "Francisco de Vitoria and the nature of colonial policy," *Catholic Historical Review* 35 (1949), 129-162.

Kuppens, M. "Les origines de la doctrine catholique du droit a la colonisation," *Miscellanea moralia* (ed. A. Janssen), 1958, 405-448.

LaCugna, C. "The Relational God: Aquinas and Beyond," *Theological Studies* 46:4 (December, 1985) 647-663.

Lesetre, H. "Esclavage," *Dictionnaire de la Bible*. Paris: Letouzey et Ane, 1912, II, col. 1918-28.

Lewis, E. "Medieval Thought and Western Political Tradition," *Thought* 37 (1962), 173-193.

Lyall, F. "Roman Law in the Writings of Paul: the Slave and the Freedman," *New Testament Studies* [London] 17 (1970), 73-79

McGarry, W. "St. Paul and the Slave," *Thought* 10 (Dec. 1935), 374-90.

MacQueen, D. "St. Augustine's Concept of Property Ownership," *Recherches Augustiniennes* 8 (1972), 187-229.

Maldonado, E., "Tomas de Aquino, Bartolomé de las Casas y la controversia de Indias," *Studium* 14 (1974) 519-542.

Maraval, P. "L'eglise du IV siecle et l'esclavage," *Studia Moralia* 8 (1970), 319-346.

Markus, R. "Two conceptions of Political Authority: Augustine, 'De Civitate Dei, xix, 14-15,' and some thirteenth century interpretations," *Journal of Theological Studies* 16 (1965), 68-100.

Masson, P. "Essai sur la conception de l'usufruit en droit romain," *Revue Historique de Droit Francais et Etrangere*. 4th ser., 13 (1934), 1-47.

Maxwell, J.F. "Le developpement de la doctrine catholique sur l'esclavage," *Justice dans le monde* 11 (1970), 147-195; 291-326.

Mayer, C. "Augustins Aufflassung uber die Sklaverei, Wurdigung und Kritik," *Augustinianum* 17 (1977), 237-247.

Molinero, M., OFM. "El concepto de ley en fray Alfonso de Castro," *Verdad y Vida* (1959), 31-74.

Mueller, H. "Morality of Slavery in Holy Scripture," *American Ecclesiastical Review* 151 (1964), 298-306.

Munier, C. "El concepto de 'dominium' y 'proprietas' en los canonistas y moralistas desde el s. xvi al xix," *Jus Canonicum* 2 (1962), 469-479.

Nieto Velez, A. "Teologos y juristas frente a la conquista y a la independencia de America," *Revista Teologica Limensiana* 8 (1974), 105-113.

Overbeke, P. "St. Thomas et Droit: II-II, q. 57," *Revue Thomiste* 55 (1954-55), 519-565.

_____. "Droit et morale. Essai de synthese thomiste," *Revue Thomiste* 58 (1958), 285-338.

Pfaff-Giesberg, R. "Sklaverei," *Staatslexikon.* 4, col. 1584-1591.

Pijper, J. "The Christian Church and Slavery in the Middle Ages," *American Historical Review* XIV, no. 4 (1909), 675-695.

Pinckaers, S., OP. "La théologie morale au déclin du Moyen-Age: Le nominalisme," *Nova et Vetera* 52:3 (1977) 209-221.

236

_____. "Le role de la fin dans l'action morale selon saint Thomas," *Revue des sciences philosophiques et théologiques* XLV (1961) 393-421.

Robleda, O. "La nocion tomista de la ley en relacion con las ideas romanas," *Gregorianum* 48 (1967), 284-301.

Ruiz-Maldonado, E. "Tomas de Aquino, Bartolomé de las Casas y la controversia de Indias," *Studium* 14 (1974), 319-342.

_____. "Bartolomé de las Casas y la justicia en Indias," *La Ciencia Tomista* 101 (1974), 345-410.

Smith, I., OP. "St. Thomas and Human Social Life," *New Scholasticism* (1945), 285-321.

Spanneut, M. "Les normes morales du stoicisme chez les peres de l'eglise," *Studia Moralia* 19 (1981), 153-175.

Spicq, C. "Notes de Lexicographie Philosophique Medievale: Dominium, Possessio, Proprietas chez S. Thomas et chez les juristes romains," *Revue Des Sciences Philosophiques et Théologiques* 18 (1929), 269-81.

_____. "La notion analogique de dominium et le droit de propriété," *Revue Des Sciences Philosophiques et Théologiques* 20 (1931), 52-76.

Stanley, D. "Freedom and slavery in Pauline usage," *Way* (1975), 83-99.

Swiezawski, S. "Quelques Deformations de la pensee de St. Thomas dans la tradition thomiste," in *Aquinas and the Problems of His*

Time. Ed. M. Verbeke and D. Verhelst. The Hague: Leuven University Press, 1976.

Tonneau, J., OP, "Justice," in *The Virtues and States of Life*, vol. 1, ed. A.M. Henry, OP. Chicago, IL: Fides, 1957.

Vignaux, P. "Nominalisme," *Dictionnaire de Théologie Catholique*. Paris: Librairie, Letouzey et Ane, 1924, XI, col. 717-784.

del Vigo Gutierrez, A. "Las tasas y las pragmaticas reales en los moralistas espanolas del siglo de oro," *Burgense* 22 (1981), 427-470.

Watts, W. "Seneca on Slavery," *Downside Review* 90 (1972), 183-195.

Wilberforce, R. "The church and slavery," *Catholic International Outlook*. n. 210, 1-29.

Willems, S. "De jure servitutis," *Collegio Brugensis* 30 (1930), 27-36; 60-65.

Willoweit, D. "Dominium und proprietas: Zur Entwicklung des Eigentumbegriffs in der mittelaltlichen und neuzeitlichen Rechtswissenschaft," *Historich Jahrbuch* 94 (1974), 131-158.

Wolff, H.W. "Masters and Slaves. On Overcoming Class Struggle in the Old Testament," *Interpretation* 27 (1973), 259-272.

Zagar, J. "Aquinas and the Social Teaching of the Church," *Thomist* 38 (1974), 826-855.